BLACK BELT C++
THE MASTERS COLLECTION

Bruce Eckel

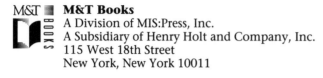

M&T Books
A Division of MIS:Press, Inc.
A Subsidiary of Henry Holt and Company, Inc.
115 West 18th Street
New York, New York 10011

Library of Congress Cataloging-in-Publication Data

Eckel, Bruce.
    Black belt C++: the masters collection / Bruce Eckel.
        p.   cm.
    Includes index.
    ISBN 1-55851-334-5
    1. C++ (Computer program language)   I. Title
    QA76.73.C153E23   1994
    005.13'3--dc20   94-40099
                                                                                          CIP

97   96   95   94   4   3   2   1

Development Editor: Alla Efimova
Copy Editor: Suzanne Ingrao
Technical Editor: Nancy Nicolaisen
Production Editor: Patricia Wallenburg

TABLE OF CONTENTS

FIRST ENCOUNTER WITH C++

SPECIAL MEMBER FUNCTIONS AND PROGRAMMING TECHNIQUES
Bruce Eckel   183

DESIGNING C++ CLASS LIBRARIES
Thomas Keffer   217

C++ Under the Hood

MEMORY MANAGEMENT IN C++

Nathan C. Myers   267

THE DIFFICULTIES OF USING OBJECT-ORIENTED TECHNIQUES: PERCEPTIONS OF C++ DEVELOPERS

Steven D. Sheetz   281

INTRODUCTION

Bruce Eckel

When I took over the C track for the Software Development Conference in 1991, it was clear (in my imagination only) that everyone wanted it to become the C++ track—why else would they want *me* to do it? Since SD had started as a C conference, there was some surprise when the change came about but it soon turned to pleasant surprise, since the track became the largest draw in the conference (sometimes eclipsed by its companion track on Windows programming, also heavily C++ oriented). In this book you'll see what makes the track so popular.

I believe that people (or rather, their companies) don't pay a lot of money to come to a conference to see things that they can find in books. The preconference tutorials provide a grounding in the language, but for the conference proper I strive to have topics that fill the gaps in your knowledge using novel and well-crafted approaches. In addition, I feel that most of the talks should push you beyond the boundaries of what you normally think about in programming. I've personally found that if I exceed my boundaries, I learn techniques that give even the most mundane of tasks an elegant solution. When you come to a conference like SD, you shouldn't return just "trained," but instead lifted to a whole new programming plane. While this book won't produce the same experience you get from attending the conference (especially the hallway conversations) it draws you into deeper thinking about the language just as the conference does.

The authors in this book are all experts in their subjects. They share my lack of tolerance for inaccuracy. But these authors are more than just technical experts: they're good presenters. I believe a good conference—and a good book—should be entertaining. One thing you'll notice is that the voice of each author is distinct: I've made a point to leave the personality in their writing (including their code formatting style). So you won't be bored in these pages.

Although I've met many of the people in this book through conferences, some I've come to know under more interesting circumstances. I worked with Tom Keffer for a year as a researcher while he was at the University of Washington School of Oceanography where both of us did our original C++ work. His company Rogue Wave (referring to an oceanographic phenomenon) continues to lure scientists and engineers away from FORTRAN by providing useful C++ class libraries. Scott Meyers and I have climbed Half Dome (not the face, the backside) in Yosemite together. I first met Dan Saks at the organizational meeting for the ANSI/ISO C++ committee in Washington DC where he volunteered to be secretary. At the time I thought it was insane, and I'm regularly amazed at his endurance in the position. Tim Gooch first appeared in one of my presentations, embarrassing me by asking very intelligent questions (that boomed from the back of the room, carried on his actor-trained voice) that I couldn't answer. Steven Sheetz appeared at an entrepreneur's conference for *Midnight Engineering* magazine, looking for guinea pigs for his doctoral dissertation. And as you'll discover through their writing, each of the authors in this book is unique.

Overview

The first two chapters, *Moving to C++* by Hank Shiffman, and *A C Programmer's First Encounter with C++*, by Steve Ross, at first seem to cover basic topics. However, you'll soon see that Hank's chapter looks at the nooks and crannies of C++ as a "better C" and aspects of C++ as a general programming language that most texts ignore (or worse, don't understand). Steve's chapter is valuable because he's dealt with a lot of people considering the change to C++. Not only does it fill in some of your knowledge and provide design techniques, but it gives answers to questions you'll be asked when trying to motivate your own company to move to the language.

When you begin reading Scott Meyers' *Examining C++ Development Tools*, you may think you've wandered into a strange universe where the humor columnist Dave Barry knows about computer programming. Yet Scott's questions, as always, are right to the point. Reading this before a trade show will provide hours of entertainment with embarrassing questions for C++ tool vendors.

The easiest way to deal with multiple inheritance is to "just say no." Tim Gooch's *Using Multiple Inheritance Effectively* sidesteps the ongoing debate about whether MI should be in the language (it's there, and it won't go away) and instead looks at the best way to use it in your designs, a topic which doesn't get nearly as much coverage. You may still choose to avoid MI after reading this chapter, but you'll have a much better view of the issues.

In *Compilation Firewalls*, Dan Saks discusses a problem everyone discovers when separating the interface from the implementation: C++ only goes part way. The "compilation interface" includes all the private members because the compiler has to see them, even though the end user really only wants or needs to see the public interface. This also means that changes to the underlying implementation cause recompilations even though the use of the class doesn't change. Dan solves this problem by demonstrating techniques to more completely separate the interface from the implementation and to reduce needless recompilation during development.

My chapter is a potpourri of subjects and techniques, including a brief introduction to containers and iterators; overloading `new`, `delete`, and changing the `new-handler`; modifying `new` and `delete` for arrays; smart pointers; automatic type conversion; pointers to members; the function call operator; selecting member versus friend when overloading operators; and the programming techniques of "wrappers" and inheriting from C `structs`, reference counting, "virtual constructors," and approaches to debugging.

As mentioned earlier, Tom Keffer is president and founder of Rogue Wave, which specializes in the development of C++ class libraries. In his chapter *Designing C++ Class Libraries*, he provides some insight into what he's learned about the creation of robust, reusable classes.

Jan Gray makes the Microsoft C++ compiler tick. In *C++ Under the Hood*, you'll learn what makes it tick, too, in particular, the way objects are laid out, how members are accessed, and how member functions are called. He doesn't stop at the simple stuff, of course: the explanations cover the thorny topics of multiple inheritance and exception handling.

Nathan Myers is in charge of Rogue Wave's heap++ dynamic memory allocation package. In *Memory Management in C++* you'll learn what he knows about the implementation and use of alternate memory-management techniques, as well as the limitations of the built-in versions.

Finally, no book is complete without some treatment of the thorny topic of design methodology. But instead of the usual approach of endorsing one particular methodology, Steven Sheetz looks at the general problem of using *any* methodology with C++, based on interviews and "cognitive mapping" techniques to explore the way people create mental models about conceptual systems. If you're considering an analysis and design methodology, you need to read this chapter first.

I sincerely hope you will come away from this book with new and fresh insights on the language and a greater understanding of subjects that were previously fuzzy or unknown. In one way of looking at the world, a person is defined by their actions, so I hope this book will help you become a better programmer.

MOVING TO C++: IT'S NOT JUST OBJECTS

Harris Shiffman

INTRODUCTION

C++ started life as a set of object extensions to C. Because of this history and the tremendous interest in object-oriented techniques for analysis, design and programming, most people associate C++ with objects and vice versa. This is a pity for two reasons: first because C++ is not the purest, most flexible or most powerful language for object-oriented programming; and second because C++ offers tremendous benefits to C programmers whether or not they buy into an object-oriented style of programming.

When he started designing the C With Classes language that became C++, Dr. Bjarne Stroustrup made several decisions that distinguish it from other popular object-oriented languages. Foremost among these were the desire to maintain compatibility with C, to build on top of existing C facilities instead of inventing new ones and to design every feature so as to avoid any overhead unless the feature is actually in use. The result is a language that often seems more like a collection of good ideas than the product of a single vision.

Taken as a whole, C++ is a complex language with enough idiosyncrasies to trap even the most experienced programmer. It is helpful to look at the language not as a huge set of features that must all be mastered at once but instead as layers of capabilities that build upon each other. The following Figure 1.1 shows one admittedly arbitrary way of breaking C++ into a set of languages, which start with a safer version of C and go on to offer steadily more sophisticated capabilities.

A good guiding philosophy for both learning and using C++ is to work with only as much of the language as is required by the problem at hand. Many C++ programs simply use the language as a better, more convenient C. Others take advantage of C++'s ability to support programmer-defined data types without needing object-oriented features like inheritance. Even fully object-oriented programs don't often make use of sophisticated and error prone features like multiple inheritance.

This paper examines all of the different languages that are part of C++ and discuss the benefits offered by each.

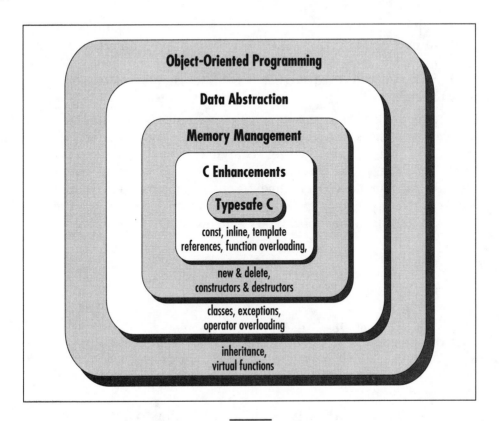

Object-Oriented Programming

Data Abstraction

Memory Management

C Enhancements

Typesafe C

const, inline, template
references, function overloading,

new & delete,
constructors & destructors

classes, exceptions,
operator overloading

inheritance,
virtual functions

FIGURE 1.1

C++ As a Typesafe C

Traditional Kernighan & Ritchie C was designed around a simple and horribly flawed assumption: that we programmers always know what we're doing. A simple example may serve to demonstrate just how easy it is to violate that assumption:

```
float x2 (value)
   float value;
{ return (2 * value); }

void main ()
{ int a = 10;
   float b = x2 (a); }
```

The function called x2 accepts a floating point value, multiplies it by 2 and returns a floating point result. In the main procedure you call this function with a value of 10, storing the result in the variable b. If you examine b you will discover that it contains a value of zero, not the expected answer of 20.

The problem here is that you called x2 with a value of type int, whereas x2 declares its argument to be of type float. The semantics of K&R C say that x2 will interpret its argument as the declared type of float, regardless of the type of the value passed to it. It is the responsibility of the programmer (with no help from the compiler) to make sure that every call to every function passes the types of values the function expects, with explicit casts to the proper type where necessary:

```
void main ()
{ int a = 10;
  float b = x2 ((float)a); }
```

K&R C assumes that argument type mismatches are intentional and compiles the program without providing any hint that something may be wrong. It is generally very easy to get a K&R C program to compile. Most of the work comes later when we sit in the debugger trying to figure out why it produces the wrong results.

C++ was designed to catch errors like this during compilation. Here is the same piece of code in C++:

```
float x2 (float value)
{ return (2 * value); }

void main ()
{ int a = 10;
  float b = x2 (a); }
```

Notice the difference in the declaration of x2. In C++ you place the types of a function's arguments in the argument list. This change in syntax is accompanied by a change in semantics: Where K&R C interprets any value passed to x2 as a float, C++ tells callers of x2 that it expects a float; every call to x2 will convert the value it passes to the proper type automatically. In the C++ version of the example, the variable b gets the value of 20 you expect.

This function prototype feature does more than handle data type conversions for us. It also detects situations where data of the wrong type is passed to a function:

```
float x2 (float value)
{ return (2 * value); }

void main ()
{ int a = 10;
  float b = x2 ("1234"); }

$ CC -o x2 x2.cc
"x2.cc", line 6: Error: Formal argument value of type float
in call to x2(float) is being passed char*.
```

It generally takes more effort to get a C++ program to compile without errors than it would for a similar C program. However, the C++ program is much closer to working correctly, which translates to less time in the debugger. Prototypes are particularly useful where pointers are involved. They permit the compiler to identify both missing and extraneous pointer dereference operations.

C++'s function prototypes were considered such a valuable feature that the ANSI committee for the C language took the idea and included it in their C standard, a rare situation where something became part of Standard C without first appearing in some other implementation of C. (C++ also includes several small features lifted from Standard C.) It could be argued that the rapid success of Standard C owes far more to the advantages of function prototypes than to any desire on the part of its users to adhere to a standard.

One important difference between C++ and Standard C is that C++ requires the use of function prototypes, while Standard C offers them as an option. For compatibility with existing code, Standard C continues to accept the K&R style of function declaration (and continues to permit type mismatch errors like the one shown above). This difference also leads to a difference in the way that Standard C and C++ interpret function declarations like this one:

```
extern float x2();
```

To Standard C, x2 is a function that returns a float. The empty parentheses indicate that nothing is known about the argument list. Standard C will permit x2 to be called with any combination of arguments (or no arguments at all) and will do no type checking on the values passed.

C++, on the other hand, interprets the same declaration as a function which accepts no arguments. The right declaration for x2 for both Standard C and C++ would be:

```
extern float x2(float);
```

Both Standard C and C++ permit argument types in function declarations to be followed by dummy argument names. This helps to document the values the functions expect and the proper order:

```
extern int copy_until_eof (fstream *outstr,
                           fstream *instr);
```

NOTE For most C code, a move to C++ will mean little more than a conversion of function declarations to the new prototype syntax. This is the most significant of the very few changes required for C code to be acceptable to a C++ compiler.

C++ As an Enhanced C

Along with major changes like function prototypes, C++ offers many small convenience features. Most of these have no effect on the efficiency of code. Instead, they make it possible to write code that is just a little bit easier to read, understand, and maintain. Although most of these were included in the language to support its object-oriented features they turn out to be quite useful on their own.

One improvement C++ made to C was to relax the requirement that all local variables be declared before the first executable statement in a block. This requirement can put many lines of code between a variable's declaration and the first reference to it, making it more difficult to determine the relationship between a variable's creation, assignment, and use. C++, on the other hand, permits variables to be declared closer to the point where they are used. One popular use of this feature is for defining index variables for loops:

```
int sumsq (int n)
{ for (int i = 0, sum = 0; i < n; i++)
```

```
    sum += i * i;
 return sum; }
```

In this example, the variables i and sum are declared at the start of the for loop. Variables declared in the initialization clause of a for statement exist until the end of the block in which they are declared (the sumsq function), rather than the scope of the for loop itself, which is why you can refer to the value of sum in the return statement that follows the loop. (Note: The lifetime is narrowed in the new C++ Standard.)

C++ also permits the use of default values in function argument lists. This is of particular use during program maintenance. Sometimes you need to add an extra argument to a function to handle a new capability. In C this would require changing every caller of this function to add the new argument. C++ makes life easier by letting us provide a default value:

```
void show_entry (int *table, int element,
                 int use_bg=FALSE);
```

Callers that need the new capability can specify a value for this argument:

```
show_entry (sort_table, x, TRUE);
```

Existing calls to this function need not be modified:

```
show_entry (sort_table, y);
```

A function may declare default values for any number of its arguments. However, all defaulted arguments must appear at the end of the argument list. Also, callers may not leave out arguments from the middle of the argument list. Finally, it is important to note that insertion of default values occurs at the function call and not in the called function. If a function declares 20 arguments with default values, every call to that function will have to pass 20 values. Default values are not a good substitute for a variable argument mechanism.

C++ also defines a second syntax for *casting*. The new style of cast uses the syntax of a function call. The C style of cast may also be used:

```
int window_width  = int(xv_get (window, XV_WIDTH));
int window_height = (int)xv_get (window, XV_HEIGHT);
complex c = (complex)5.3 * complex(5.3);
```

As in C, C++ uses the term *cast* to represent two different concepts: data type conversions and changes in interpretation. You can use the two types of cast to help indicate your intentions to readers of your code:

```
/* Reinterpret result of malloc (void *) as a double *.
*/
double *dp = (double *)malloc(sizeof(double));
*dp = 1.0 / 3.0;
/* Convert intermediate result from double to int.   */
*dp = int(*dp * 10) / 10.0;
```

Some situations will require a specific style of cast. Casts to a type with multiple words in its name must use the C syntax. Casts in C++ can involve multiple arguments; these require the function syntax. (You'll see these when you learn about class constructors.)

```
int a = (unsigned short) -1;
complex i = complex(0, -1);
```

const & inline

Because of limitations in C, programmers have been forced to do some of their work in a second language: that of the C preprocessor (cpp). C++ adds many of cpp's capabilities directly to the language, among them the ability to declare constant values and the inline expansion of procedures.

Like Standard C, C++ provides the const declaration for read-only values. This declaration can be used in two ways: (1) to provide names for constant expressions (like the #define directive); and (2) in function argument lists to identify arguments that will not be modified:

```
const max_width = 640; // Type is int by default
const float world_factor = 5.5;
extern int strcpy (char *, const char *);
```

NOTE Notice the use of const with a pointer in the declaration of strcpy. This indicates that the second argument to strcpy is a string whose contents will not be modified. When const is combined with a pointer, the meaning depends on where the const keyword appears:

```
char *p;
const char * q = p;          // Can modify q but not *q
char * const r = p;          // Can modify *r but not r
const char * const s = p;    // Can't modify s or *s
```

C++'s inline directive can be used in place of another major use of cpp: to improve performance by replacing calls to small functions with in-place expansion of their code. Instead of rewriting functions as cpp macros to reduce function calling overhead, you can simply insert the inline keyword:

```
inline int max (int x, int y)
{ return x > y ? x : y; }

void main ()
{ int a = 10, b = 25;
  int result = max (x, y); }
```

The inline directive has one other advantage over cpp macros: inline functions behave like regular functions. Unlike cpp macros, inline functions don't have problems with multiple evaluation of their arguments. C++ also permits pointer operations on inline functions by creating a separate copy of the function:

```
void main ()
{ int (*max_func) (int, int) = max;
  printf ("%d",  max_func (75, 33)); }
```

Variable References

A common problem for C programmers involves passing values to functions that expect pointers and pointers where they expect values. As you have already seen, C++ is much better than K&R C at detecting such errors. However, C++ offers another mechanism called *variable references*, which can eliminate much of the problem.

Consider a simple function to swap the values of two integer variables. Because C calls functions with copies of the values provided by the caller, you would need to pass the addresses of the two integer variables. The function itself would operate on pointers to integers, as in the following code:

```
void swap (int *x, int *y)
{ int temp = *x; *x = *y; *y = temp; }

void main ()
{ int a = 5, b = 7;
  swap (&a, &b); }
```

In C, a caller of a function needs to know which arguments might be modified and to pass the addresses of those values. (Unless the arguments are character arrays, in which case the value is already a pointer. Sorta.) Does the programmer exist anywhere who has used a function like scanf and who has not forgotten the ampersand in front of its arguments at least once? Or placed one in front of a character array where it didn't belong?

C++ addresses this problem with a new data type: the variable reference. By declaring a function's arguments as references you get the call by reference behavior of languages like FORTRAN. Here is the same piece of code using references instead of pointers:

```
void swap (int &x, int &y)
{ int temp = x; x = y; y = temp; }

void main ()
{ int a = 5, b = 7;
  swap (a, b); }
```

NOTE   Notice the differences: you no longer need to dereference pointers inside the swap function, nor do you need to remember to pass addresses of our integers in the function call. The compiler takes care of all of that.

References have one other advantage over pointers: the opportunity for greater efficiency. A major challenge for C compiler writers is to produce high performance code in a language with pointers. Pointers make it extremely difficult for a compiler to know when different variables refer to the same location, which prevents them from generating the fastest possible code. Since a variable reference points to the same location during its entire life, a C++ compiler can do a better job of optimization than it can with pointer-based code.

References can also be used on the result types of functions. Functions that return references can be used as both *lvalues* (values on the left side of an assignment) and *rvalues* (values on the right side). This function treats an array of one hundred integers as a matrix of ten rows and columns:

```
int& matrix (int array[], int x, int y)
{ return array[x * 10 + y]; }
```

When the function is used as an rvalue, it behaves exactly as it would without the reference:

```
static int a[100] = 0;
void main ()
{ int b = matrix (a, 4, 3);    // same as "int b = a[43];"
```

It is when the function appears on the left side of an assignment that the reference matters. In this case the function returns the location of the selected element instead of its value:

```
matrix (a, 5, 7) = b; }     // same as "a[57] = b;"
```

This use of references is an essential part of C++'s support for user-defined data types, as you will see later.

Memory Allocation

C++ adds two new operators to the list supported by C: new and delete. These operators handle creation and destruction of dynamic data and can be used in place of malloc and free. new is more convenient than malloc, as this example demonstrates:

```
int *ip1 = (int *) malloc (sizeof (int) * 20);
int *ip2 = new int[20];
```

Where as malloc accepts a byte count and returns a void pointer that you must cast, new takes a data type and the number of objects to create and returns a pointer of the appropriate type. User-defined data types can define initialization functions (constructors), which new will call after it allocates memory for the new data item, as well as cleanup functions (destructors), which delete will call before reclaiming the space.

An important feature of new and delete is that we can write our own implementation of them for specific data types. This makes it easy to define special memory collection schemes for certain kinds of data without requiring anything of the user of that data. This customization of new and delete is made possible by a C++ feature called *overloading*.

Overloading

Overloading permits you to write many functions with the same name. This lets you reduce the size of your function namespace by grouping functions that perform the same operations on different arguments under the same name.

As an example, consider a set of functions to return the larger of two values. Function overloading permits you to define several of these functions for different data types. Callers need only remember one function name regardless of the types of values to be compared:

```
int max (int x, int y)
{ return x > y ? x : y; }

double max (double x, double y)
{ return x > y ? x : y; }

void main ()
{ int    a   = max (10, 3);
  double b = max (7.5, 13.3);
  int    a   = max (3, 5.5); }
```

Overloaded functions are selected based on the number of values passed to the function and their types. The first call to max above is resolved as a call to the first (int, int) version of the function. The second call resolves to the second (double, double) version. This selection is done at compile time. Function overloading introduces no run time overhead to the program.

The last call to max above generates a compilation error. The compiler could use the (double, double) version of max by casting the first argument. Alternatively, it could use the (int, int) version of max by casting the second argument. In ambiguous situations like this C++ refuses to choose. It is up to the programmer to identify the correct function to use, either by casting one argument explicitly or by defining another version of max that accepts an int and a double.

Ambiguity can also arise when overloading is combined with default values for function arguments. Here is a third version of max that accepts three ints with default values:

```
int max (int x=INT_MIN, y=INT_MIN, z=INT_MIN)
{ return x > y ? (x > z ? x : z) : (y > z ? y : z); }
```

This new max function prevents the program from compiling. Although it is the proper choice for calls to max with three, one, or no values, it creates ambiguity when max is called with two values. This third version of max cannot exist in the same program as the first max. One of them must be deleted.

Overloading introduces an interesting implementation problem. Although C++ permits many functions to share a single name, most operating systems do not. C++ works around the limitations of the systems on which it runs by employing a scheme known as *mangling*. (Really!) When we write a function called `max` that accepts two `int`s the C++ compiler actually generates a function with a name like `__OFDminiTB`. C++ development environments automatically convert between the source (unmangled) and internal (mangled) names as needed, so programmers generally don't have to deal with those horrible mangled names.

There is one time when programmers do have to worry about function name mangling: when they need to interact with C code. If every call to a function called `draw_text` actually turns into a call to something like `__OFJdraw_textUliTCPc`, what do we do when we really want the C function called plain ordinary `draw_text`?

C++ addresses this with a function declaration called `extern "C"`. If a function is declared `extern "C"` the compiler knows not to mangle references to it. This declaration can be used to make C functions callable from C++ or to make C++ functions callable from C. Because it turns off name mangling, functions declared `extern "C"` may not be overloaded.

Overloading can be applied to C++ operators as well as to functions. This lets us create new data types that look and behave like built-in data types. We will see examples of this later.

Function Templates

A recent addition to C++ is the *template* mechanism. Templates address an inconvenience that we have already seen with our `max` function: Where a C programmer could write one C preprocessor macro that would work with any kind of data, a C++ programmer would have to write separate functions for each combination of argument types. (Of course, a C++ programmer could fall back to the preprocessor as well.)

Templates permit us to write one source definition that can produce multiple functions. Here is a definition of a function which uses the Quicksort algorithm to sort a table of double-precision floating point numbers:

```
void quicksort (double *table, int l, int r)
{ double x, temp;
  int i = l, j = r;
  x = table[(l + r) / 2];
  do {
```

```
    while (table[i] < x) i++;
    while (x < table[j]) j--;
    if (i <= j) {
      temp = table[i];
      table[i++] = table[j];
      table[j--] = temp; }
  } while (i <= j);
  if (1 < j)
    quicksort (table, 1, j);
  if (i < r)
    quicksort (table, i, r); }
```

To convert this function to a template we simply add a `template` declaration. The `template` declaration identifies data type names, which are place holders. Then we use these place holder names in the function:

```
template <class Type>
void quicksort (Type *table, int 1, int r)
{ Type x, temp;
```

(The rest of the function is identical to the previous one.) In this example, the place holder `Type` will be replaced by the actual type of the array passed in each call to `quicksort`: `int`, `double`, `unsigned short`, `signed char` and so on. A new version of `quicksort` will be compiled for each different data type passed to it:

```
void main ()
{ int ia[50000];
  double da[100000], da2[40000];

  quicksort (ia, 0, 49999);
  quicksort (da, 0, 99999);
  quicksort (da2, 0, 39999); }
```

In this case, two versions of `quicksort` will be created: one that sorts an array of `int`s and a second for arrays of `double`s. This second version will be used for both the second and third calls to `quicksort`.

A sort function created from a template is identical in size and performance to one created for a specific data type. This is a big win over previous attempts to produce a general purpose sort function like the Standard C `qsort` on SunOS. `qsort` took as arguments the array to sort, the size of each element, and a comparison function. `qsort` was harder to write, harder to use, and at least five times slower than the simple quicksort function you see here.

The combination of the `template` and `inline` directives gives us everything we need to write a single definition for `max`. Instead of writing a cpp macro like this:

```
#define max(x,y) ((x) > (y) ? (x) : (y))
```

we write a template function like this:

```
template <class Type>
inline Type max (Type a, Type b)
{ return a > b ? a : b; }
```

This definition of `max` has one problem that it shares with the macro: Neither one works for character strings. If we use either one to compare two strings, we'll discover that they return the one at the lower memory address, not the one that is first alphabetically.

Templates can be overridden where necessary for specific data types. We can create a separate max function that operates on character strings, which will be used instead of the template definition for that particular data type:

```
char *max (char *a, char *b)
{ return strcmp (a,b) > 0 ? a : b; }
```

As before, each use of `max` with a new data type will create another function. Versions of `max` will also be created for user-defined data types, which need to define a meaning for the ">" operator used by `max`.

```
void main ()
{ int a = max (5, 7);          // Creates max (int, int)
  double b = max (3.3, 4.2);   // Creates max
                               // (double, double)
  char *c = max ("ab", "cd");  // Uses max (char *, char *)
  int d = max (4, 2);          // Uses max (int, int)

  mytype e(a), f(b);
  mytype g = max (e, f); }     // Creates max (mytype,
                               //  mytype)
```

NOTE

Templates give us an easy way to reuse source code for new kinds of data. In addition to their use with functions, templates can be applied to the definition of new data types. You will see this second use of templates later.

Exceptions

Most C++ implementations now include support for templates. Fewer compilers support exceptions, an important addition to the language for writing error and condition handlers.

N O T E

> This situation can be expected to change. By 1995 it will be the rare C++ product that doesn't support exceptions.

Exceptions give the builders of code libraries a way to indicate when anomalies occur inside their code, while letting users of the libraries decide when and how to deal with them.

Exceptions add three new keywords to C++: throw to signal that an exception has occurred, try to identify a block of code in which exceptions are to be handled, and catch to associate a handler for a particular kind of exception with the try block it follows.

Here is a simple function that divides one int by another. If its second argument is zero it throws an exception, a character string containing an error message:

```
int div (int a, int b)
{ if (b != 0)
    return a / b;
  else
    throw "Division by zero"; }
```

Now we call this function from one which prints the result of the division:

```
void printdiv (int a, int b)
{ printf ("%d / %d = %d", a, b, div (a, b)); }
```

We'll call this function with several pairs of numbers to be divided. Here we can see how a try block and a catch block are combined to handle exceptions:

```
void main ()
{ try {
    printdiv (57, 3);
    printdiv (5, 2);
    printdiv (3, 0);
```

```
    printdiv (10,3); }
catch (char *err) {
   fprintf (stderr, "Error: %s", err); }
printf ("That's all, folks!"); }
```

The `try` block surrounds the code in which exceptions are handled. The `catch` block will be executed if a value of the specified type (`char *`) is thrown. The variable `err` will contain the argument to the `throw`. When this program is run we get the following output:

```
$ div
57 / 3 = 19
5 / 2 = 2
Error: Division by zero
That's all, folks!
```

The first two divisions are successful. The third causes the exception to be thrown. Control immediately moves from the `throw` statement in `div` to the first `try` block that has a `catch` for a `char*`. The `catch` block prints the error message. Control then transfers to the statement after the `catch` block.

 The last call to `printdiv` did not occur. If you want to make sure that all of the divisions take place, you could add a `try`/`catch` pair to `printdiv`. If `printdiv` handles the exception it will not be passed back to main.

NOTE

What happens if an exception is thrown for which there is no handler? If you remove the `try` and `catch` from our example, you see the following:

```
$ div
57 / 3 = 19
5 / 2 = 2
Run-time exception error; current exception: char *
        No handler for exception.
Abort(coredump)
```

As we can see, an exception that isn't handled will cause the program to terminate. This is intended to prevent situations in which a program neglects to check for an error and continues executing with invalid data.

Exceptions are most useful when combined with data abstraction and inheritance. We will revisit this feature as part of those discussions.

All of these features provide benefits to C programmers without requiring major changes in the way they design their applications. For many experienced C programmers, they provide more than enough justification for switching to C++.

C++ AS A DATA ABSTRACTION LANGUAGE

Programming languages can be divided into categories based on the programming model or models they support. Most languages fall into one of four categories based on their facilities for managing data: procedural, data hiding, data abstraction, and object-oriented.

Procedural languages are the ones with which most of us are familiar. Languages like C, FORTRAN, Pascal, and COBOL focus on operations and algorithms. Programs are described as a set of procedures that call other procedures. Data are dragged along from procedure to procedure. Encoded in each procedure is detailed knowledge about the structure of the data it manipulates and its relationship to other data in the program. Consistency among the procedures that manipulate the same piece of data is difficult to achieve in such languages. It should shock us to realize that COBOL, the language used to manipulate most of the world's data, provides no facilities to ensure data consistency.

One of the first languages to attempt a solution was Modula-2. Using an approach called *data hiding*, Modula-2 attempted to build a firewall between the details of a data structure and its users. The hope was that hiding such detail from programmers would keep them from building so many assumptions about the data into their code. This would permit changes to be made to the structure of data without breaking all of the code that used that data. Although Modula-2's data hiding provided insufficient benefit to attract a wide audience, it was a step in the right direction.

Data abstraction languages like Ada let programmers create their own data types that have the properties of built-in data types. Every type provided by a language has an allowable range of values (0 to 255 for a char, -32768 to 32767 for a short, etc.) and a set of permitted operators (addition and subtraction for shorts but not dereferences or subscripting). In a data abstraction language like Ada, a programmer can create a new data type for a stack and define the set of operators that can act on one: push, pop, check for empty, and so on. C's typedef capability does not restrict the range of values a new type can have or the operations that are valid on it.

Object-oriented languages like Smalltalk, Objective C, and C++ take data abstraction even further by permitting us to define new data types (object classes) in terms of existing types. These new classes inherit all of the structure and the set of operations (an object's behavior) from the class's ancestor. Object-oriented languages also support a feature called *polymorphism*, which permits us to write a single piece of code that can operate on many different kinds of objects.

Associated with data abstraction and object-oriented programming is a new style of object-oriented analysis and program design. Traditional analysis and design methods have been likened to breaking big rocks into little rocks. These methods begin with the problem to be solved, breaking it down into smaller and smaller modules. Eventually these modules get small enough so that they can be assigned to a programmer.

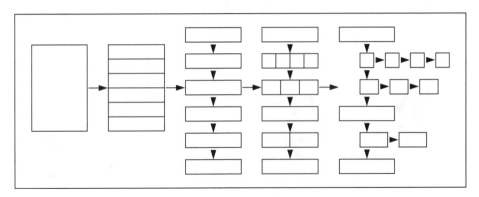

FIGURE 1.2

The difficulty with this approach is that it does nothing to reduce the complexity of the problem. Breaking a big rock into lots of little ones doesn't make the rock any simpler. And looking at a bunch of pebbles doesn't tell you much about the rock they came from.

Similarly, a procedural approach does nothing to reconcile the high level and detail views of the project. The high level view doesn't go down to the level where duplicated operations can be identified. And a detailed low level focus on a subset of the project loses track of other places where the same operations may be performed. There is nothing to tie the two views together. There is nothing to assure consistency.

Object-oriented design starts with the data. Operations on an object are associated with the object, rather than with the user of the operation. The implementation of an object, both structure and procedures, are hidden from its users. This reduces complexity for the user, who need know only the interface to the object and can ignore implementation details. It also reduces the likelihood that the user will build their code around assumptions about the object's implementation, which might be violated at some point in the future.

Imagine an employee records system that employs such a black box model of its objects. Programmers on this project would be told about the functions that make up the interfaces of the different objects. They would know that every employee object has a Get Name operation associated with it. Performing this operation would return a character string with the employee's name.

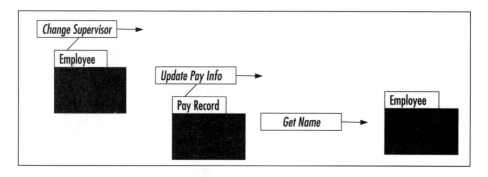

FIGURE 1.3

How does the Get Name operation work? Is the name stored in the employee object? Does the object contain a pointer to the name string? Does the operation perform a database lookup? Does it call the employee and ask for her name? Users of the object neither know nor care how Get Name produces its answer. All that matters to them is the operation's inputs, outputs, and any side effects.

A DATA ABSTRACTION EXAMPLE

To see the value in creating new abstract data types, consider the following program. This program reads text from standard input into an array, sorts the array using a Bubblesort and prints the result.

Bubblesort was chosen here for the length of its implementation, which is about its only virtue.

NOTE

Each line of input is stored in a string that strdup creates on the heap.

```c
#include <stdio.h>
#include <malloc.h>
#include <string.h>

int linecnt = 10000;

void swap (char **x, char **y)
{ char *temp = *x; *x = *y; *y = temp; }

void main ()
{ char *lines[10000], buffer[255];
  int i, j;

  for (i = 0; i < wordcnt; i++)
    if (gets (buffer) != NULL)
      lines[i] = strdup(buffer);
    else {
      linecnt = i;
      break; }

  for (i = 0; i < linecnt - 1; i++)
    for (j = i + 1; j < linecnt; j++)
      if (strcmp (lines[i], lines[j]) > 0)
        swap (&lines[i], &lines[j]);

  for (i = 0; i < linecnt; i++) {
    puts (lines[i]);
    free (lines[i]); }}
```

Now let's look at a second implementation of the same code. This new version will use a character string data type called a Charstr. We'll go through this version a little at a time and point out the differences.

```
#include <stdio.h>
```

Here is the first difference. A header file that contains the Charstr definition. Data type definitions are usually stored in their own header files. Also notice that we don't include the malloc and string header files. Charstr.h includes the functions we used from them.

```
#include "Charstr.h"

int linecnt = 10000;

void main ()
```

Here is the second difference. Both lines and buffer are defined as objects of type Charstr. The declaration for a Charstr can have two arguments: an initial value and a size for the string memory.

```
{ Charstr lines[10000], buffer("", 255);

    for (int i = 0; i < linecnt; i++)
        if (gets (buffer) != NULL)
```

Here we see another difference. In the original program we used strdup to create a new string and copy the contents of buffer into it. Here we use a simple assignment. Assigning a string to a Charstr automatically allocates the memory required to hold the characters.

```
        lines[i] = buffer;
    else {
        linecnt = i;
        break; }
    for (i = 0; i < linecnt - 1; i++)
        for (int j = i + 1; j < linecnt; j++)
```

The original code used strcmp to identify the string with the higher value. Here we can use a simple greater-than, since Charstr includes an implementation for this operator:

```
        if (lines[i] > lines[j])
```

Charstr also implements its own swap function so that the program doesn't have to define one. Notice that we don't have to pass addresses to this function. swap uses variable references for its arguments.

```
        swap (lines[i], lines[j]);
    for (i = 0; i < linecnt; i++)
```

The original program used the free function to release each character string after it was printed. The new program doesn't need to free its strings. As soon as lines goes out of scope the string memory associated with each Charstr will be reclaimed automatically.

```
        puts (lines[i]); }
```

The new program is a little bit shorter and simpler than the original. Significantly, this simplicity was achieved without any penalty in program size or performance.

Implementing a Data Type

We have just seen how we might use a Charstr data type in a program. Now we will go through the steps required to create one. We begin by defining the data items that make up the structure of a Charstr, just as we would for a struct in C:

```
struct Charstr {
  char *ptr;
  int max;
};
```

Each Charstr contains two slots: ptr, a pointer to a memory area where the characters are stored and max, the size of that area. This gives us the ability to detect attempts to overflow the string area.

To this structure definition we add declarations for all of the functions that make up the behavior of a Charstr. We divide our structure and behavior into two categories: private items, which may only be used by other members of the Charstr definition; and public items, which are accessible to users (the public interface to the data type):

```
class Charstr {
 private:
  char *ptr;
  int max;
```

```
  void grow (int size);

public:
  Charstr ();
  Charstr (char*, int = -1);
  ~Charstr ();
  operator char* () const;

  Charstr& operator = (const Charstr&);

  friend int operator > (const Charstr&, const Charstr&);
  friend void swap (Charstr&, Charstr&);
};
```

NOTE

We have changed `Charstr` from a `struct` to a `class`. This change is purely cosmetic. There is only one difference between a `struct` and a `class` in C++: items in a `struct` are `public` by default while items in a `class` are `private`. Since we declare the parts of our definition `private` and `public` explicitly, whether we call our `Charstr` a `struct` or a `class` is a matter of philosophy.

Our `Charstr` definition has several new elements: two functions with the same name as the class itself, a third function whose name begins with a tilde, three functions with the word `operator` in their names, a function with the `const` keyword outside the argument list, and two `friend` functions. You will see how all of these are used to build our class.

We'll start with a member function called `grow`. This function is called when we need to store a string that's bigger than our `Charstr` can hold. It allocates a new string area, copies the existing characters to it, and releases the old area:

```
void Charstr::grow (int size)
{ if (this -> max < size + 1) {
    /* Always grow by a few bytes more than we need. */
    char *new_ptr = new char[this -> max = size + 9];
    if (this -> ptr != NULL)
      strcpy (new_ptr, this -> ptr);
    delete this -> ptr;
    this -> ptr = new_ptr; }}
```

We precede the name of the function with the class to which it belongs: `Charstr::grow`. This identifies the function as the same one we declared in the `class` statement.

Member functions are called using the same dot syntax we use for data in a `struct`: for example, `a.grow()`. This can be interpreted as sending the `grow` message to the `a` object. The object that precedes the dot does not appear in the argument list. A pointer to this object (the recipient of the request) is available in a special local variable called `this`. In the `grow` function the expression `this -> max` refers to the `max` slot in the `Charstr` which received the `grow` request. (We can refer to the complete object with `*this`.)

Access to the slots of an object is such a common operation in member functions that C++ simplifies it for you. Instead of having to refer constantly to `this -> slot`, you can simply refer to the name of the slot:

```
void Charstr::grow (int size)
{ if (max < size + 1) {
    /* Always grow by more than we need. */
    char *new_ptr = new char[max = size + 9];
    if (ptr != NULL)
      strcpy (new_ptr, ptr);
    delete ptr;
    ptr = new_ptr; }}
```

Inside the grow member function any appearance of `max` or `ptr` refers to those slots on the `Charstr` which was requested to `grow`.

N O T E

We declared the `grow` function in the `private` area of `Charstr`. We do not want users of `Charstr` to manipulate its available memory themselves. This is an implementation detail that we will manage for them. By declaring a member function `private`, you make it accessible only to other functions declared as part of the class.

Constructors and Destructors

As I've mentioned a few times before, C++ provides a mechanism for initializing newly created objects and for cleaning up when they are destroyed. Constructor and destructor functions have the same name as the class to which they belong. (The destructor precedes the class name with a tilde, since destruction is the complement of construction.) Here are constructor and destructor functions for the `Charstr` class:

```
Charstr::Charstr ()
{ ptr = NULL; max = 0; }

Charstr::Charstr (char *str, int size)
```

```
{ ptr = NULL; max = 0;
  int slen = strlen(str);
  grow (slen > size ? slen : size);
  strcpy (ptr, str); }

Charstr::~Charstr ()
{ delete ptr; }
```

> Notice that constructors and destructors do not have return types. Also, we may have many constructors for a class with different (overloaded) argument lists. A class may have only one destructor.

N O T E

Constructors are invoked whenever we create an object of that type, whether by creating a variable or by filling a pointer with an object allocated on the heap with `new`. In the same way, destructors are invoked when an object leaves scope or is destroyed by a `delete` statement. Here are some examples of `Charstr`s being created and destroyed:

```
void main ()
{ Charstr fred("fred"), *jptr; // fred constructed
  jptr = new Charstr("joe");   // *jptr constructed
  { Charstr ralph = "ralph";   // ralph constructed
    fred = ralph;
  }                            // ralph destroyed

  delete jptr;                 // *jptr destroyed

}                              // fred destroyed
```

Destructors save us the trouble and grief of reclaiming the space used by our objects. If a `Charstr` is destroyed either automatically or manually, its character string space will be reclaimed. This reduces the likelihood of memory leaks in our programs.

Making Friends

There will be times when a function that needs access to the internals of our class can't be a member function. The function that swaps the values of two `Charstr`s is such a function. For obvious aesthetic reasons we would prefer writing

```
swap (lines[i], lines[j]);
```

   to

```
lines[i].swap (lines[j]);
```

The `friend` declaration gives a function that is not a member of a class access to its internal structure and behavior. Like member functions, every friend of a class must be declared in the `class` statement. Having declared `swap` a friend of class `Charstr` we define it like any other function:

```
inline void swap (Charstr& a, Charstr& b)
{ char *temp_ptr = a.ptr; a.ptr = b.ptr; b.ptr = temp_ptr;
  int   temp_max = a.max; a.max = b.max; b.max = temp_max;
}
```

There is a second reason that we need the `friend` declaration. Member functions will not cast their implied first argument. Consider a greater-than member function for the `Charstr` class:

```
inline int Charstr::greater_than (const Charstr &b)
{ return strcmp (ptr, b.ptr) > 0; }
```

This function can be used to compare two `Charstr` objects (with the same aesthetic argument against it as for `swap` above). It can also be used to compare a `Charstr` to a `char*`: the compiler will use the `Charstr` constructor to make a `Charstr` from the `char*`. What it can't do is compare a `char*` to a `Charstr`. Calling a member function on a data item that isn't a member of the class yields a compiler error.

The solution is to write `greater_than` as a regular function and declare it a friend of the `Charstr` class. This technique implements `operator >` which follows.

Overloading Operators

As was mentioned during the discussion of function overloading, C++ also provides a mechanism for defining the meaning of C++ operators on user-defined data types. Most operators can be overloaded, including casting operators like `operator int` and the `new` and `delete` operators previously mentioned. The Charstr class declares three such operators: assignment, greater-than comparison, and casting to a char*.

Overloaded operators are written just like functions. The name of the function uses the reserved word operator followed by the operator itself. Here is how we define the assignment and comparison operators:

```
Charstr& Charstr::operator= (const Charstr& s)
{ grow (strlen(s.ptr));
  strcpy (ptr, s.ptr);
  return *this; }

inline int operator > (const Charstr &a, const Charstr &b)
{ return strcmp (a.ptr, b.ptr) > 0; }
```

Casting operators are a little bit special:

```
inline Charstr::operator char * () const
{ return ptr; }
```

Notice that, although there is no return type specified, the function does return a value. (The return type for a casting operator is inherent in the function name.) Also notice the const keyword after the argument list. This specifies that the object to be cast (the recipient of the request, a.k.a. *this) is not modified by the cast operation. Normally, the const keyword would precede the argument to which it applies. Since the argument we want to declare const doesn't appear in the argument list, we put the keyword at the end of the declaration.

The Charstr class defines only the operations necessary for our example. (A proper class would define the rest of the comparison operators, as well as concatenation, substrings, string searches, and more.) It may not be obvious why we need operator char* in our example. Its use occurs on the last line of the program:

```
puts (lines[i]); }
```

This statement calls puts, a function that accepts a char* and prints it to standard output, passing it lines[i], a Charstr. C++ automatically inserts a call to operator char* to convert lines[i] to the type of value puts expects.

Since we define a cast from Charstr to char*, why don't we have one to go the other way? The answer is that we have already done so with the Charstr constructor: Since it can accept a char* and create a Charstr from it, it serves the purpose of a casting operator.

There are some important restrictions in the use of operator overloading. You are not permitted to override operator behavior for built-in data types, to change the number of arguments to operators (no unary "=" or binary "!" operator), or to define additional operators (no "+−" operator). You can, if you wish, define operators that behave in surprising ways, like a "+" operator that modifies its arguments or that does subtraction. If you do this you deserve whatever horrible fate comes your way.

A Type of I/O

C++ includes a set of data types that use operator overloading to implement formatted input and output. The `iostream` package overloads the bit shift operators ">>" and "<<" for input and output, respectively. They offer a less efficient but more flexible and frequently more convenient alternative to the `stdio` (standard I/O) package C++ gets from C. This example shows the use of both I/O packages:

```
#include <stdio.h>
#include <iostream.h>

void main ()
{ int a = 1; float b = 2.5; char *c = "String";

  scanf ("%d", &a);
  printf ("%d, %f, %s", a, b, c);

  cin >> a;
  cout << a << ", " << b << ", " << c << endl; }
```

This example reads an integer value into the variable a and then prints the values of a (an `int`), b (a `float`) and c (a character string). `cin` and `cout` are streams that are attached to standard input and output. There is also a `cerr` stream attached to standard error.

Notice that the `iostream` code does not need a format string like `scanf` and `printf`. Instead it uses the types of the variables to determine formatting. This keeps us from making the common error of mismatches between directives in the format string and the arguments to the function:

```
printf ("%f, %s", a, b, c);
```

The `iostream` package also has the advantage of permitting new formatting functions to be written for user-defined data types, like this one for an `array` data type:

```
ostream& operator << (ostream& o, const array& a)
{ o << "(";
  for (int i = 0; i < size(a); i++) {
    if (i > 0)
      o << ", ";
    o << a[i]; }
  return o << ")"; }
```

With this operator defined, you can print an `array` as easily as we would an `int`:

```
#include <iostream.h>
#include "array.h"

void main ()
{ array a(10);
  for (int i = 0; i < 10; i++)
    a[i] = i + i * i;
  cout << a << endl; }
```

Running this program (with the rest of the `array` definition) produces the following:

```
(0, 2, 6, 12, 20, 30, 42, 56, 72, 90)
```

Similarly, we can create specialized input and output routines for each new data type we create. These are especially useful in debugging, since our print routine can provide just the information needed in the format that is most useful to us.

Class Templates

The template mechanism you used with function definitions can also be used with class definitions, letting you use one definition to create several classes which differ only in the types of data they manipulate. An example is this linked list class:

```
#include <iostream.h>
```

```
template <class Type>
class list {

  private:
   Type val;
   list *fwdptr;

  public:
   list (const Type new_value, list* next)
      { val = new_value; fwdptr = next; }
   Type value () const          { return val; }
   int is_eol () const          { return fwdptr == NULL; }
   list *next () const          { return fwdptr; }
   friend ostream& operator<< (ostream&, const list<Type>&);
};

template <class Type>
ostream& operator<< (ostream& o, const list<Type>& l)
{ o << "[";
   for (const list<Type> *n = &l; !n->is_eol();
       n = n->next())
     o << n->value() << " ";
   return o << n->value() << "]"; }
```

We can use this one definition to create linked lists for many different types of data. The following example creates and prints three lists for int, double and char* data:

```
#include <string.h>
#include <stdio.h>
#include "tstack.h"

void main ()
{ list<int>    *ilp = NULL;
   list<double> *dlp = NULL;
   list<char *> *clp = NULL;

   for (int i = 0; i < 10; i++) {
     ilp = new list<int> (i, ilp);
     dlp = new list<double> (i + i / 10.0, dlp);

     char chars[20];
     sprintf (chars, "%.2f!", dlp->value());
     clp = new list<char *> (strdup(chars), clp); }
   cout << (*ilp) << endl << (*dlp) << endl << (*clp) <<
   endl; }
```

Running this program produces the following:

```
$ tlist
[9 8 7 6 5 4 3 2 1 0]
[9.9 8.8 7.7 6.6 5.5 4.4 3.3 2.2 1.1 0]
[9.90! 8.80! 7.70! 6.60! 5.50! 4.40! 3.30! 2.20! 1.10!
0.00!]
```

NOTE

Notice that when you refer to a `list` type in your code you must always include the complete type: `list<int>`. Unlike functions, data types in C++ do not support overloading. Also note that a template definition does not give you the ability to create a single list that can handle values of multiple types.

Classes of Exceptions

Abstract data types can also be combined very naturally with exceptions. Instead of reporting an exception with a character string, you can return an object with more detail on the specific conditions that caused the problem. Here is a definition for a division by zero exception. It includes a member function for generating a formatted error message:

```
class ZeroDivideError {
  private:
    int d1, d2;
  public:
    ZeroDivideError (int a, int b)
      { d1 = a; d2 = b; }
    void report (ostream& o)
      { o << "Division by zero: " << d1 << " / " << d2 <<
        endl; }
};
```

When you detect a problem you signal it by throwing a `ZeroDivide-Error` object:

```
int div (int a, int b)
{ if (b != 0)
    return a / b;
  else
    throw ZeroDivideError (a, b); }
```

The exception handler can detect specific types of exceptions. Here we add a handler for `ZeroDivideError` that uses the class's `report` member function to print the error message to the standard error stream:

```
void main ()
{ try {
    printdiv (57, 3);
    printdiv (5, 2);
    printdiv (3, 0);
    printdiv (10,3); }
  catch (DivByZeroError &err) {
    err.report (cerr); }
  printf ("That's all, folks!"); }

$ div2
57 / 3 = 19
5 / 2 = 2
Division by zero: 3 / 0
That's all, folks!
```

C++ exceptions and abstract data types also combine to solve a major problem with setjmp and longjmp, functions that C programmers use to implement non-local exits: releasing resources held by the functions that are being exited. If we open a file or allocate a chunk of memory in a function and then exit using an exception, how do we make sure that the file is closed or the memory is freed?

The answer can be found in class destructors. C++ guarantees that destructors will be called for any object that goes out of scope, even if it happens as the result of an exception. For example, we can write a trivial class that will automatically close an open file:

```
#include <stdio.h>

class AutoClose {
 private:
  FILE *fp;

 public:
  AutoClose (FILE *f)    { fp = f; }
  ~AutoClose ()          { if (fp != NULL) fclose(fp); }
};
```

We create a new AutoClose variable right after we open each file:

```
{ fp = fopen (SAVE_FILE, "r");
  if (fp == NULL) {
    if ((fp = fopen (SAVE_FILE, "w")) == NULL) {
      printf ("Can't create %s\n", SAVE_FILE);
      return; }
    printf ("File %s does not exist - creating it\n",
            SAVE_FILE); }

  AutoClose ac1(fp);
```

As soon as the block containing the declaration of ac1 is exited the file pointed to by fp will be closed. Even a thrown exception won't leave the file open. We can use simple classes like this to guarantee that every resource we allocate gets cleaned up at the appropriate time.

Summary

What we have seen in this section is only a subset of C++'s facilities for creating new kinds of objects. In many cases the ability to define new abstract data types is all we need to build our applications. Abstract data types are also easy to reuse, which makes them important in improving the productivity of development teams working on a single application or sharing code across multiple applications.

C++ As an Object-Oriented Language (Finally!)

In this last section we cover the facilities C++ provides that go beyond data abstraction into an object-oriented programming language. First, we'll take a moment to explain what we mean by the term object-oriented and what a language needs to qualify.

Like data abstraction, object-orientation begins with classes and objects. A class or data type specifies the structure (the slots or data members) and behavior (the methods or member functions) shared by every object that belongs to that class. Every instance of a class has exactly the same set of data members and the same set of functions that operate on it.

To this object-orientation adds the concept of inheritance. Inheritance permits new classes to be defined in terms of existing ones. These child classes may define new data members and member functions, in addition to those they inherit from their parent class. A child class may also have different behavior associated with a particular member function than it inherits from the parent. However, child classes may not delete structure or behavior that they inherit; they may only add to or modify it.

Inheritance makes it possible to build hierarchies of related classes and share much of their structure and behavior. For example, a set of different types of motor vehicles might be built on top of a common ancestor, with everything sharable defined in the parent and everything unique in the children:

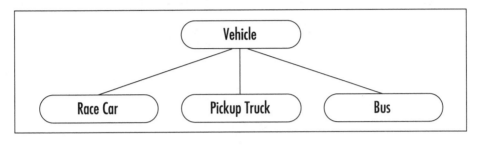

FIGURE 1.4

Note that we are using the term *inheritance* differently than we do in normal speech. Generally we think of characteristics inherited from individual to individual: my mother's eyes or my father's wide feet. Object-oriented languages use inheritance to describe characteristics inherited by groups from higher level groups: All mammals have spinal columns; dolphins are mammals; dolphins inherit all of the attributes of mammals, including the spinal column.

Object-orientation also demands polymorphism, the ability for a single procedure to operate on many different types of objects. Some object-oriented languages provide only a compile-time kind of polymorphism that resembles C++ overloading. Other languages can defer the choice of member function to call until runtime. Such languages can be used to write generic functions that switch their behavior based on the different types of objects they are given.

Object-oriented languages differ in the other facilities they support. Most provide some scheme for creation and initialization of new objects and for reclaiming their space when they are no longer in use. These range from C++, with its constructors, destructors and customizable new and delete operators, to languages like Smalltalk and Lisp, with their sophisticated garbage collectors.

Languages also vary in their support for encapsulation: the ability to customize inherited behavior by adding pre- or postprocessing to it. C++ is relatively weak in this regard, while Smalltalk's super-send and the Common Lisp Object System's :BEFORE, :AFTER and :AROUND methods make it easy to partially override inherited behavior.

Some languages, C++ among them, support multiple inheritance. Multiple inheritance permits a class to inherit the characteristics of several existing classes, as in the case of an amphibious car that has the properties of both car and boat:

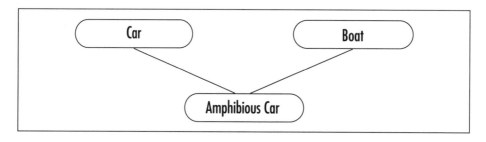

FIGURE 1.5

(Multiple inheritance is used in few C++ programs and necessary in even fewer. Dr. Stroustrup refused to include this feature in C++ until he was convinced that it was needed and could be implemented well and efficiently. There are those who believe he gave in too soon.)

Some object-oriented languages permit the behavior of a class to change during program execution. Some even permit an object to change from one class to another, with a corresponding change in its structure. Aside for their use in exploratory programming or to model a caterpillar's metamorphosis into a butterfly neither facility is of general use. C++ supports neither.

An Object Example

To understand C++'s implementation of objects we will consider a graphics application. This program will manipulate many kinds of shapes: circles, squares, triangles, rhombuses and so on. All of these shapes have some common structure: the position of the object's center and a color. We will also want to maintain all of our shapes on a long linked list, so each shape will contain a pointer to the next shape in the list.

Our shapes also have a common set of interfaces: a function to draw the shape on the screen, a function to erase the shape, a function to move the shape to a new location and one to rotate the shape in place. With so much in common, it seems logical to build our shapes around a common base class:

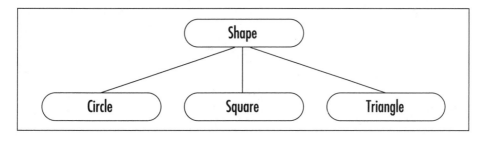

FIGURE 1.6

The Shape class defines all of the structure shared by all shapes:

```
class Shape {

private:
  Shape *next;

 protected:
  Point center;
  Color col;

 public:
  Shape (Point, Color, Shape *=NULL);
  ~Shape();
};
```

In addition to the private and public member categories we saw earlier, Shape uses a new category for its center and col data members: protected. A protected member is accessible to members of this class and its children. A private member like the next pointer is accessible only to members defined in Shape itself.

Each class based on Shape identifies its parent class at the beginning of the class statement. Here's a declaration for the Circle class, along with definitions for the move and rotate member functions:

```
class Circle : public Shape {

 protected:
  float radius;

 public:
```

```
Circle (Point, Color, radius=1, Shape *=NULL);

void move(Point to)   { erase(); center = to; draw(); }
void erase();
void draw();
void rotate(double)   { }
};
```

Each Circle object will contain four slots: the next, center and col members it inherits from Shape and the radius slot defined on Circle. next is accessible to members of Shape, center and col to members on Shape or Circle and radius only to members of Circle.

Every child class of Shape will define the same basic set of member functions:

```
void move(Point to);
void erase();
void draw();
void rotate(double);
```

Some of these functions will even be implemented the same way in each class. Every Shape will move itself by first erasing itself from its present location, changing the value of center and then redrawing itself in its new location:

```
void move(Point to)   { erase(); center = to; draw(); }
```

Of course, the function used to erase and draw a Circle will be different than the ones used for a Rectangle.

In addition to reusing the implementation of common routines like move, we would like to be able to write generic code that can operate on any Shape:

```
void main ()
{ Point p(20,17), q(5,73);
  Shape *sp = new Circle(p, 5);
  do_something(sp);
  /* At this stage does sp point to a Circle? */
  sp->draw();
  sp->move(q); }
```

C++ provides runtime polymorphism through its virtual function mechanism. If a class has virtual functions C++ will insert type information into every object of that class. This type field is used to select the right member function for an object, rather than relying on the type of the variable in which it is stored.

Here is a new definition for Shape:

```
class Shape {

 private:
  Shape *next;

 protected:
  Point center;
  Color col;

 public:
  Shape (Point, Color, Shape *=NULL);
  ~Shape();

  void move(Point to)  { erase(); center = to; draw(); }
  virtual void erase();
  virtual void draw();
  virtual void rotate(double);
};
```

With erase and draw declared as virtual functions we can define move once in Shape and have all of the other classes inherit it. move itself does not need to be virtual, since its calls to erase and draw will use runtime polymorphism to assure that the right functions are called.

C++ attempts to be as efficient as possible about polymorphism. In the example below it knows at compile time that the variable c contains a Circle. As a result the call to c.draw() is translated to a standard function call. Since move is not virtual, its call also becomes a standard function call. (The calls to erase and draw inside move must still be resolved at runtime.)

```
void main()
{ Circle c(p, green, 5.0);
  c.draw();
  c.move(q); }
```

If the class of an object can't be known at compile time and a virtual function is called, that call cannot be resolved until runtime. In this example both calls to draw are resolved at runtime. (The calls to move are still translated to standard function calls.)

```
void main()
{ Shape *sp = new Circle(p, red, 10.0);
  sp->draw();
  sp->move(q);
  delete sp;

  sp = new Square(p, blue, 5.0);
  sp->draw();
  sp->move(Point(25, 0)); }
```

With virtual functions we can write truly generic routines. For example, we might add the following function to the class definition for Shape to permit all of our shapes to be drawn with a single call:

```
void drawAll()
  { draw(); if (next) next->drawAll(); }
```

This function will work with any list of shapes we create:

```
void main ()
{ Shape *shape_list;

  shape_list = new Square (x, red, 10);
  shape_list = new Circle (y, blue, 5, shape_list);
  shape_list = new Rectangle(z, green, 8, 12, shape_list);

  shape_list->drawAll(); }
```

When drawAll is called it will use the type information to determine the right draw function to use for each object: first Rectangle::draw, then Circle::draw and finally Square::draw:

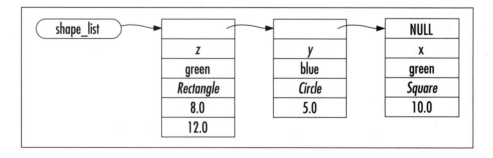

FIGURE 1.7

Hierarchies of Exceptions

Inheritance hierarchies are a natural way of describing exception classes. Here is a simple inheritance hierarchy for errors that might occur when working with a class of small integers:

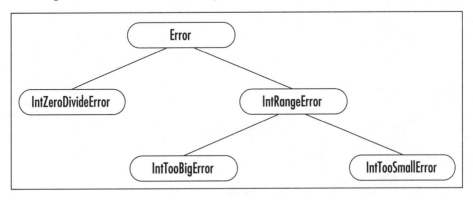

FIGURE 1.8

By grouping exceptions under a parent we permit users to write handlers for individual exceptions or entire categories of exceptions. We can also provide a virtual error reporting function for use by the exception handlers.

This piece of code employs an int100 class to perform arithmetic on integers in the range of zero to one hundred, catching and reporting any errors that occur:

```
#include "int100.h"

int main ()
{ int100 a, b;

  while (1) {
    try {
      cout << "Enter a and b: " << flush;
      cin >> a >> b;
      if (cin.eof())
        return 0;
      cout << a << " + " << b << " = " << (a + b) << endl;
      cout << a << " - " << b << " = " << (a - b) << endl;
      cout << a << " * " << b << " = " << (a * b) << endl;
      cout << a << " / " << b << " = " << (a / b) << endl;
    }
```

```
catch (IntRangeError &err) {
  err.report (cerr); }

catch (Error &err) {
  err.report (cerr);
  return 1; }}}
```

Here's a sample run:

```
$ int100

Enter a and b: 15 4
15 + 4 = 19
15 - 4 = 11
15 * 4 = 60
15 / 4 = 3

Enter a and b: 73 10
73 + 10 = 83
73 - 10 = 63
73 * 10 = Error in multiply: Value 730 greater than limit
100

Enter a and b: 16 25
16 + 25 = 41
16 - 25 = Error in subtract: Value -9 less than limit 0

Enter a and b: 14 0
14 + 0 = 14
14 - 0 = 14
14 * 0 = 0
14 / 0 = Error in divide: Zero divisor (dividend = 14)
$
```

Notice that this example attaches two catch blocks to the same try. The first
catch block handles all IntRangeError conditions (IntTooSmallError
and IntTooBigError) by reporting the error and continuing with the next
problem. The second handles any Error conditions not handled by the first
(IntZeroDivideError) by reporting the error and terminating execution.
The order of catch blocks is important: if these two were reversed the
IntRangeError handler would never execute.

C++ Is Not Smalltalk

To appreciate both object-oriented programming and C++'s approach to it, we must accept a painful truth: that C++ is not Smalltalk and that any attempt to apply Smalltalk design and programming approaches to C++ is doomed to disappointment.

The differences between these two languages are many: C++ is a strongly typed language, which gives it the ability to detect many errors during compilation that Smalltalk programmers can only detect during execution. Strong typing also permits most function calls to be resolved at compile time, avoiding extra overhead during execution.

C++ programs typically employ many small inheritance trees, rather than the single tree for all objects (including built-in data types) available in Smalltalk. All of this makes it more difficult to write truly generic code in C++, like a single linked list that can hold values of many different types.

C++ was designed for the C world of file level compilation and linking. Its memory requirements and execution time are close to those of C. Smalltalk systems typically trade some amount of runtime efficiency for greater programmer productivity. C++ was designed less to improve productivity of individual developers than to reduce integration and maintenance efforts of groups of developers working on large projects.

Finally, the biggest difference of all: Smalltalk is object-oriented from the ground up. As we have seen, C++ offers benefits both to object-oriented developers and to procedural developers who just want a better C.

ADDING IT ALL UP

A programming language is more than the sum of its individual features. The benefits of C++ go beyond the advantages of specific language details. Foremost among these is ease of integration. A project is typically only half done when all of the developers have completed their individual modules. Pulling all of those modules together and dealing with all of the incompatibilities can take just as long as it did to write them.

Teams working in C++ can reduce integration time dramatically. By taking advantage of C++ classes and hiding their implementation behind private members, they can define solid interfaces to their objects and be confident that everyone adhered to those interfaces. Well-defined interfaces can reduce much of the integration headache caused by inconsistent manipulation of the internal structure of data.

The benefits to integration recur when an application needs to be maintained. If any changes need to be made to the internal workings of a class, the class declaration provides a complete list of those function which have knowledge of those internal workings and might need to be modified. This is both simpler and faster than having to go through the entire program looking for places where such knowledge might be buried.

Classes with clean, separable interfaces and implementation also promote code reuse. There are C++ class libraries available for purchase, as well as free libraries from a number of different sources. With inheritance and encapsulation it becomes possible to take advantage of the work of others and customize it for our particular requirements.

Object-oriented programming promises to help us write simpler, better organized, more understandable and more maintainable code, promises that were once made for structure programming. The ability of a specific language to deliver on this promise depends on much more than its ability to support objects. The many languages contained in C++ make it a good choice for developers, whatever their stand in the great object debate.

FIRST ENCOUNTER WITH C++

Steven Ross

INTRODUCTION

When a C programmer first encounters C++, certain parts of the language make a great deal of sense and others are a complete mystery. Most people have developed a learning style that allows them to grasp familiar concepts before going on to unfamiliar territory. Consequently, the C programmer may choose a set of C++ features that do not immediately enhance productivity.

This chapter started out when I wandered by Denis Gilbert's office to complain about something or other. (Denis is the Business Unit Manager for Microsoft Visual C++ Business Unit.) The phone rang and he listened for a while, then he turned to me and said, "Steve, you know something about C++, don't you?" I innocently replied that I did, and was signed up to do a talk at C++ World. I have since presented the same talk at several Software Development Conferences, and each time have received invaluable feedback from the attendees.

The original goal of this information was to explain what sort of problems an accomplished C programmer could expect when moving to C++. In talking to you, and in revisiting this material, I've discovered that it's... well, to put it bluntly, it's hard to talk about C++ without talking about C++. One of the advantages of having this set in print is that you can underline a section of technical nonsense, look in some authoritative reference and understand it, then come back to my material. But, be forewarned, my material is littered with lots of "C++ness." Don't let *virtual functions*, *constructors*, or *inheritance* intimidate you. If you don't understand the exact implications of something in here, as I said, underline it, read by it, and look it up in your favorite C++ language reference.

Following that thought a bit, I'd like to encourage you *not* to take this chapter as more than a thumbnail sketch of places to remain alert as you learn C++. Nothing teaches like experience, and if you approach that learning process forearmed with this and other information contained in this book, I'm confident you'll find C++ a far preferable language to C.

THE C++ RICH FEATURE SET

When programmers learn C++ and the object-oriented programming model, they do so with the following goals in mind:

◆ Improve software quality

◆ Speed development

◆ Reduce bug count

◆ Decrease the bug-find time

The previous list is a broad-brush description of the advantages of object-oriented programming. However, learning the object-oriented "religion" at the same time one is assimilating the syntactic and semantic differences between C and C++ can be confusing. A neophyte C++ programmer may write less readable code than if he or she were writing in C. Furthermore, new C++ programmers are almost certain to compromise design efficiency or extensibility.

WHAT *Is* AN OBJECT?

There is a good deal of literature dedicated to object-oriented programming and design. This literature tends to offer only the slightest hint of how to identify and implement meaningful objects for your own problem domain. One of the most offensive examples of this was a book that stated (and I'm paraphrasing) "objects are everywhere." As a C programmer, it can be particularly frustrating to read something like that, only to return to an object-oriented design that isn't quite working out.

Object-oriented programming, more than anything else, is an exercise in patience. Most programmers don't get it right at first. Patience, however, is rewarded with an ability to pick objects that describe meaningful programmatic elements. A particularly good way to learn object-oriented design is to derive classes from a well-designed class library. This will lead you to think about why that class library is good and what sorts of design decisions you might have made differently.

A more detailed discussion of picking out objects, together with a few practical examples, is presented later in this chapter (after we get through the nuts and bolts of what C++ *is*).

COMMONLY ASKED QUESTIONS

There is a set of questions I frequently hear concerning "taking the plunge" into C++. Here are the answers I usually give.

Q: How long does it take to learn C++? Estimates on the time to become proficient with C++ vary. I've heard numbers like 4 to 6 months fairly frequently. My observation is that a good C programmer who spends this much time with C++ is very likely to become a decent C++ programmer. Becoming a C++ wizard can take a bit longer. Note that this is not total dead time where no work is getting done—it's just that even great C programmers don't hit full steam with C++ for a while.

Q: Can any C programmer learn C++? My answer has always been yes. C++ is different but anybody with an open mind and a desire to learn can become proficient in C++. There is a prevailing sentiment that only the brightest computer scientists should really use C++. In practical application, the new features that C++ adds are extremely effective at reducing the number of errors that "sneak" into code. This is significant because it leads me to believe we have a more helpful compiler—one that catches errors far earlier in the development process.

Q: Are C++ programs slower than C programs? Not inherently so. Or, rather, not so much that you'd notice. Quantifying something like this is difficult because a C program compiled with a C++ compiler or translator doesn't use any of the C++ features that might affect speed. At the same time, using C++ features precludes compilation with a C compiler. In any case, you can't get a good apples-to-apples comparison. The original mission of C++ was to have performance attributes very similar to those of C. A few features of C++ lead to slightly slower programs in isolated areas, but overall your programs should be just fine.

Q: Are C++ programs bigger (execution working set) than C programs? Generally, yes. The footprint of a C++ program is often somewhat heftier than a similar program written in C. As with the previous question, a good apples-to-apples comparison is difficult to obtain, but if you use C++ as it was meant to be used, you will incur "behind the scenes" overhead that you wouldn't have incurred using C. The other side of this particular coin is that the overhead isn't useless baggage: It provides you with capabilities you wouldn't have had in C.

The answers to this and the previous question might be "your mileage may vary," because how wisely you use C++ will ultimately have a great impact on the size and speed attributes of your application. It's been said that with C++, you don't write the same code as often so you have more time to tune the code you *do* write.

Q: Generally speaking, do you write fewer lines of C++ than C for the same application? The short answer is yes. C++ tends to favor code-factoring, so you will recognize two immediate benefits: 1. fewer lines of source code; and 2. a single implementation of a given service instead of multiple ad-hoc instantiations of the same code. If you elect to use a class library as the basis of your application, the answer is yes! You'll write far fewer lines of code.

PROBLEMS IN TRANSITION FROM C TO C++

Programmers have expectations when moving from one language to another, presumably "better," language: Improved productivity; more compact code; more robust systems.... These expectations are not always met. In addition to some initial disappointment because of expectations not being met, the learning experience is made more difficult by the fact that C and C++ *look* almost identical. There are semantic differences that can be very difficult for experienced C programmers to understand because they are so used to looking at these constructs. Consider, as a simple example, the subtle difference between initialization and assignment shown below:

```
/* C code */
int a = 7;
```

All C programmers know that a is simply being defined and assigned a value of 7. There are no other side effects. In C++, however, you have two different cases whose syntaxes look very similar:

```
// C++ code
MyType t = 7;    // This is an initialization

t = 9;           // This is an assignment
```

The mechanisms for accomplishing assignment and initialization are completely different in C++. Assignment is carried out using a special function called the *assignment operator*, whereas initialization is carried out using a function called a *constructor* (constructors are explained in more detail later). To muddy the waters still further, these functions may either be compiler-supplied *or* user-defined, so the difference between an assignment and an initialization can be critical. The C++ code, therefore, can be viewed as follows:

```
MyType t;        // This is fake because of course the constructor
t.MyType( 7 );   // is called implicitly when the object is created.

t.operator=( 9 );
```

NOTE

Although I've faked the above code, the difference between C and C++ is that in C++ you are implicitly calling functions but you don't *see* those function calls.

The basis of C++'s object-orientedness is the *class*. You'll soon discover that a `class` is just another name for a `struct`. As a savvy C programmer, you'll look at the syntax and some examples and pretty soon say "I get it"! Although what I've said about classes being structs in disguise is true, what I didn't say is that both classes and structs have lots of new capabilities. Among these capabilities are

♦ **Functions.** Structs and classes can contain functions as well as data. "Contain" is an odd word in this context because the code does not occupy space in objects of your new type; however, the code is taken to refer to an object of this new type.

♦ *User-defined operator functions*, so that you can assign semantics to the familiar C operators.

♦ *User-defined conversion functions* (a special case of the above), so that you can precisely control how data of one type is converted to another type.

♦ *Construction and destruction functions* that perform orderly initialization and cleanup of user-defined type objects.

Let's look at an innocent class that has the potential to cause a good C programmer hours of headache:

```
class String
{
public:
    String( const char *szInit );          // Construct from char *
    const char *operator const char *();   // Convert to const char *
    int operator==( String& s );           // Compare two Strings
// Other member functions and state variables
};
```

The previous class declaration provides a method to construct a String from a char * so you can write code like:

```
String str1 = "Hello, world!";
```

It also provides a means to get a char * from an object of type String for use in C run-time functions like this:

```
if( strchr(str1, 'q') )     // strchr takes a char * first argument so
    Quit();                 // the conversion operator function is
                            // called.
```

In practice, this class will probably not break code right away, but if your program contains the following code it breaks:

```
String str = "Hello";   // Define a string
if( str == "Hello" )
    // Do something
```

The problem with the previous code is that in the comparison, there are multiple options available to the compiler: The equivalence test can invoke the operator== function by constructing a temporary variable of type String from "Hello", then binding it to a reference.

```
// Option 1 shown in terms of function calls
if( str.operator==( String("Hello") )
```

The compiler detects another equally acceptable option: It can obtain a
`const char *` from `str` using the conversion operator. It can then use
pointer comparison to detect if they are equivalent (the programmer probably didn't mean this).

```
// Option 2 shown in terms of function calls
if( str.operator const char *() == "Hello" )
```

This, then, is an ambiguity the compiler cannot resolve and results in a
compile-time error. Such ambiguities can be foreseen after some experience, but early in the learning process they are to be expected.

To avoid such ambiguities, consider the kinds of conversions you'll
need very carefully before supplying them. (This includes both conversion
by construction and conversion using conversion, or "cast" operators.)

CONSTRUCTORS

You've already heard some things about constructors. Here is a more complete discussion. The orderly construction and destruction facilities provided
by C++ are features experienced C programmers appreciate immediately. By
writing constructors and destructors, programmers can provide for complete
initialization of every object in the program, and for the orderly take-down
of these objects (destructors are covered in the following section).

The syntax for a constructor is:

```
classname::classname(arg-listopt)
```

So, for my `String` class from above, I can declare constructors in the class
declaration as follows:

```
class String
{
public:
    String();           // Declare a default (no args) constructor
    String(const char *); // Declare a constructor with args
};
```

The definition of these constructors might be

```
String::String()
{
    // Do something like allocate memory
}

String::String(const char *sz)
{
    // Do something and initialize from sz
}
```

It's quite common to have more than one function—especially constructor function—with the same name, as shown above. This is called *overloading* and is discussed later in this chapter.

C programmers face two temptations in writing constructors:

◆   The temptation to ascribe too much responsibility to the constructor. The constructor's responsibility is to "make an object out of a bunch of raw bits." Just that, and no more. A constructor that has sweeping side-effects is normally poor programming practice because constructors can be called by the compiler when you least expect it. This can introduce exposure to buggy behavior or inefficiency.

◆   The temptation to write a constructor to create an object of a user-defined type from just about any other type imaginable. Conversion by construction is not bad, but it is important to define what sort of conversions make sense up front.

The first of these points contains words to live by. You should seriously limit what your constructors do because every time an object of your class type is created, whether temporary or not, the constructor is called. As an example of why side-effects in constructors can be troublesome, consider the following code:

```
#include <iostream.h>

class T
{
public:
    T() { cout << "constructing object\n"; }
    T(const T&) { cout << "constructing by copying object\n";
```

```
    }
    ~T() { cout << "destructing object\n"; }
};

T func()
{
    T aT;

    return aT;
}

void main()
{
    T mainT;

    mainT = func();
}
```

The previous program doesn't seem to do much—and in fact, it *doesn't* do much—but the following output shows that it makes more function calls than you might imagine:

```
constructing object
constructing object
constructing by copying object
destructing object
destructing object
destructing object
```

Imagine what would happen to your program's efficiency if these constructors did things like opening files and performing a read-ahead!

If you look at the declaration of the previous constructors, you'll notice that they don't specify a return type. That's because constructors can't return a value. Put bluntly, there is no direct way to tell the client code that construction failed. There are a few ways for the application to discover that construction failed. For example,

◆ Have the constructor throw an exception on failure

◆ Move to a two-phase construction architecture

The cleanest of these alternatives is to throw an exception. It is cleanest because it places the least burden on the user code (that is, the client of your class), but not all implementations of C++ support exception handling.

Using Exceptions to Indicate Failure

```
// Constructor failure example  #1
// Skeleton for a fictitious "String" class that allocates memory
// on the fly for the string it stores.
class MemoryException{/* some members */};

class String
{
public:
    String() { szBuffer = NULL; }
    String(const char *szInitFrom) throw(MemoryException);

private:
    char *szBuffer;
};

String::String(const char *szInitFrom) throw(MemoryException)
{
    szBuffer = new char[strlen(szInitFrom) + 1]; // Allow for '\0'

    // If the buffer was not allocated properly, fail
    if( szBuffer == 0 )
        throw MemoryException();
}
```

The above code has a few new syntactic wrinkles. Instead of using malloc to allocate memory, I've used the new operator. C++ has a built-in operator for memory allocation and a corresponding one, delete, for freeing memory. These operators can be overridden for memory-leak tracking and so on. Like malloc, the new operator returns a zero value if it can't find a suitable block of memory. Our program tests for this condition and "throws an exception." An exception is not an error so much as an exceptional condition. In this case it was insufficient memory. To see how this exception might be processed in user code, examine the next code snippet:

```
try
{
    String aString = "Hello";
    // Other statements
}
catch(MemoryException m)
{
    // Not enough memory
    cerr << "Not enough memory to continue\n";
    Cleanup();
    return;
}
```

Everything in the try block is in what's considered a *guarded block*. That is, you have programmatically stated that you know something might go wrong and you will specifically handle one of these things: a MemoryException. That's what you said in the catch statement. The flow of control is that if there is enough memory, the catch block is not executed. If the out-of-memory exception occurs, however, none of the other statements after the declaration of aString are executed, and execution transfers to the first statement in the catch block.

> Throwing exceptions is not limited to use inside constructors. It is, however, a complicated syntax compared to the parsimonious C syntax.

NOTE

C++ exception handling is one of those areas where "behind the scenes" overhead can affect your program's performance. Here are two ways:

◆ The compiler has to track all objects that are allocated on the frame (automatic variables). This can be expensive both in terms of setup and takedown, in terms of memory footprint, and in terms of the raw number of instructions required to perform the task. This tracking is done so that all objects can be destroyed correctly if an exception occurs

◆ Compilers may not be able to optimize as aggressively where guarded blocks are concerned. Code motion and safe exception handling don't mix too well

Using Two-Phase Construction Architectures

Two-phase construction has been a hotly debated topic in some circles. Using this technique you write constructors that perform essentially default actions. These constructors are highly unlikely to fail because of their simplicity and near zero resource demands. The first phase is called "construction." The second phase, which completes the process, requires the client program to call a Create function to perform initialization. The responsibility of the Create function is

1. **Check the state of the object.** If it is not internally consistent, return a failure code.

2. **Initialize the object.** If any step of initialization fails, return a failure code.

Naturally, the idea of writing two functions to perform the work of one is unpopular. It does, however, provide a safe implementation and excellent performance. Consider the following example:

```
// Constructor failure example  #2
// Skeleton for a fictitious "String" class that allocates memory
// on the fly for the string it stores.

class String
{
public:
    String() { szBuffer = NULL; }
    int Create(const char *szInitFrom);

private:
    char *szBuffer;
};

int String::Create(const char *szInitFrom)
{
    szBuffer = new char[strlen(szInitFrom) + 1]; // Allow for '\0'

    // A return value of 0 means that the allocation failed;
    // any non-zero value means that the allocation succeeded.
    return ( szBuffer != 0 );
}

// ...and in the client code...

    String aString;      // Next statement can't fail,
                         // so not guarded by a try{}

    if( aString.Create("Hello") == 0 )
    {
        cerr << "Not enough memory to continue\n";
        Cleanup();
        return;
    }
```

What Part of an Object Is Being Constructed?

Another area that is confusing about constructors is what part of the object the constructor is operating on. Objects are constructed from the "inside out." That is, they are constructed from the base class, in inheritance graph order, to the most derived class. No constructor can perform operations on a part of the object of a more derived type than its own. Therefore, virtual function calls in constructors are interpreted to mean: "call the virtual function for the object of the type currently under construction." Consider the following class hierarchy:

```
class A{};

class B : public A {};

class C : public B {};
```

In the following diagram, the conceptual memory layout of an object of type **C** is as pictured at right. When the constructors are called, they are called as follows:

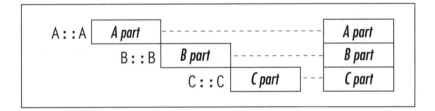

DESTRUCTORS

Destructors allow your class to clean up any resources your object has allocated at the end of its "duration" or lifetime. This typically involves freeing memory, closing files, and other tidying-up activities. The syntax for destructors is

```
classname::~classname()
```

An example serves better:

```
class DtorEx
{
    ~DtorEx();    // Declaration
};

DtorEx::~DtorEx()
```

```
{
    // some destruction semantics
}
```

Destructors are almost exactly the inverse of constructors, but note the *almost*. As with constructors, destructors destroy only the part of the original object that is currently being destroyed. Objects are destroyed from the "outside in"; that is, from the most derived part of the object down to the base as shown below (for an object of type **C**, described in the previous section):

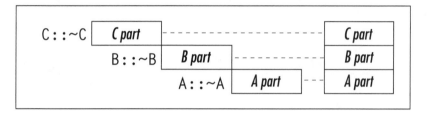

Unlike constructors, however, destructors can (and often should) be declared as virtual. By using a virtual destructor, an object can invoke the correct destructor, even if it is referenced using a pointer to a base class. Note, however, that destructors are among those functions that the compiler can "quietly" generate calls to without your expressly coding one. This is a point to bear in mind if your destructor does lots of work.

Inline Functions

Inline functions are wonderful for code tuning. For the C programmer, however, there is a temptation to declare functions as `inline` without examining whether it's really called for. Possibly one of the worst functions to declare as `inline` is a constructor—especially a default or copy constructor—because these functions are called behind the scenes by the compiler. That means that the code expansion can be horrendous.

Use inline functions for the following reasons:

♦ Type-safe wrapper functions or accessor functions.

♦ Short functions that you discover, by using a profiling tool, are causing performance hits because of the function-call overhead.

When you inline a function, good compilers have more opportunities for optimization. You also eliminate the overhead of a function call. These optimizations can produce dramatic performance increases for very short functions. For a longer function the impact of function call overhead and the opportunities for global optimization is outweighed by the impact on code size. Most optimizers work only on code in a given function. That means if your function is out of line (in a separate function), as opposed to inline, the chance for a simple optimization might be missed. Consider the following code snippet, which calls a function, fact, that recursively evaluates the factorial of its argument:

```
inline int fact( int );

void main()
{
    int i = fact( 5 );
    cout << "Factorial of 5 is " << i << endl;
}

int fact( int nF )
{
    return (nF > 1) ? nF * fact(nF - 1) : 1;
}
```

This is an $O(n)$ algorithm—that is, its expected completion time is expected to correspond directly with n, which can be a reasonably large number for higher values of n. Although it is a trivial example, it is a useful example of how inlining can move the burden of this evaluation into the compiler:

```
;|*** void main()
;|*** {
; Line 10
    *** 000000  55              push    bp
    *** 000001  8b ec           mov bp,sp
    *** 000003  83 ec 02        sub sp,2
;    i = -2
;|***       int i = fact( 5 );
; Line 11
    *** 000006  b8 78 00        mov ax,120   ;0078H
;|***       cout << "Factorial of 5 is " << i << endl;
```

As you can see above, the code emitted for line 11 simply moves the value 120 into the ax register; the compiler took the following steps:

◆ It inlined the function `fact`. This was done to a depth of 5, because the compiler chosen for this example is capable of inlining recursive functions.

◆ It then was able to use constant propagation to substitute 5 for `nF` in the first conditional, 4 in the next, and so on.

◆ Finally, it noticed that the resultant expression, 5 * 4 * 3 * 2, is a constant, so it evaluated that and came up with 120.

As mentioned earlier, this is a contrived example, but it serves to illustrate how relatively small functions can be inlined and how the optimizer might take advantage of the inline expansion.

OVERLOADING FUNCTIONS

Overloading functions is a process whereby you can write more than one function with exactly the same name that takes different argument lists. This may seem like a snooze so far, but consider an issue like writing a `Print` function. In C, typical approaches were

1. To write multiple specialized functions with different names such as `PrintChar`, `PrintPChar`, `PrintShort`, `PrintUShort`, and so on. This works great just as long as you can remember what you *called* the correct `Printxxx` function.

2. To write a single "does everything" function like `printf` that interprets varying amounts of anonymous-typed data according to a user-supplied format specification. Again, this works well, but has the drawbacks of being error-prone and completely inextensible.

C++ overloading is really much more like the first of these options: You write a lot of functions; you just don't give them different names! The trick is, you tell the compiler to print and it figures out if there is a `Print` function available for the object. What you're doing is moving the problem of remembering all of the possible names of Print functions from your plate onto the compiler's.

At first glance, this seems like a godsend: figure out neat groups of like functionality and write a cluster of overloaded functions. In many cases, it's that easy, but in some cases, you'll have difficulties. While it's hard to say exactly what will go wrong, you must remember that the rules the compiler uses for selecting an overloaded function are exacting and complex. If you are not in sync with the way your compiler performs overload resolution, you might get some surprising results. A simplified statement of how overload resolution is performed is contained in the next sections, "Argument Type Differences," "Restrictions on Sets of Functions," "Declaration Matching," and "Argument Matching"(and even simplified it isn't easy).

Argument Type Differences

The arguments to a function are said to be of different types if they take *different initializers*. I've emphasized this because, for example, a given type and a reference to that type take the same initializer (references are discussed later in this chapter). In code

```
void func(int n);
void func(int& n);
```

are considered the same because int and reference to `int` (`int&`) take the same initializer. Other pieces of the language, such as `const` and `volatile`, when qualifying a reference modify this rule slightly. For example, `const char *` is considered a discretely different argument type from `char *`.

Another example of two derivative types that are considered the same is "array of" and "pointer to." That is, `char *` and `char []` are considered the same.

Restrictions on Sets of Functions

These are kind of "rules to overload by."

◆ No two functions in a set of overloaded functions may have the same argument list. (This is being relaxed somewhat in newer compilers that can overload solely based on return type.)

◆ Don't rely on a compiler implementing overloading solely on the basis of return type (yet).

◆ typedefs don't define new types; they are synonyms for types in the existing system. Consider the following code:

```
typedef int * PINT;

BOOL Print( PINT pi );
BOOL Print( int *pi );  // Error, identical in type system
```

◆ enums are distinct types; you can overload on them. Consider this code:

```
enum first  { left, right, center };
enum second { left, right, center };

BOOL Print( char *szArg, first Alignment );
BOOL Print( char *szArg, second Alignment );
```

Although both first and second clearly describe the same kind of data, they are considered different types.

Declaration Matching

This essentially refers to the compiler's process of figuring out the scope of the functions that might be overloaded. For example:

◆ If you declare a function in a base class and then in a derived class, you have not overloaded the function, you have hidden the base class implementation for all members of the derived class (and classes derived from that derived class)

```
class base
{
public:
void func();                  // no arguments
};

class derived : public base   // derived from base
{
public:
    void func(int);           // One argument of type int
};
```

```
void main()
{
    derived aDerived;
    aDerived.func();     // Error. This function is hidden
}
```

◆   Scopes nest, and the innermost declaration of a function is consid-
    ered the declaration against which matching takes place. The fol-
    lowing example illustrates this concept:

```
// Declare a couple of classes. Note the number of
// arguments the constructors take.
class RECT
{
public:
    RECT(int, int, int, int);
};

class POINT
{
public:
    POINT(int, int);
};

// Define two Draw functions
void Draw( RECT& s )
{
}

void Draw( POINT& upperLeft, POINT& lowerRight )
{
}

void main()
{
    // No nested redeclarations, so...
    Draw( RECT(3, 3, 10, 10) );          // OK
    Draw( POINT(3, 3), POINT(10, 10) );  // OK
    {
            // Redeclare in local scope
            void Draw(POINT& upperLeft,
                    POINT& lowerRight );

    Draw( POINT(3, 3), POINT(10, 10) );  // OK
    Draw( RECT(3, 3, 10, 10) );          // Error, hidden
    }
}
```

In the previous sample, instead of supplying variables (or *objects*) of the specified types, I created them on the fly. This is a common C++ coding practice, and it helps in creating exactly the type you want.

Argument Matching

Argument matching is the method most people consider when they think of overload resolution. As I said earlier, the resolution of a function name to an appropriate version of your function generally happens "magically"—that is, the compiler does it. But, as a programmer, it's still your responsibility to understand *how* this takes place so you can exert more precise control over the compiler's behavior.

To make this aforementioned "magic" occur, the following (conceptual) process occurs:

◆ The compiler examines sets of functions that are determined to be candidates for this overload. These candidates are determined using declaration matching. Functions are initially considered that are visible in the scope of the call and that have the same name.

◆ The compiler then eliminates those functions that have the wrong argument count from the candidate list.

◆ A set of candidate functions is created for each argument, positionally.

At this point, let's look at an example of a fictitious `Cash` type where you need to implement a function to add money to an account:

```
Cash& Add( Cash& amt, long increase );      // overload 1
Cash& Add( long increase, Cash& amt );      // overload 2
Cash& Add( Cash& amt, Cash& increase );     // overload 3
```

In the previous set of functions, you implement the cases where you are adding an integral value to a `Cash` object, a `Cash` object to an integral amount (commutative behavior), and two `Cash` objects. These seem like reasonable things to do, especially considering you can substitute `operator+` for Add and get proper semantics for the addition operator. Moving along, say you write the following code:

```
Cash OnHand, InBank;

InBank = Add(OnHand, 150);
```

What we're trying to do here is to add $150 to our cash on hand and store it in the bank (this bank is giving a $150 cash bonus with the first deposit!). The compiler constructs a list of candidate functions.

1. The compiler does declaration matching and discovers that all functions have the correct number of arguments and they are all visible at the point of the function call.

2. The compiler prunes the list of candidate functions to include only those whose first argument is of type Cash. That prunes out overload 2.

3. Then the compiler prunes the list constructed in step 2 to include only those whose second argument is of type int. This would normally produce an empty set, but there is a standard conversion from type int to type long, so the remaining function in the set is overload 1.

NOTE It is possible, especially in a language that allows for user-defined conversions, to have more than one function in the remaining set. This is considered an ambiguity, as the compiler has no good way of breaking ties—C++ does not implement a "do what I mean" operator.

Ambiguities are common problems and sometimes can be difficult to predict when you are implementing. The reason for this difficulty is that an ambiguity is not manifest until the point where this whole mechanism kicks into gear: the function call point. If a function is not called (say you defined an overloaded function you thought you might use later) or if it is not called with a particular set of arguments, then the ambiguity lies hidden, waiting to bite you later. Subtle changes in your environment—for example, adding a user-defined conversion to a class because you think it will clarify your code—can kick up a certain amount of dust elsewhere in your program in terms of ambiguous overloads.

Default Arguments

It may seem odd to treat a subject like default arguments in a section on function overloading, but I believe that in practice C++ provides two ways to overload functions: writing functions with different argument lists and writing functions with default arguments. In a C++ sense, only the first of these is called overloading. However, new C++ programmers do not always know they can write a function with default arguments that behaves just like *n* overloaded functions, where *n* is the number of default arguments + 1. By writing the function once and supplying sensible defaults, the programmer writes only one unit of code. Once that unit is tested, all of its functionality resides in the same place. This strategy eliminates some of the need for "helper" functions. Let's consider an example of how one might use default arguments to advantage (this example stolen from the Microsoft Foundation Classes):

```
LRESULT SendMessage(UINT message, WPARAM wParam = 0,
          LPARAM lParam = 0);
```

Notice that a good number of Microsoft Windows messages do not use the `wParam` or `lParam` arguments. User messages often follow this pattern. The above default argument usage might be

```
BOOL fChecked = (BOOL)SendMessage(BM_GETCHECK);
```

It the previous example, the last two parameters are not only unused, the documentation explicitly says "must be zero," so by supplying these sensible defaults, you are reducing the opportunity for error.

OVERLOADING OPERATORS

Overloading operators is probably better stated as "supplying user-defined operators." The primary reason for supplying a user-defined operator is to allow for easy manipulation of an object of user-defined type. Some user-defined types map well onto the arithmetic model that the C operators express, but many do not. A common problem new C++ programmers encounter is defining every possible operator, whether it makes sense or not. For example, what does it mean to multiply a `Window` by an `int`?

While this issue is hotly debated, there is a growing sentiment that the original semantic meaning of the operator should be retained in over-loaded operators. That is, you should use an overloaded operator when your user-defined type expresses an arithmetic concept. It is appropriate to use `operator+` to express translation on a `Rectangle` or `Point` type, but not (for example) a `Window`.

In addition to retaining the semantics, it is desirable to retain the original associativity and commutativity of the original operator. This can require some care in coding, especially when writing subscript and assignment operators.

One strategy that can help is to start out not overloading operators, but rather using operator-type functions such as `GetAt()`, `SetAt()`, `AddTo()`, and so on. These can later be wrapped by an inline overloaded operator without incurring additional overhead.

USING CONST

Many good C programmers are used to indicating that a variable is non-modifiable using the `const` keyword. `const` is a way of making a promise that a data item is nonmodifiable. Better, it is a way of having the compiler enforce that promise. C++ introduces some (at first) confusing new syntactic constructs related to the use of `const`. Consider the following two declarations for member functions:

```
char *MyType::GetBuffer() const;
const char *MyType::GetBuffer();
```

These two declarations are very different. In the first one, the programmer has promised that code in the `GetBuffer` function (or any function it calls) will not modify the *object*. The `const` keyword, then, applies to the `this` pointer. In the second declaration, `GetBuffer` is free to change the state of the object, but the returned value is a nonmodifiable `char *` (that is, it's a safe buffer).

The concept of "`const` correctness" is an important C++ issue because:

◆ The "constness" of an object is considered part of its type for compile-time type checking.

◆ Use of `const` on reference type arguments explicitly states the programmer's intent to pass a nonmodifiable object by reference.

◆ In many cases, a `const` object can replace a #`define` in a C program with a type-safe entity.

The best way to achieve `const`-correctness is to be explicit about everything that is to be `const`, including member functions. This can require some patience on the part of a C programmer who is unused to the seemingly disjoint semantic implications of applying `const` on functions as opposed to data.

You should always use `const` on objects (global and member data), and on return values that are never to be modified. Here are some tips on using the `const` keyword to modify the `this` pointer in function declarations. Consider the following member function declaration:

```
T SomeMemberFunc() const;
```

The previous declaration is a "promise" not to modify the object as a side-effect of `SomeMemberFunc`. The `const` applies to the object itself, and means that for the duration of the function, the object will not be changed. By making these syntactic promises, you can increase the robustness of your software because you are explicitly specifying under what circumstances your object can be changed. You are also making it possible for the compiler to detect the error, rather than relying on some run-time consistency tests or worse, black-box testing.

NOTE

Remember: The earlier in the development cycle an error is detected the less costly it is to fix.

Explicitly declare as `const`:

◆ All by-reference arguments that are not to be modified.

◆ All reference or pointer type return values that are not to be modified.

◆ All member functions that can promise not to have *any* side-effects on the object's state.

Designing `const`-correctness into a program is far less expensive from a development perspective than retrofitting an existing program. I recommend you make it a goal to incorporate this concept in all new code and when time permits, migrate it back into old code.

USING STATIC

static members are used in several cases:

◆ When a local object must persist beyond the scope of a given function (just as in C).

◆ When you want to constrain the linkage of an object to a given translation unit (just as in C).

◆ When a single instance of class-member data must be shared among all instances of the class.

The most important tricks to using static correctly are as follows:

◆ static data members are always *declared* in class scope but *defined* outside of class scope. For example:

```
class HasAStaticMember
{
public:
    static int aStaticMember;           // Declaration, not definition
};
int HasAStaticMember::aStaticMember = 5;  // Definition and initialization
```

◆ static member functions need not be associated with an object. So, for example, you can implement a Time class:

```
class Time
{
public:
    static time_t GetTime();
};
```

You can invoke the member function GetTime with or without an associated Time object:

```
time_t now = Time::GetTime();  // Invoke without associated object
Time theTime;
now = theTime.GetTime();       // Invoke with associated object
```

◆ Static member functions cannot access nonstatic member of their class because they do not have a `this` pointer. So, for example, the following code is erroneous:

```
class Time
{
public:
    static time_t SetTime(time_t t)
    {
            return m_lTime = t;   // Error: accessing nonstatic data
    }
private:
    time_t m_lTime;
};
```

However, by making m_lTime static, we can fix it to be correct:

```
class Time
{
public:
    static time_t SetTime(time_t t)
    {
            return m_lTime = t;          // Ok, m_lTime is static
    }
private:
    static time_t m_lTime;
};
time_t Time::m_lTime;
```

◆ Remember that global static objects are constructed prior to entering `main()`. They are destroyed after exit, usually as the result of `atexit` or `onexit` processing. Side-effects that result from construction or destruction, therefore, take place outside of traditional program boundaries. When writing a constructor or destructor, be aware that not every object in your program will be completely initialized. Here is an example:

```
#include <iostream.h>

class LogState
{
public:
    LogState(){ cout << "Constructing LogState object\n"; }
    ~LogState(){ cout << "Destructing LogState object\n"; }
};

LogState aLogState;
```

```
void main()
{
    cout << "Entering main\n";
    cout << "Exiting main\n";
}
```

Because aLogState is implicitly static, the resultant output is:

```
Constructing LogState object
Entering main
Exiting main
Destructing LogState object
```

The rule of thumb here is not to rely on any particular order of construction for global statics.

REFERENCES

References are a language element in C++ that does not exist in C. The declaration notation is similar to that for pointer types, except that where an asterisk is used for a pointer, an ampersand is substituted:

```
char *pChar;     // Pointer to char
char &rChar;     // Reference to char
```

Reference types are derivative types, like pointers. Unlike pointers, a reference type is accessed (syntactically) exactly like an object:

```
char aChar;
char &rChar = aChar;    // Reference bound to aChar
char *pChar = &aChar;   // Pointer pointing to aChar

aChar = 'z';            // Assign to object
*pChar = 'z';           // Assign through pointer
rChar = 'z';            // Assign through reference
```

The above three statements are identical in effect: They all put a z in the variable aChar. Note, however, that the pointer version requires explicit syntax (*pChar).

The underlying implementation of references is the same as pointers. The implications of this "under the hood" implementation are

◆ References can be less expensive to pass around as arguments, especially for large objects. They can, therefore, be used for some code tuning. There is an implicit ("trivial") conversion from any type to a reference to that type, perhaps for this reason. Consider this code snippet:

```
struct BigStruct
{
    // Lots of stuff
};
BigStruct aBigStruct;

func( &aBigStruct );
```

Most C programmers are used to calling functions, passing pointers because it reduces function calling overhead. With references, this can happen automatically!

```
void func( BigStruct &b );     // declaration

func( aBigStruct );            // Function call
```

In the example above, aBigStruct—an object—is converted to a reference to type BigStruct, then passed by reference to func.

◆ Function returns can be lvalues. That is, you can conveniently make an assignment to a function call:

```
int& GetX() { return m_x; }   // GetX returns member variable by reference

anObject.GetX() = 7;          // Assign to lvalue return
```

◆ Objects that appear to have been passed to a function by value can be passed by reference. They are, whatever the programmer's original intent, therefore modifiable unless explicitly declared as const.

Using the example func(aBigStruct), we passed an object using by-reference semantics. While convenient, it means that this object is implicitly modifiable in the function func. That is not immediately apparent to the C programmer's eye.

Reference types were originally implemented to make operator overloading possible. To ease into using references, you can start out using references only for operator overloading (where the operator has to return an lvalue) and copy constructors. After you are more comfortable with references, you can use them for tuning, but *always state your intent with respect to modifiability* (maintain const-correctness).

Don't Step on Your Objects

You already know that C++ classes are implemented "on top" of the C struct. In fact, earlier in this chapter, I said that a class is another name for a struct. Well, that's not exactly true. Classes can have behavior—functions—as well as data members. These functions normally don't take up any data space, but they have several implications. Most C programmers are used to file I/O where they suck a struct or array of structs into memory at one time as follows:

```
struct Example
{
    char c;
    DWORD  dwStuff;
    char   szMoreStuff[44];
}
Ex1, Ex2;

// ...intervening code...

nBytesRead = fread(&Ex1, nBuffers, sizeof(Example), fp);
```

We've all learned that for performance reasons compilers will generally lay out a structure like the one defined above as follows:

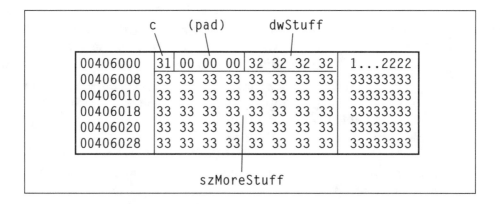

FIGURE 2.1 STRUCTURE LAYOUT IN C.

Of course, such a layout made writing data to disk and reading it back in perfectly safe, as they are inverse operations and rely on the same packing (hence, the same alignment pads). Extending our knowledge, it would seem perfectly sensible that the following code would work perfectly well:

```cpp
class Example
{
public:
    // Construction/Destruction
    Example();          // Implementation for these
    virtual ~Example(); // functions presumed elsewhere
private:
    char c;
    DWORD  dwStuff;
    char   szMoreStuff[44];
}
Ex1, Ex2;

// ...intervening code...

nBytesRead = fread(&Ex1, nBuffers, sizeof(Example), fp);
```

However, the layout of this structure can, and often *is* different from that of a raw struct. Why? Because C++ needs to keep tables for virtual functions and virtual base classes. In the previous case, I declared the destructor to be virtual—a common thing to do in C++. The resultant layout in the Microsoft Visual C++ (for Windows NT) implementation is

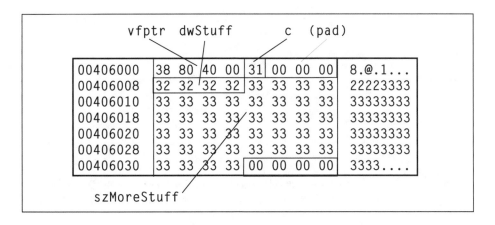

FIGURE 2.2 STRUCTURE LAYOUT IN C++.

In contrast to Figure 2.1, you'll notice that the compiler has inserted some extra stuff in the memory associated with this object. Specifically, the compiler has inserted a "hidden" field in your structure to point to the virtual function table. As a result, if you treat the C++ object the same as a struct in an fread, you'll trample the virtual function pointer, causing two problems: You won't be able to call your virtual destructor; and the data you read in will be in the wrong place, offset by `sizeof(__vfptr)`.

This problem can occur when using any function that treats memory anonymously. A few functions you should exercise care in using are listed in Table 2.1.

After the preceding "skull and crossbones" depiction of C++ objects, you might be wondering if there is any way to avoid getting poisoned. In this particular case, there are happy workarounds.

Embedding Structs In Classes

Use C structs *with absolutely no C++ behavior* when you want to preserve C behavior. Here is a simple way to do that:

TABLE 2.1 RUN-TIME FUNCTIONS THAT TREAT MEMORY ANONYMOUSLY.

Function	Comment
memccpy	Copy may overwrite virtual function or virtual base pointers
memchr	Offset may be meaningless
memcmp	Objects whose data is identical are not required to binary compare
memcpy	Copy may overwrite virtual function or virtual base pointers
memicmp	See note under memcmp
memmove	See note under memcpy
memset	Certain to destroy virtual function or virtual base pointers
fread	Read may overwrite virtual function or virtual base pointers
fwrite	Virtual function or virtual base pointers serialized to disk are meaningless, as they point to functions in a given loaded execution image. Subsequent execution images (in memory) may relocate the tables elsewhere in memory

continued

Function	Comment
_read	See note under fread
_write	See note under fwrite
bsearch	bsearch takes **void** * arguments. Unless you are meticulous about casting back to the original type, you will break the type system and risk using invalid offsets when you retrieve your data.
_lsearch	See note under bsearch
qsort	See note under bsearch

```cpp
class Example
{
public:
    Example();
    virtual ~Example();
    size_t Read();
private:
    struct{
            char c;
            long dwStuff;
            char szMoreStuff[40];
    } m_example;
    FILE *fp;
}
Ex1, Ex2;

Example::Example()
{
    m_example.c = '1';
    memset(&m_example.dwStuff, '2', sizeof(long));
    memset(m_example.szMoreStuff, '3',
        sizeof(m_example.szMoreStuff));
}

Example::~Example()
{
}

size_t Example::Read()
{
    return fread(&m_example, sizeof(m_example), 1, fp);
}
// ...intervening code...

nBytesRead = Ex1.Read();
```

The previous example shows that you can still pull your structures off disk as before, just not arrays of structures.

Implement "Streaming" or Serialization

Another approach that is sometimes used is that of streaming information to and from disk on a per-member basis. This is used in the Microsoft Foundation Classes Serialize functions. Consider the following code:

```
class Example
{
public:
    // Construction/Destruction
    Example();          // Implementation for these
    virtual ~Example(); // functions presumed elsewhere
    BOOL Read(ifstream& ifs);
private:
    char c;
    DWORD  dwStuff;
    char   szMoreStuff[44];
}
Ex1, Ex2;

BOOL Example::Read(ifstream& ifs)
{
    ifs >> c;
    ifs >> dwStuff;
    ifs >> szMoreStuff;
}
```

The approach of writing out each item separately might seem inefficient until you consider the fact that the run-times and operating systems always buffer reads and writes into reasonable sized blocks. That means you are simply using a more straightforward, possibly more explicit means of expressing the read or write operation. There are efficiencies to be gained by optimizing I/O, but you have to be careful where you take them.

PICKING OUT OBJECTS

Although there is no magic to picking out objects from your problem domain, some guidelines or examples of "prior art" are of immense benefit.

Models of the Real World

Objects that model things in your immediate problem domain—especially things that you can see—are the most intuitive to pick out. An example of such an object is a window in a windowing operating system. To create a class that describes a window, you need to think about several categories of information:

- **Attributes.** What information does this object need to "know" about itself. For example, is it important for a window object to remember its location? Its size? These attributes ultimately become member variables in your class.

- **Operations.** These are ways you might want to manipulate an object of this type. Get*xxx* and Set*xxx* functions are operations, as are overloaded operators. Other methods for manipulation are Move, Resize, and so on.

- **Construction/Destruction.** Some people like to consider these apart from operations. By doing so, they are able to determine what the responsibility of the constructors and destructors should be in setting the initial state and cleaning up after an object dies.

Models of a Service

Many programmatic "entities" function as services to other programs or parts of programs. Making a service into an object helps improve its robustness. Here is an example of a service: a file-system encapsulation.

File Encapsulation

A file system, while not strictly speaking a "real world" object, is a perfect thing to encapsulate using object-oriented technology. A file system is a collection of files and directories. A directory is a collection of files and directories, and a file is a collection of anonymous bytes. There are a limited number of operations one performs within a file system, but many variations on each operation.

Finding a file in the file system

The VMS file system is different from the MS-DOS file system, which is, in turn, very different from the Macintosh file system. Abstracting the operation of finding a file means that your application can ignore what operating system it runs on top of.

Opening a file

We commonly rely on the C run-time library to abstract this concept, but do you use `fopen` or `_open` for opening files? Or if you program for Windows NT, do you use `CreateFile` or `OpenFile`? In some cases, this can be important. In most cases it isn't. In C, files are usually opened explicitly with one of the calls mentioned earlier. In C++, you can rely on your file object's *constructor* to open a file for you, eliminating one more area of concern (did I remember to open the file?). Constructors are discussed previously in "Constructors".

Sharing a file

Again, we normally rely on the C run-time library to abstract this concept. However, once we have a file open, how can we tell what sharing mode we used? If this kind of information is important, you can cache this kind of setting and provide inquiry (or "accessor") functions to return the state.

Closing a file

It's important to close the files that you open. In a program with a long lifespan that has to access many different files, the failure to close files once you're done with them can cause system degradation and finally program failure. In a C++ abstraction of file services, you might rely on your file object's *destructor* to close the file automatically, as soon as the object goes out of scope. (See "Destructors" for more information about destructors.)

Reading data

This is one of the most straightforward things you can do in C, but it is not type safe. In C, you read chunks of data into an anonymous buffer. You, the programmer, supply the buffer and the size *each time you do the read*. In C++, you can "teach" the file objects about the types of data in your program. Alternatively, you can teach your new classes about the file services such that you need only enter a line of code like

```
SomeType myObject;

myFile >> myObject;
```

The data on disk is interpreted using the extraction (>>) function defined for SomeType.

MOVING SUBSTANTIAL C CODEBASES TO C++

A common issue in moving from C to C++ is that of existing codebase. Some systems are so significant that rewriting in C++ is prohibitive. The question is what strategies have been effective in *migrating* to C++? Here are a few answers that I've found from personal experience and from talking with others who have done the same thing.

Creeping C++

As I said before, some existing systems are so extensive that rewriting from scratch in C++ is out of the question. For such programs, a phased move to C++ is appropriate. I call this "creeping C++." What you do is assume C is a proper subset of C++, and that no semantic differences exist. We know that semantic differences *do* exist, but as a first operating assumption, it gets you a long way down the road.

1. Rebuild your entire project—every C file—specifying that you want the compiler to assume C++. This will cause a number of compile-time warnings and errors. I recommend that you use a high warning level, and try to cull the offending code from your program using the compiler to locate suspicious code. This exercise is not terribly time-consuming, and when complete, you're almost certain to have eliminated at least one or two quiet bugs in your code.

NOTE

If you have a compiler that is sensitive to file extensions, it's usually better to make a copy of your source files, renaming the .C files to .CPP or .CXX, whichever your compiler understands. This should automatically imply to the compiler that it should compile as C++.

As you scan the error list, you'll notice that they fall into categories. If you have old K&R style function headers, C++ compilers will gag on them. More interesting are subtle anomalies in your typing system.

For example, in C++ signed and unsigned types are considered different, as are const/nonconst and volatile/nonvolatile. You'll get errors or warnings when you mix these.

There are several other things to watch out for: Added C++ keywords may conflict with variable or function names. Any variable or function named `catch`, `class`, `delete`, `friend`, `inline`, `new`, `operator`, `private`, `protected`, `public`, `template`, `this`, `throw`, `try`, or `virtual` will be disallowed.

2. Once your project compiles and links, you actually *have* a C++ program, although you haven't added any of the new C++ features to it.

3. As you have to make changes to your program, feel free to integrate any C++ features you need or want. If you have a chance to rearchitect a single subsystem in a more object-oriented way, that will give you a good feel for the level of effort involved.

Over time, the C++ will "creep" into your program, and at a certain point (if the program lives on long enough), it will begin to predominate.

Rearchitecting Using an Application Framework

Rearchitecting applications to use application frameworks (or class libraries) is getting popular for several reasons:

◆ Good application frameworks are extensively tested, relieving you of the burden of writing and testing some relatively tricky code.

◆ These frameworks are made with reusability in mind. They have a structure that promotes building reusable components, and help you with decisions on how to design your class hierarchies.

◆ The code in the frameworks can sometimes be shared among multiple applications on the same computer. This saves on redundancy and reduces the on-disk size of your executable image.

◆ Application framework code is often highly tuned for the target platform, especially when the implementors of the framework knew something about the compiler they were expecting to use. This gives you a solid base for an optimized application before you write your first line of C++.

As a result of the benefits I've listed, you may find that rearchitecting your application is a better choice than preserving the C code intact. It's possible you have organized your code around certain object-oriented principles already. If so, the migration may be less work than you expect. Here is an example of how Microsoft moved a very large body of existing C code to C++, using the Microsoft Foundation Classes.

> **The Problem:** The Microsoft Visual C++ Visual Workbench was written in C. This code had become brittle over time and was increasingly difficult to extend without interactions elsewhere in the system. For the most recent revision, the decision was made to port the whole thing to C++. Over the span of the project, several trends emerged.

> **The Strategy:** Visual C++ is a Windows program, so we focused, initially, on windows objects. The steps (broad brush) were as listed in Table 2.2:

The result of this exercise was to:

◆ Add more new features in less time than this team ever has before.

◆ Introduce fewer regressions during bug fixing.

◆ Allow for future extensibility consistent with the direction of the Microsoft Foundation Classes.

Of particular note is the fact that lots of the "one-off" implementations were tossed completely: for example, toolbar, status bar, multiple document interface, and document handling code. This is all provided for nicely by the Microsoft Foundation Classes, so we inherited their work. Where necessary, we overrode their implementations to suit our particular needs, but in large measure we were able to leverage a great quantity of tested code.

Depending on the class library or application framework you use, your results will be different. It is crucial to pick a library that is well suited to the application you are building. Once you understand the underlying architecture of that class library, you can formulate a strategy similar to ours, but specific to your application and framework choices.

TABLE 2.2 COST/BENEFIT FOR C++ MIGRATION.

Task	Cost (How Hard)	Benefit
Compile everything with C++. In this step, we got everything to compile cleanly in C++.	*Moderate.* As mentioned above, the things to watch for are subtle inconsistencies in the type system.	A C++ program. This is analogous to running Lint over your program with all the floodgates open.
Use AppWizard to generate a new skeleton for the application.	*Almost none.* AppWizard generates a skeleton (do-nothing) application, based on some settings you specify in dialog boxes. This amounts to a fair amount of source code, but you don't have to write it!	The framework provided facilities for such things as MDI window management, toolbars, status bars, and idle-time processing, all of which were being handled in special-case code.
Plug window procedures into **CWnd** objects.	*Substantial.* MFC implements an abstraction on the Microsoft Windows concept of a window in a class called **CWnd**. The problem you face in doing this with applications of any complexity is that you have lots of windows. You therefore have to figure out what functions are handled by the framework automatically and what you have to implement.	Document/View architecture, multiple views, document templates, dirty file tracking, File.Open and File.Save, etc.
Change WndProc cases to message maps.	*Low.* MFC implements message routing via a scheme called message maps. There is a one-to-one correspondence between messages creceived and handler functions.	Instead of a monolithic window procedure with a long switch statement, you now have many small, self-contained message-handling functions. At this point, you can start using the ClassWizard to maintain and extend the user interface.

Examining C++ Development Tools

Scott Meyers, Ph.D.

INTRODUCTION

No C++ programmer works without development tools. At the very least, you use a text editor and a compiler, and the odds are pretty good that you use a debugger, too. However, outside of the C++ compiler, the tools you're using may well be leftovers from your days as a C hacker, and you may have discovered that the tools that served you so well in the land of Kernighan and Ritchie fall short of the mark when you work in the realm of Stroustrup. There are important technical reasons for this state of affairs[5], but rather than prattle on about what's wrong with C tools when you program in C++, I'm going to devote this chapter to bringing to your attention some of the things you should consider when you evaluate various kinds of tools for C++ programming.

I've chosen to organize my presentation as a list of questions you can use to grill tool vendors, because the unfortunate fact of the matter is that things are often not as they appear. For example, you might think that if you have a compiler that implements templates, you'd be able to separate template declarations (.h files) and definitions (.C or .cc, etc. files) in the usual manner. Unfortunately, the price you pay for this kind of thinking can be bitter disappointment: Some compilers make templates much easier to use when you put both the declaration *and* the definition in the .h file; if you choose to separate the declaration from the definition, you have a lot more work to do. Suddenly the game becomes clear: You can have templates and you can have separate compilation, but there is a substantial surcharge for wanting both at the same time.

In view of this regrettable state of affairs, you need to ask much more specific questions about tools than you might think. What follows are questions you might want to consider adding to your inquisitorial quiver when you go shopping for C++ development tools.

The material in this chapter appeared in an earlier form in the October 1992 and January 1993 issues of *The C++ Report.*

COMPILERS

Next to your text editor (a tool to which most programmers have an attachment that is best described as umbilical), a compiler is your most frequently used development tool. It's the tool most intimately related to your existence as not just a generic software developer, but as a *C++* software developer. Here are a few questions to ask when looking at a compiler.

♦ *What language features does it support?* This is the most basic of questions, and the answer can be remarkably confusing. C++ has been publicly available less than a decade, and already we've seen versions 1.2, 2.0, 2.1, and 3.0, all of which are incompatible in some way or other, and most (perhaps all) of which are still available from one vendor or another. Adding to the fun is the fact that these are USL release numbers, so they have no official meaning (AT&T was the original purveyor of all things C++, but they have since sent their promising brainchild off to Unix Systems Labs, which was subsequently purchased by Novell). Unfortunately, people think they have meaning. That's why we're told that version 2.2.2 of one C++ compiler (which is also a C compiler and an Objective C compiler, but don't get confused) is roughly the same as USL's 3.0, while another vendor's brand spanking new C++ compiler (which was also the latest release of their C compiler, but don't get confused) was version 7 and was roughly the same as USL's 2.1. Clearly, release numbers mean nothing, so don't be fooled.

　　Ask instead about features. For example, ask about nested types, templates, exceptions, and the recently added language support for run-time type identification (RTTI) and namespaces. Except for RTTI and namespaces, each of these is already in the unofficial language specification (the ARM[1]), so an ideal C++ compiler should support each of them. By determining which of these fundamental language features is supported by the compiler, you can come to a basic understanding of how up to date the compiler is.

♦ *Ha, ha! No, really, what features does it support?* Don't stop at the general questions, because the fact that features A and B are supported does *not* necessarily imply that A and B can be used together. I've already discussed one example of this irritating set of circumstances: that of templates and separate compilation in one compiler. As a second example, consider nested types. Many compilers claim to support nested types, but in fact they frequently exhibit "transitional" behavior that attempts to reconcile C's support for nested types (none) with C++'s fairly good support for the concept, with the end result that the actual behavior of the compiler manages to correspond to nothing in either language's specification. Frankly, I think that such behavior is better termed schizophrenic than transitional, but perhaps that's why I'm not in marketing.

Similarly, some compilers' support for exceptions boils down to macros that call `setjmp` and `longjmp`, which is an exception-handling strategy exhibiting many of the serious shortcomings that exceptions were designed to eliminate in the first place. In particular, executing a `longjmp` fails to call destructors for objects in the scopes being exited, and this can lead to disaster in C++ programs.

Templates are more or less commonly available now, and you'd think that a compiler either supports templates or it doesn't, but in fact many compilers *sort of* support them. Coming from the Pascal tradition as I do (so sue me), I naturally think in terms of nested classes. I was therefore surprised—to put it mildly—when I discovered that my C++ compiler wouldn't allow me to nest classes inside templates classes. How annoying! And here's a completely legal template class that lots of compilers will turn their computational noses up at:

```
template<class T>
class Derived: public T {};    // inherit from
                               // template arg
```

Your best defense against such limitations is a good offense: know precisely which features of the language you plan to use and in which combinations, then grill prospective compiler vendors about their support for those features and combinations of features. If a vendor's compiler lacks support for the things you need, do your best to make the vendor feel self-conscious and inadequate; with luck, we can shame the compiler vendors into supporting the full language as quickly as possible.

Note to compiler writers: I sympathize with your plight. I know it's a difficult language to implement (especially the parts that aren't yet well defined) but this business of releasing half-baked support for major language features has really got to stop.

◆ *What kinds of optimizations are performed?* What you're really interested in here are optimizations that are specific to C++. Sure, loop unrolling, constant folding, and strength reduction are wonderful things, but C++ presents new optimization problems that need solutions in their own right. For example, ask compiler vendors how they minimize the generation of temporaries. Do they perform the return-value optimization described in Section 12.1.1c of the ARM? Do they guarantee that they will never generate more than one copy of a class's virtual table? Do they optimize away virtual calls when the dynamic type of the object can be determined by static analysis?

Here's an opportunity for optimization I'd like to see exploited in C++ compilers: Sharing of code by template class member functions that differ by only a constant template parameter. For example, here's a class I used in *Effective C++*[6]:

```
template<class T, int size>
class Buffer {
   private:
      T buffer[size];

   public:
      ...
};

Buffer<int, 10> bufferOf10Ints;
Buffer<int, 20> bufferOf20Ints;
```

Look at this closely. Wouldn't it be downright *immoral* if the compiler generated two sets of functions, one for buffers of size 10 and the second for buffers of size 20? It would indeed, but, as Tom Cargill pointed out to me, most compilers will blithely do just that. Sure, programmers can redesign their code to eliminate such sets of almost-identical functions, but wouldn't it be nice if the compiler did it for them?

Let me hasten to add that I'm not seriously suggesting that this particular optimization is the be all and end all of C++ optimizations. Rather, I'm arguing that traditional optimizations, useful though they are, should be viewed as no more than a starting point for C++ compilers. C++ offers new optimization opportunities by the veritable *gaggle*.

◆ *How well does the compiler work with other tools?* You'll pardon my single-minded fascination with templates, I hope, but I've found that they have all kinds of hidden facets just *waiting* to be discovered. One of the more interesting implications of the automatic instantiation of template classes and functions is that dependency tools like make no longer work as you expect them to. For example, suppose that I declare a template function in functions.h,

```
template<class T>
bool operator==(const T&, const T&);
```

I implement it in functions.C,

```
template<class T>
bool operator==(const T& lhs, const T& rhs)
{ return &lhs == &rhs; }
```

and I use it in appl.C:

```
void eatLikeAPig(const Refrigerator& r1,
                 const Refrigerator& r2)
{
    emptyAndConsume(r1);
    if (r1 == r2)          // really only one
                           // refrigerator?
        return;            // shucks, we're done
    emptyAndConsume(r2);   // hooray, more food!
}
```

Suppose that the executable generated from all these files is called application. To generate this executable, the operator== template has to be instantiated for the type Refrigerator. Many compilers do this by generating a hidden file, say functions_h.C, containing this:

```
bool operator==( const Refrigerator& lhs,
                 const Refrigerator& rhs)
{ return &lhs == &rhs; }
```

This is compiled into functions_h.o, which is then magically linked with all the other object files to generate application.

This is all fine and dandy, except for one thing: How is make to detect the dependency between the executable file application and the intrinsically generated source file functions_h.C? You might say that you should just add a dependency to make indicating that application is dependent on functions_h.C, but in general, that's not true. After all, changes to functions_h.C can only affect the behavior of application if application contains an *instantiation* of a template defined in functions_h.C. But there is no way for make to determine whether such an instantiation exists. (To its credit, at least one compiler vendor has recognized this problem and is planning to enhance its compiler so that the dilemma can be circumvented.)

The combination of automatic template instantiation with make, then, can leave you feeling like Odysseus approaching Scylla and Charybdis: If you use the tried-and-true rules for make, you may end up with an executable that make thinks is up to date when in fact it is not; but if you add a dependency between your source files and the template definition files, you may end up recompiling even when you don't need to. Such fun, this C++, no?

DEBUGGERS

In a perfect world, there would be no need for debugging, but as things stand now, software defects are not only as certain as death and taxes, they are also more time-consuming for most programmers. That being the case, it's worth subjecting candidate debuggers to particularly intense scrutiny. Here are some questions to ask.

◆ *Can it hide name-mangling?* Name-mangling is the process whereby the compiler takes your oh-so-carefully chosen identifier names and, well, mangles them. The primary reason for this is that the overloading of function names tends to make linkers rather cranky. They view with disdain more than one function having the same name. Hence, your helpful C++ compiler assigns all your functions unique names in the code that it generates. (Contrary to the belief of many, there is no standard for name mangling[10], so different compilers mangle names in different ways. Even different versions of the same compiler may mangle names in different ways.) This is inconvenient, but the payoff is greater than just pacified linkers; you also obtain the benefits of type-safe linkage[15].

You don't want to debug your code in terms of mangled names. You want to debug it in terms of the names you chose. (Well, truth be told, you don't want to debug it at all, but that's another story.) This means your debugger must be able to both demangle names (when displaying them to you) and mangle names (when mapping your debugger commands to operations on the program's functions), and if it can't do that, it's not really a C++ debugger, it's a C debugger.

◆ *Can it cope with overloaded function names?* This is related to, but is not the same as, the issues of name mangling and demangling. The problem is that you may specify an ambiguous function name when specifying a breakpoint, and the debugger has to have a reasonable way to make sense of your command. For example, suppose you ask to set a breakpoint in function foo, but there are three different overloaded functions with that name. Does the debugger reject the command, does it present you with a list of signatures to choose from, or does it take some other tack? You *will* want to do this kind of thing, so a debugger that won't let you should cause you to raise your eyebrows until they form a profile of the Alps.

◆ *Can it print the dynamic types of pointers and references?* What with the wonder of inheritance and all, it's not uncommon to have a pointer or a reference to a base class that actually points (refers) to an object of a derived class. For example:

```
BaseClass *p;
...
p = new DerivedClass;
```

Your debugger should be able to tell you that the dynamic type of p in this example is DerivedClass*, not BaseClass*. Furthermore, if you ask to see what p points to, i.e., for the debugger to display *p, you should see all the fields declared in *both* BaseClass and DerivedClass, not just those declared in BaseClass. If your debugger does not offer this kind of behavior, it doesn't support inheritance, and you'll find that limitation to be crippling.

◆ *Can it set breakpoints and/or step through inline functions? Virtual functions? Member initialization lists? Template classes and functions?* This is a multifaceted question, but C++ is a multifaceted language, and a good debugger will deal with all facets equally well. Most debuggers have no trouble with breakpoints and single-stepping as long as they're on familiar C-like turf, but some of them develop a noticeable limp once you leave the playing field they were raised on. Consider inline functions. They're functions, which means you'd like to be able to step into them, set breakpoints on entry and exit, and so on, but they're not functions, because the function isn't supposed to actually exist. This puts debuggers in a tough position: it's difficult to step into a function that's not there. Nonetheless, the notion of dealing with inline functions as "normal" functions is sensible, so your debugger should have a reasonable policy. One approach to the problem is to have a compiler switch that disables inlining, thus forcing the compiler to generate out-of-line functions and calls for all functions in that translation unit. A different approach is to disable breakpoints and/or single-stepping for functions that have been inlined. A less reasonable approach is to disallow debugging of code containing inlined functions.

One of my favorite questions for debugger people is whether they support breakpoints in virtual functions, including pure virtual functions. What this means is that I have a pointer or a reference to a base class, and I want to set a breakpoint at the entry to the function that is actually called, even though I don't know at the time I set the breakpoint which function this will be. After all, to program the function call, I just call the base class virtual function, so in the debugger, I should be able to just set a breakpoint in the base class virtual function, too. Some debuggers let you set a single breakpoint to do this, others require that you manually set a breakpoint in each function to which the call might resolve at runtime. The latter approach can be acceptable if there is an easy way to set all the breakpoints (e.g., by specifying a regular expression that describes all the functions to receive a breakpoint), but if you need to type in *n* breakpoint commands for *n* virtual functions, you'll find that you tire of the game rather quickly.

Member initialization lists can be troublesome for debuggers, because they may contain arbitrarily complex expressions, yet they're not inside a function body. For example, if you're maintaining the code of a String class that was written by someone determined to demonstrate their initialization-list machismo, you might be faced with something like this:

```
class String {
private:
    char *data;

public:
    ...
};

String::String(const String& rhs)
: data(strcpy(new char[strlen(rhs.data)+1],
        rhs.data))
{}
```

This is gross, but legal. Now suppose you'd like to check the return value of strlen or new as String's data field is initialized. How will you do it if you can't step into the code in the member initialization list?

Finally, templates create all kinds of interesting problems for debuggers, because the source code that you write for a template is *not* the code that is compiled into executable instructions. Instead, the template you write is *instantiated* into C++ that you (theoretically) never see, and it is this invisible source that the compiler uses to generate executable code. A fundamental question, then, is this: What source code does your source code debugger show you when you're debugging a template? Does it show you the template code *you* wrote, which means you won't have the benefit of seeing the arguments used to instantiate the template, or does it show you the code *it* wrote? For simple template arguments, the difference may not be significant, but when you get into templates like this,

```
template<class Key, class Value>
class Map { ... };

...

Map<String, Map<String, String>*> symbolTableMap;
```

you may be able to figure out what's going on a lot easier if you can read the C++ source that the compiler actually saw.

♦ *Can it display all the members of an object, including those that are inherited?* This question is pretty straightforward, but be sure to ask specifically about members inherited from virtual base classes. The most common implementation of such classes uses pointers in derived classes[1], and you *don't* want to see the presence of such pointers (unless you're debugging your compiler, which, I'm happy to report, is becoming less and less necessary for many compilers). More importantly, you *do* want to see the members of the virtual base classes, and that means that the debugger needs to automatically dereference the pointers to virtual bases and show the members it finds there. Needless to say, the members of a virtual base class should only be displayed *once* per object. (Actually, it's not needless to say; that's the whole point of this chapter.)

♦ *Does it understand about static members?* Static members sometimes confuse debuggers due to their dual nature. In many ways they act like global variables (which, for C++ to C translators, is how they are typically implemented), but they still obey class access restrictions, etc. Debuggers that cheat sometimes don't recognize fully qualified references to static data members (e.g., "print MyClass::myStaticMember," or they won't allow static member functions to be called from inside the debugger. You want to steer clear of such debuggers.

CLASS BROWSERS

Surely you know the old joke about technical standards: The nice thing about them is that there are so many to choose from. A similar situation exists regarding browsers, because there's not really any widely accepted definition of the term. Let us sally forth anyway, with the general under-standing that a browser is a program that provides information about a C++ software system in both graphical and textual form. Most people expect a browser to have at least enough graphical capabilities to draw a pic-ture of the inheritance graph and/or the call graph for a C++ program. Often a browser allows users to specify queries about particular aspects of the sys-tem, such as showing all the public members of a class (including inherited members). Here are some questions to consider when evaluating browsers.

◆ *Can the browser provide reasonable graphical displays of inheritance hierarchies employing multiple inheritance?* Let's get one thing straight right from the start: Drawing single-inheritance hierarchies (i.e., trees) is easy, but drawing arbitrary inheritance graphs (i.e., directed acyclic graphs) is so hard as to be an open research prob-lem[9]. So anybody who says their program will always produce beautiful pictures of arbitrary hierarchies is simply lying to you. The class browser we developed in our research at Brown University[13] offers eight different layout algorithms, each with numerous options, and it is still not uncommon to encounter a (multiple) inheritance graph whose automatic display is less than fully satisfactory.

Still, some approaches to graph layout are better than others. For example, some browsers assume that all inheritance hierarchies are basically trees, and they just draw extra lines when this assump-tion is violated. Such browsers offer lip-service support for multiple inheritance, but fundamentally they aren't trying. Other cop-out approaches include offering only manual layout (tedious for large graphs, and it puts the burden on you to solve the very difficult lay-out problems that can arise from multiple inheritance) and display-ing only a restricted portion of the graph (which makes it impossi-ble to get a complete overview of your inheritance structure).

The ideal solution would probably be to automatically generate a graph layout using one or more algorithms, then to allow users to selectively move elements of the graph around until they were satis-fied with its appearance. Unfortunately, I am not aware of any browser that offers this approach. In the meantime, look for browsers that acknowledge the existence of multiple inheritance and that make a genuine effort to display it in an informative manner.

◆ *Are different kinds of inheritance relationships depicted differently?* A public inheritance relationship between classes is very different than a private inheritance relationship between those same classes[6], so it's important for a browser to distinguish between different kinds of inheritance. Similarly, a virtual inheritance relationship is quite different from a nonvirtual inheritance relationship, so a browser should depict those relationships differently, too. Baldly put, just knowing that one class inherits from another doesn't tell you much, no matter how pretty the picture.

◆ *Can you navigate through the inheritance graph by zooming and panning?* Often it is quite useful to see only a class and the classes to which it is related. You don't want to be stuck looking at a graph containing a googol of classes when the only ones you care about are the half-dozen you wrote last week.

◆ *Can the browser display class relationships other than inheritance?* One look through a text on object-oriented design[8,14,16] will convince you that inheritance does not a complete world model make. Can the browser show friend relationships? Has-a relationships? Is-implemented-in-terms-of relationships[6]? Uses relationships? The more relationships a browser can show graphically, the easier it is to get a fix on how the different components of your program interact. It's worth noting that these other relationships may result in arbitrary graphs, making the problem of drawing them nicely that much more difficult and important.

◆ *Can it show templates and instantiations?* A class template is not a class, so perhaps it shouldn't be in a class browser. On the other hand, a class template instantiation is a class, so perhaps it should be in a class browser. On the third hand, if a class template doesn't go in a class diagram, where does it go? Analogous issues arise for function templates in browsers for call graphs. Quite simply, it's not clear how templates and template instantiations should interact in class and function browsers, but they certainly must interact in *some* way. For the browsers you're considering, find out what the interaction mechanism is, and see if it makes sense to you.

◆ *Can it display all the members of an object, including those that are inherited?* One of the most irksome hurdles to overcome when maintaining a C++ program is what I call the *distributed interface problem*: The complete interface for a class is usually distributed over a number of .h files, one for the class and one for each class from which it directly or indirectly inherits. A good browser should be able to synthesize a single interface for a class, generating a list of all the members contained in the class, no matter where they come from. As in the case of debuggers, check closely to make sure that virtual base classes are handled correctly.

◆ *Can the information displayed be filtered by users?* Maybe you don't care about classes declared in iostream.h. Maybe you'd just as soon forget about private members. Perhaps static members give you heartburn. Your browser should allow you to shield yourself from the aspects of a system you don't want to see. A decent rule of thumb is that you should be able to filter on any combination of a member's attributes (e.g., private, protected, public, static, virtual, const, volatile, inherited, etc.), and even better is also being able to filter on the basis of class and member names, typically by providing one or more regular expressions that specify which names should be included or excluded.

◆ *Can it provide information about incomplete and/or incorrect programs?* It is a fact of life that complete programs start out as incomplete programs. For example, you might not get around to writing main until many of your classes have been developed. It is also a fact of life that, try as we might, we invariably write code that contains bugs. Some of them are even simple things like syntax errors. Many browsers get put off by incomplete and/or incorrect programs, yet it is often when our programs are far from finished that we need the most help with them. A browser that can display, say, the inheritance hierarchy of a program that won't compile is substantially more useful than is one that balks at source code the compiler refuses to sanction.

Both kinds of browsers are available. The more flexible browsers employ what has been called "fuzzy parsing,"[7] which really means that they ignore constructs that they don't care about. This is a time-honored tradition for pretty-printers, but the technique has paid off for class browsers, too. Fuzzy parsing is not only more flexible than strict parsing, it's usually faster, too. The downside to fuzzy parsing is twofold. First, it can yield incorrect information, due to the fact that it is really parsing a language that is different than C++. For example, a class browser employing fuzzy parsing might ignore nested classes, in which case it might depict all classes as being at global scope, even though in the program some of them were actually nested inside other classes. Whether this is a disaster depends on the kind of information you are interested in. The second drawback to fuzzy parsing is that it tends to gather much less information than a strict parse; hence, it usually causes tools to omit information that is actually present in the program. Again, whether this is troublesome depends on the particular context in which the browser is used.

In general, strict parsing is to be preferred to fuzzy parsing, but there have been times when I was working on a program whose structure was (to put it euphemistically) "in transition" and would therefore not compile, and I would have given my eye teeth to see a picture of its inheritance structure. At that point, only a browser employing fuzzy parsing could help me. The bottom line, then, is it's nice to have access to fuzzy parsing when strict parsing is not a possibility.

Development Environments

You can think of a development environment as a combination of a compiler, a debugger, a browser, and more, so all the issues I raised about these tools apply equally well to environments, too. However, here are some additional questions to think about when looking at a development environment.

◆ *How big a system can it handle with decent speed?* Put another way, does the environment scale well? If you find the environment useful for a 25,000-line application, you'll probably find its facilities downright *essential* when you start in on the maintenance of a 2,500,000-line behemoth. When things get that big, you don't want to be stuck behind the wheel of an environment whose speed can accurately be characterized as glacial.

◆ *Can it show dynamic aspects of the system's behavior?* Most software development tools for C++ focus on the static structure of the program. However, you also need insight into the dynamic behavior of a system if you're ever going to truly understand what makes it tick. Often it is possible to enhance views of a program's static structure to also display some dynamic information. For example, a call graph might be animated to show which function is actually being called as the program runs, and an inheritance hierarchy might be animated to show which member function is executing. Both of these capabilities are present in FIELD[12], the software development environment in which we try out new research ideas at Brown University, and both have been found to yield useful information, especially when used together[11].

◆ *Can the environment work with shared libraries?* Or does it insist on everything being in a single object file?

◆ *Does it support dynamic linking?* Or does your entire application have to be statically linked in advance?

◆ *Will the environment allow you to develop mixed-language applications?* Most environments have no trouble with a combination of C and C++ (of course, you should still be sure to ask), but are they as accommodating when it comes to calling routines developed in Pascal, FORTRAN, and assembler? Do they require that the main routine be written in C++, or can you use the environment for the development of C++ utility libraries to be called from applications written in other languages?

◆ *Can you add new tools to the environment?* Contrary to popular marketing claims, no environment can possibly offer you all the functionality you'll ever need. At some point you may well want to write your own custom tool. It might be something as simple as a source code pretty-printer, it might be as complex as a symbolic evaluator for determining test coverage or a general-purpose constraint evaluator, but whatever it is, you'll find it much easier to add to your environment if the appropriate hooks are in place. For example, is there a way you can get at the information the compiler gathers when it parses your program, or will you be faced with the nearly insurmountable task of writing your own parser for C++? Don't put up with an environment that forces you into the latter situation. Remember, this is the age of openness in computer systems.

Similarly, is there a way for you to integrate third-party tools into the environment? For example, if you're a programmer whose attitude toward text editors is that you'd rather fight than switch, ask if you can use your favorite text editor instead of the one that comes bundled with the environment. If you can, make sure you know what functionality you're giving up, because nothing comes for free. For example, if your editor doesn't provide parsing on the fly, but a vendor's editor does, it will be difficult for you to insist that you gain the benefits of their on-the-fly parsing inside your editor.

Finally, when looking at environments and the tools they contain, resist the temptation to be overly dazzled by the latest rage in programming environments, namely, generators for glitzy graphical user interfaces (GUI generators). Obviously, if you are responsible for writing code for applications with graphical interfaces, you will want to find out everything you can about such generators, and for many applications, good GUI generators can save you many hours of toiling and grief. On the other hand, however, it's important to bear in mind that the guts of most nontrivial applications (compilers, operating systems, communications programs, scheduling systems, automatic layout algorithms, and so on) are not graphical in nature, and no amount of support for icons and dialog boxes will compensate for lost productivity due to poor compiler, debugger, and/or browser support for more fundamental C++ constructs.

BOOKS

Some of your most important development tools aren't executable at all; they're sitting on your bookshelf. Every good C++ programmer has a collection of books he or she consults on a more or less regular basis, and you should be no exception. Different books serve different purposes. Some describe the features of the language, others cover approaches to object-oriented design, still others provide algorithms and data structures in C++ that you can use in your applications, but before plunking down your hard-earned cash for some author's *magnum opus*, you should examine it carefully. Of course you should check the writing style to see if you can stomach the prose, but you should also consider these questions:

◆ *How current is the book?* All those lovely questions about compiler versions come back to haunt you when you look at C++ books, because a book that was current in 1991 may be of only historical interest in 1995. On the other hand, such a book might still be state of the art, so you can't do anything as simple as check the copyright date and dismiss anything older than a year or two. No, you've got to do a little digging to see what the book covers. The best place to start is the promotional blurb on the back of the book: Does it mention relatively new things, like templates, exceptions, RTTI, and namespaces, or does it announce with great fanfare that it actually covers such everyday topics as multiple inheritance?

It's worth bearing in mind that you may not really want a book that assumes you have access to the latest features of C++. After all, if you know you're not going to be using a compiler supporting exception handling for a couple of years (not everybody wants to live on the bleeding edge of technology), a book using exceptions here, there, and everywhere is likely to leave you feeling like you've downed a bit too much subtraction soup[2]: The more you read, the less you feel you have.

◆ *How general is the book?* Some people write code that has to run on everything from flying fortresses to toaster ovens (using a different compiler for each brownness setting); others know in advance that the fruits of their efforts will reside exclusively on calculators with thyroid conditions (i.e., PCs running DOS). There are books for both kinds of programmers. If you're only going to be using vendor X's compiler, you could probably make good use of the X-specific tips to be found in a book like "Transcending Mortal Limits with X's C++." On the other hand, if your code absolutely positively has to port there overnight, you'll want to avoid polluting your mind with vendor-specific keywords and class libraries. And then there's the third hand: If you have to run everywhere with maximum efficiency and you're willing to conditionally compile until the cows come home, you might want to get an X-specific book for all the Xs you'll be using.

◆ *How carefully was the code tested?* If you're just starting out in C++, it's difficult to detect technical errors in a book, but if you've mastered the basics and you're looking for a more advanced book, flip through your prospective purchase and check the code examples that cover topics you already know. Do you see any syntax errors? Do you see any stylistic blunders? Do you notice any suspect design decisions? Every book has a few errors (as an author, I can personally attest to the difficulty of producing a perfect book), but if you notice more than one or two in just a casual look through the book, you're likely to be frustrated by many more when you actually work through the material in detail. C++ is a complicated enough language in and of itself; you don't need a buggy book to further obscure matters.

WARNING

> At the same time, don't disqualify a book for errors unless you are *sure* you're right and the book is wrong. More than one person has indignantly written to comp.lang.c++ to denounce errors in a book, only to be shown that the book was correct and the poster was—how shall I put this?—less than fully informed.

◆ *Is the index any good?* If a book is valuable, you'll use it in two ways. First, you'll read through it front to back, and during that time, the index will be the last thing on your mind. Once you've completed the book, however, you'll want to refer back to it repeatedly, and when you start to use the book in that way, the index will instantly be promoted to the first rank of relevant features. Bear that in mind when you're looking through a book for the first time. Think of some topics that are important to you, then see if you can find them quickly through the index.

Different people think in different ways, so a good index will list a topic under a number of different headings. One of my benchmark examples is "pure virtual member functions," which I believe should be reachable through each of the four words. A more recent addition to my list of index-testing phrases is "conversion of pointers to members under inheritance," because I had to look up that topic just days ago.

As long as you're perusing the index, you might look up templates, exceptions, RTTI, and namespaces to see how extensively these topics are covered.

SUMMARY

Choosing effective tools for C++ software development is not as easy as it should be, although the situation is substantially better than it once was. Use the questions in this chapter to prepare yourself for the regrettably daunting task of evaluating compilers, debuggers, browsers, environments, and books. Arm yourself with as much information about your programming needs as you possibly can, because until high-quality tools for C++ development become widely available on all platforms, the best advice remains unchanged from that of centuries ago: *caveat emptor* (let the buyer beware).

ACKNOWLEDGMENTS

Jill Huchital provided valuable comments on an early version of this material in this chapter.

REFERENCES

1. Margaret A. Ellis and Bjarne Stroustrup, *The Annotated C++ Reference Manual*. Addison Wesley, 1990.

2. Norton Juster, *The Phantom Tollbooth*. Random House, 1964.

3. Moises Lejter, Scott Meyers, and Steven P. Reiss, "Adding Semantic Information To C++ Development Environments," in *Proceedings of C++ at Work-'90*, pp. 103-108, September 1990.

4. Moises Lejter, Scott Meyers, and Steven P. Reiss, "Support for Maintaining Object-Oriented Programs," *IEEE Transactions on Software Engineering*, December 1992. Also available as *Brown University Computer Science Department Technical Report No. CS-91-52*, August 1991. This paper is largely drawn from two other papers[3,5].

5. Scott Meyers, "Working with Object-Oriented Programs: The View from the Trenches is Not Always Pretty," in *Proceedings of the Symposium on Object-Oriented Programming Emphasizing Practical Applications (SOOPPA)*, pp. 51-65, September 1990.

6. Scott Meyers, *Effective C++: 50 Specific Ways to Improve Your Programs and Designs*. Addison-Wesley, 1992.

7. Walter R. Bischofberger, "Sniff: A Pragmatic Approach to a C++ Programming Environment," in *USENIX C++ Conference Proceedings*, pp. 67-81, August 1992.

8. Grady Booch, *Object Oriented Analysis and Design with Applications*, second edition. The Benjamin/Cummings Series in Object-Oriented Software Engineering, Benjamin/Cummings, 1994.

9. Peter Eades and Roberto Tamassia, "Algorithms for Drawing Graphs: An Annotated Bibliography," *Technical Report CS-89-09*, Brown University Department of Computer Science, August 1988.

10. Alex Lane, "Name Mangling in DOS," *The C++ Report*, vol. 2, no. 8, pp. 9-10, September 1990.

11. Scott Meyers and Steven P. Reiss, "An Empirical Study of Multiple-View Software Development," in *Proceedings of SIGSOFT '92: Fifth Symposium on Software Development Environments*, December 1992.

12. Steven P. Reiss, "Connecting Tools using Message Passing in the FIELD Program Development Environment," *IEEE Software*, pp. 57-67, July 1990. Also available as *Brown University Computer Science Department Technical Report CS-88-18*, "Integration Mechanisms in the FIELD Environment," 1988.

13. Steven P. Reiss and Scott Meyers, "FIELD Support for C++," in *USENIX C++ Conference Proceedings*, pp. 293-299, April 1990.

14. James Rumbaugh, Michael Blaha, William Premerlani, Frederick Eddy, and William Lorensen, *Object-Oriented Modeling and Design*. Prentice Hall, 1991.

15. Bjarne Stroustrup, "Type-Safe Linkage for C++," in *1988 USENIX C++ Conference*, pp. 193-210, 1988.

16. Rebecca Wirfs-Brock, Brian Wilkerson, and Lauren Wiener, *Designing Object-Oriented Software*. Prentice Hall, 1990.

Using Multiple Inheritance Effectively

Tim Gooch

INTRODUCTION

One of the more controversial elements of C++ is multiple inheritance. Many of the newer object-oriented languages have multiple inheritance, while many of the traditional (some would say "pure") object-oriented languages like Smalltalk, Object Pascal, and Objective C don't. Obviously, the language-designing community doesn't agree on the value of this feature.

However, whether it's "better" for C++ to have multiple inheritance is not an issue because it's already part of C++. You'll notice that this chapter isn't titled "Avoiding Multiple Inheritance." Instead, we'll look at some of the issues related to taking advantage of multiple inheritance with C++.

First, we'll review the basics of single inheritance—since an incomplete understanding of these issues can further complicate understanding multiple inheritance. Next, we'll look at some of the issues you should consider when you're trying to decide whether or not multiple inheritance is an appropriate solution to a design or implementation problem. With this in mind, we'll look at methods of analyzing the problem domain to determine whether or not multiple inheritance could be a valuable component of the solution. Along the way we'll examine some successful design techniques that use multiple inheritance.

Finally, we'll look at some of the more troublesome mechanics of using multiple inheritance in real applications. While this is the aspect that many discussions of multiple inheritance spend most of their time on, some explanations are necessary only when the reader has an incomplete knowledge of inheritance in the first place, or because someone is using multiple inheritance where it isn't appropriate.

PREPARING FOR MULTIPLE INHERITANCE

In order to use multiple inheritance in C++, you first need to understand single inheritance in C++. There are at least two ways you can view inheritance in C++: from the compiler's perspective or from the designer's perspective.

First, let's review some class terminology. In any class or struct, you can specify that data members or member functions exist within one of three access levels: public, private, or protected.

1. **Public.** Data members or member functions of the class that are visible to any part of the application that has a valid identifier for an object of this class. Many people refer to public members as the interface to a class since most of the surrounding application will use these members to communicate with an object of that class.

2. **Private.** Data members or member functions that aren't visible to the world outside this class's member functions and friends. Many people refer to private members as the implementation of the class since member functions of this class or friends of this class are the only parts of the application that can use these members. If you place the implementation details of the class in private members, you're using implementation hiding.

3. **Protected.** Data members or member functions that aren't visible to the world outside this class, but are visible to classes you derive from this class, and derived member functions and friends. If you derive a new class from an existing one, the new class won't have access to the base class's private members, but it will have access to its public and protected members. If you like to think of private members as the implementation of the class, think of protected members as the implementation of this class and any derived classes.

Now, consider what you are trying to do when you inherit one class from another. You may want to simply add additional data or behavior to the base class, you may want to change the behavior of the base class, or you may want to do a little of both.

The Compiler's View of Inheritance

From the compiler's point of view, three things happen when you derive a class from a base class:

◆ All of the data and behavior of the base class become part of the derived class's interface or implementation. In other words, the derived class gets an unnamed copy of the base class. We'll call this the inherited sub-object.

◆ The compiler will allow you to override functions from the base class. If those functions are virtual, overriding them replaces the address of the base class virtual function in a derived class object's vtable with the address of the overriding derived class function.

◆ You're telling the compiler that under certain conditions it can implicitly convert a derived class pointer or reference to a base class pointer or reference. If the base class has an accessible copy constructor, the compiler will be able to convert a derived object to a base object as well.

The Inherited Subobject

The most obvious aspect of inheritance is that the derived class "inherits" the members of the base class. In general, you can think of the base class members as composing complete, unnamed sub-object of the base class inside each derived class object.

For example, assuming that you've defined a struct `Caveman` :

```
struct Caveman
{ char Name[20];
  int  AvgBowlingScore;
};
```

a typical C++ compiler might create a memory image of a `Caveman` object that looks like this

```
| Name                  |    // 20 bytes
| AvgBowlingScore       |    // 4 bytes
```

Now, if you derive a new struct `Couple` from the base struct `Caveman` by writing

```
struct Couple : public Caveman
{ char SpouseName[20];
};
```

the compiler might create a memory image of a `Couple` object that looks like this

Name		// 20 bytes
AvgBowlingScore		// 4 bytes
SpouseName		// 20 bytes

Without any complications, you've already "reused" the data structure of the base `struct`. Each data member from the `Caveman` `struct` is as accessible as the new `SpouseName` data member from the `Couple` `struct`. Note that this form of reuse is fundamentally different from the reuse you were able to do in ANSI C. There, you would have to write

```
typedef struct Couple
{ struct Caveman man;
  char SpouseName[20];
} CoupleStruct;
```

and you would only be able to access the `Caveman` data members via the named `struct man`. In C++, this is analogous to

```
struct Couple
{ Caveman man;
  char SpouseName[20];
};
```

In each case, the memory image the compiler creates for a `Couple` object could be almost identical. The difference lies in our ability to access the `Caveman` class data members directly without using a named sub-object. Throughout this chapter, we'll revisit the differences between including a named class object within a new class (sometimes called "layering") and deriving the new class from the existing class.

In the first declaration for the struct `Couple`, you'll notice that we used the access specifier `public` in front of the name of the base `struct Caveman`. The access specifier in front of a base type's name determines the access level for the sub-object's members. Table 4.1 shows how the different access specifiers affect the access level of the sub-object members.

TABLE **4.1**

Derivation	Public members	Protected members	Private members
public	public	protected	(inaccessible)
protected	protected	protected	(inaccessible)
private	private	private	(inaccessible)

For example, if you derive `class B` from `class A` using the protected access specifier, the `public` members of `class A` will become protected members in `class B`. Likewise, if you use the `private` access specifier, the `public` and `protected` members of `class A` will become `private` members in `class B`. Members of `class A` that are `private` will never by accessible in `class B`. Figure 4.1 shows graphically how using the different access specifiers affects the access to inherited members of the sub-object.

Overriding Virtual Functions

The second characteristic of inheritance is that it allows the derived class to define new versions of base class virtual functions (this is known as overriding a virtual function). By overriding a virtual function, you allow the compiler to choose the correct virtual function from the class's virtual function table or vtable.

For example, if you specify a virtual function in the `Caveman` class named `PrintBowlingScore()`, the compiler will make a VTABLE for that class (we'll call it a CavemanVtable). Each time you create a `Caveman` object, the compiler embeds a pointer to the CavemanVtable inside each object called the VPTR. The compiler will then use the VPTR and the VTABLE to lookup the address of the function it should call.

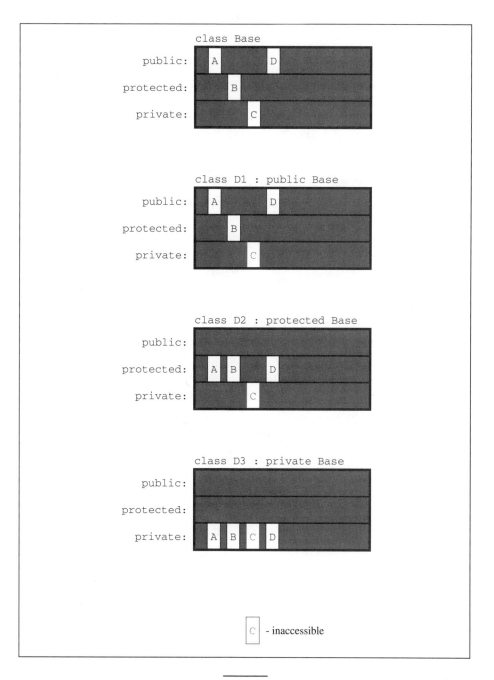

FIGURE 4.1

When you derive the new class `Couple`, the compiler will create another VTABLE for the `Caveman` class functions if the `Couple` class overrides any of the `Caveman` class's virtual functions, but the compiler will use this VTABLE only when it's calling a virtual function for the `Caveman` sub-object in a `Couple` object (we'll call this the CavemanCoupleVtable). Inside the `Caveman` sub-object of each `Couple` object, the compiler will insert a pointer to the CavemanCoupleVtable. If the couple class doesn't override the `PrintBowlingScore()` function, the compiler won't create the CavemanCoupleVtable, and it will insert a pointer to the CavemanVtable in the `Caveman` sub-object. (Less "prehistoric" compilers may choose a more sophisticated approach than this, but the end result will behave the same way.)

Therefore, the content of the VTABLE for a sub-object depends on its type and its derived class types. As you derive a class again and again, the compiler will continue to create new VTABLES as necessary. In this way, when you call a virtual function with an object of the derived class, the VTABLE for the base sub-object will contain the correct function address.

Implicit Conversions

In C++, there are a number of different ways the compiler can create an appropriate object when you use an object, pointer, or reference in a place where the compiler was expecting an object of a different type. In some cases, you'll want to specify that a conversion is possible. When you do this, you're creating a user-defined conversion.

In other cases, the compiler can create an object of the appropriate type by itself (for example, converting an `int` to a `long`) by performing implicit conversions. When you inherit one class from another, you're enabling the compiler to perform a number of implicit conversions.

Because the compiler will create a default copy-constructor for each class where you don't specify one, a derived class will usually have some level of access (`public`, `protected`, or `private`) to the base class's copy constructor (unless the the base class's copy constructor was a `private` member of the base class). This means the compiler will be able to use this copy constructor to create a copy of the base class sub-object if it needs to convert a derived class object into a base class object.

For example, if you declared a new object of the `Couple` struct by writing

```
Couple Flintstones;
```

and you declared the function `Print()` as follows

```
void Print(Caveman c);
```

calling this function with

```
Print(Flintstones);
```

will cause the compiler to call the copy-constructor for the `Caveman` `struct` to create the temporary object the function needs. Unfortunately, the temporary `Caveman` object has no way of knowing that it once was a part of a `Couple` object. The true "type" of the object is lost. This is frequently referred to as "slicing" since the compiler "slices" off everything except the base type object.

In addition to allowing the compiler to convert objects (if the copy-constructor is accessible), using inheritance gives the compiler permission to convert a derived class pointer or reference into a base class pointer or reference. However, these conversions don't occur because of a specific function like the copy-constructor. Therefore, you may be wondering whether or not the access specifiers for the base classes affect the compiler's ability to perform these conversions. In fact, they do. Instead of checking the accessibility of a particular function, the compiler allows implicit pointer or reference conversions based on whether or not the public members of the base class are accessible.

For example, if you use the `public` access specifier when you inherit `class B` from `class A`, any part of the program will be able to convert a pointer or reference to a B object to a pointer or reference to an A object. If you use the `protected` access specifier (which makes the base class's `public` members `protected` members of the derived class), only member functions or friends of `class B` or classes you derive from B will be able to convert pointers or references to B objects to pointers or references to A objects. Finally, using the `private` access specifier prevents any part of your program except member functions or friends of `class B` from converting pointers or references to B objects to pointers or references to A objects.

The Class Designer's View of Inheritance

Now that you've seen what the compiler creates when we use inheritance, let's consider how the low-level issues affect design decisions. Since designers are used to thinking in terms other than the low-level data structures we were just looking at, let's go way out. Consider a company that manufactures compact personal stereo equipment (Boom Boxes). The initial model, which plays AM and FM radio in addition to cassette tapes, is a huge success. They're planning a new model that will automatically shut off the tape when it reaches the end. Since it's unlikely that this company will create the new design from scratch, let's look at their options for reusing the previous model's design in the new model.

Layering—Adding the Sub-object

One solution may be to design a new cabinet that's just slightly larger than the existing model and then placing an old model boom box inside the case. By carefully positioning the openings and the new button assemblies, they might be able to make this approach work. (When the new model detects that the tape isn't moving via a tape motion sensor, it simulates a key press on the Stop button.)

This bizarre situation is actually somewhat similar to including a named sub-object in a new class to reuse code from an existing class. The advantage to this approach is that it requires absolutely no changes to the existing class, just as the new boom box design reuses the old model "as-is." The primary disadvantage to doing this is that the new class must replicate the existing class's functions to be able to intercept any of the member function calls destined for the sub-object. In addition, functions inside the sub-object have no way of calling member functions in the enclosing class (just as the existing boom box components have no way of knowing about the external hardware). If you use inheritance instead, you can let the derived class implement a virtual function that you declared in the base class and then call that function from other base class functions.

Private or Protected Inheritance—Overriding Virtual Functions

As an alternative, the company could use the new case, but add additional hardware inside the existing boom box. To do this, they'll need to have access to a number of signals and controls (for example, to electrically initiate the Stop function).

This is somewhat similar to using `private` inheritance in a software design. By inheriting a new class privately from an existing class, you'll have an unnamed object of the existing class, and the ability to intercept any of the existing class's functions and change their behavior.

Unfortunately, you'll still have to re-create the existing class's functions if you want them to appear in the new class.

One inheritance topic that's not discussed very often is the difference between `private` and `protected` inheritance. As we mentioned earlier, if you derive a new class using the `protected` access specifier, `public` and `protected` members of the base class will become `protected` members of the derived class. However, if you derive from this class, those members will still be accessible. Further derivations from here could continue to change the behavior of the `protected` base class.

 NOTE If you use private inheritance, you'll only be able to make changes to the private base class in the first derived class. For further derivations, the private base class members won't be accessible. Consider using protected inheritance instead of private inheritance unless you don't want further derivations to change the private base class's behavior.

If you use `private` or `protected` inheritance, you can change the visibility of a member by using an access declaration. For example, if you privately derive `class B` from `class A`, and `class A` contains a public member function `foo()`, you can make `A::foo()` available in `class B` by placing the fully qualified name `A::foo` somewhere in the declaration for `class B`. In this way you can selectively make some of the `class A` members part of the `class B` interface, and some of them part of the `class B` implementation.

Public Inheritance—Allowing Implicit Conversions

Instead, the boom box company may decide to add the new hardware inside the existing boom box case design. Again, they'll need access to the internal signals and controls in the existing system.

This situation corresponds somewhat to `public` inheritance in a software design. By inheriting a new class publicly from an existing class, you'll have an unnamed sub-object of the existing class, the ability to intercept any of the existing class's functions and change their behavior, plus you'll have the same interface as the existing class (implicit conversions).

Example—The Simple Bank

Now let's look at a completely different type of problem. Imagine that you're implementing a system that will manage all of the accounts for a small bank (you'll also need to imagine that this type of application hasn't already been written). For the moment, the bank's accounts are relatively straightforward, consisting of the usual checking accounts and savings accounts.

The primary responsibilities of this system are twofold: to maintain accurate balances for each account, and to provide an up-to-date balance report for all accounts. To begin, we decide to create a `BaseAccount` class that defines or names the common activities of the two accounts.

```
class BaseAccount {
 public:
  BaseAccount(long int an) :
    accountNum(an) {}
  ~BaseAccount();

  virtual void
  deposit(double);

  virtual void
  withdraw(double);

  virtual double
  balance() = 0;

  long int
  AccountNumber() { return accountNum; }
 private:
  long int accountNum;
};
```

Next, we decide to derive a checking account class from the `BaseAccount` class. In addition to the base class functions, this class will also provide a function to withdraw funds to another bank (writing a check).

```
class CheckingAccount : public BaseAccount {
 public:
  CheckingAccount(long int an) :
    BaseAccount(an) {}
  ~CheckingAccount();

  void
  ProcessCheck(long int bankNumber,
               long int acctNumber,
               double amount);

  virtual double
  balance();
};
```

In a similar manner, we decide to derive a savings account class from the BaseAccount class. In addition to the base class functions, this class will provide a function to calculate the interest on the account.

```
class SavingsAccount : public BaseAccount {
 public:
  SavingsAccount(long int an, double rate) :
    BaseAccount(an) {}
  ~SavingsAccount();

  void
  CalcInterest();

  void
  SetRate(double rate);

  virtual double
  balance();

 private:
  double interestRate;
};
```

Let's consider for a moment why we might decide to derive these classes publicly from the BaseAccount class instead of using layering, protected, or private inheritance. First, we know that every account will need to have an account number. Because there isn't anything in the BaseAccount class that we don't really need, we'll want to have a BaseAccount object as a sub-object of each CheckingAccount or SavingsAccount object. To achieve this we could use public, protected, or private derivation, or we could use layering.

However, we also know that we're going to need to keep an identifier for each account—checking and savings—in a single list. From a C++ perspective, it's reasonable to consider keeping a list of BaseAccount pointers or references to manage all of the account objects. This and our desire to override virtual functions in the BaseAccount class eliminates using layering (or suggests that we rethink our class design), and leaves us with either using public, protected, or private inheritance.

The easiest way for us to decide this is to ask "who needs to be able to use a CheckingAccount or SavingsAccount object as if it were a BaseAccount object?" If the CheckingAccount and SavingsAccount classes and their friend classes are the only parts of the program that need to be able to perform these implicit conversions, we can use protected or private inheritance. Since it's unlikely that we'll make the list of all accounts part of that group of classes (or classes derived from those), we used public inheritance.

CONSIDERING MULTIPLE INHERITANCE

Now, let's look at some of the things you'll want to keep in mind when you're considering whether or not you should use multiple inheritance in a particular situation. In general, you should think of multiple inheritance as a two-edged sword. The best part about multiple inheritance is that you can inherit from more than one class. On the other hand, the worst part about multiple inheritance is that you can inherit from more than one class.

Revisiting the Boom Box Company

Back at the boom box company, they've decided that they need to create a new version of the boom box that will also play CDs. In all likelihood, this company has the technical expertise to design and add the CD hardware to the new boom box. In fact, elsewhere in the company, they manufacture a home CD player. Unfortunately, to add the types components to the boom box that exist in the home unit will require a considerable investment in time from the in-house CD expert.

Layering

To get the product to market quickly the company realizes that it could simply manufacture a subframe for the boom box that would hold the home CD player. By adding a power inverter (to convert the 15 volts DC from the batteries to 110 AC) and an RCA cable (to route the CD output to the Auxiliary input), the company can now have a portable boom box CD system. The purchase price for the unit will be high (home CD + boom box + subframe + power inverter), and the battery life will be short, but they will be able to get the product on the market quickly.

If by now, you think that the company has lost its collective mind, don't worry. They haven't yet tried to ship a product using this design. However, this design is not that much different from some software designs that use layering to reuse code. While this may seem to be an acceptable way to reuse behavior from an existing class, it's important for you to remember that your new class will be carrying the "baggage" of this object.

If the overhead of the additional object is slight, there's a good chance for this approach to work. Unfortunately, layering has a number of limitations.

For example, imagine that our electronics company wants to incorporate some form of synchronized recording between the CD subsystem and the boom box's cassette recorder. What the marketing department wants is this: If you set the cassette system to record and then press the Pause button, pressing the Play button on the CD control panel will cause the CD to start playing and the cassette system to start recording.

Back in object-oriented terms, the marketing department has just asked us to override a function of the CD player. If the CD player's circuitry was built with such flexibility in mind (unlikely), it would be roughly equivalent to an existing class containing a virtual function.

Parasitic Inheritance

If instead, the new CD boom box retains all of the controls of the old boom box, users will know how to use the CD version right away (except for the new CD specific controls). If the company decides to add CD capability by including only those CD hardware components that are appropriate for portable use, the price will go down and the battery life will go up. On the down side, this approach may require extensive testing since the CD section of the boom box is essentially a new product.

Creating the new CD boom box this way is similar to deriving a new class using public inheritance and then adding just the new members we need for additional functionality. We'll call this parasitic inheritance since the derived class members become parasites to those of the base class (they attach to the base class object and cannot exist as a unit without it).

Multiple Inheritance

In another development, one of the design engineers has noticed that personal CD players themselves are becoming popular items with young adults. The engineer recommends that the company design a CD player chassis that would be suitable for a personal CD system in addition to providing the CD capabilities for the new model boom box and a redesigned version of the Home CD player.

What the engineer has done is a very important technique in considering whether or not to apply multiple inheritance in a specific software solution. First, the engineer recognized that there was common behavior and attributes between different pieces in the product line. Second, this person noticed that there were additional opportunities to use this common behavior and attribute set.

Multiple Inheritance and Design

A child thinks nothing of asking hundreds of questions every day (sometimes about more than one topic). In general, this is a good practice when you're analyzing a problem and designing a software solution. First, let's look at some questions you can ask when you're considering using multiple inheritance. Then, we'll look at some common situations where you may want to use multiple inheritance.

Design questions

One of the first questions you should ask is "How will the program use the different types of objects?" If the program will need to keep homogeneous lists or collections of objects that have different capabilities but share some common fundamental behavior or attributes, you'll probably want to consider deriving the different object types from a common base class. Another way of looking at this is by asking "will the program need to convert a pointer or reference to a given type of object into a pointer or reference to a base class object?" If the program will need to perform this type of conversion, you need to specify that one class inherits from the other.

The next question you should ask is: "Will some of these objects need to appear in more than one list or collection?" If the answer is yes, the program may need to perform implicit conversions to more than one base class. This is one of the most obvious benefits of multiple inheritance. Finally, make sure that you ask this question: "Will some of these objects need to override virtual functions from more than one class?" This is a sure sign that you should consider multiple inheritance.

Addin Classes versus Parasitic Inheritance

When you first begin identifying classes within the problem domain of an application, look for common behavior/attribute combinations—even in unrelated parts of the program. These behavior/attribute combinations may be suitable candidates to become *addin* classes. In an inheritance graph, you can picture addin class as one that suddenly appears off to the side of one or more of the classes and then simply "hangs on" its behavior and attributes.

Unfortunately, to know what to look for, you'll have to understand the problem domain thoroughly. For example, when the engineer at the boom box company recognized that there might be two products that both played music from CDs, the engineer immediately found a third possible product that could benefit from having this subassembly because he or she knew the market where the company was trying to sell products. The engineer also had enough technical knowledge of subassemblies and CD hardware to know that it was a practical possibility.

Whenever you're about to consider a base/derived relationship between two classes, take a close look at how the derived class affects the behavior or attributes of the base class. Does the derived class change the behavior and attributes of the base class, or does it merely add new ones (parasitic inheritance)? If some of the derived class members don't change the base class behavior or communicate with the base class in any way, you may want to consider moving those members into a separate class and then deriving a new class from that class and the existing base using multiple inheritance.

For example, if you were creating an employee payroll application, and you already had a `Person` class that defined the usual name and address data, you could derive a new `Employee` class from this class with something like

```
class Employee : public Person
{
 public:
  Employee(unsigned long num);
  void PrintEmployeeNum();  // Not a function in the
                            // in the base class

 private:
  unsigned long EmployeeNumber;
};
```

The data and member function we define in this class are purely supplemental to the `Person` class. Instead, we could create another class with something like

```
class EmployeeData
{
 public:
   EmployeeData(unsigned long num);
   void PrintEmployeeNum();

 private:
   unsigned long EmployeeNumber;
};
```

Then, we could derive the `Employee` class with

```
class Employee : public Person, public EmployeeData
{
 public:
   Employee(unsigned long num);
};
```

There are two primary advantages to moving code to an addin class this way. First, we'll be able to debug and refine the `EmployeeData` class as a unit. Second, we'll be able to later use the `EmployeeData` class to create some other non-`Person` employee classes (for example, a `SubContractorCompany` class). Third, if there are parts of the program that don't need to use anything other than members of the `EmployeeData` class, we can refer to `Employee` objects via an `EmployeeData` pointer or reference. This will help communicate what that section of the program is doing with those objects, and will allow us to hold pointers or references to any `EmployeeData` derived class (like `Employee` or `SubContractorCompany`) in a list of `EmployeeData` objects.

Another excellent place to use addin classes is when you're implementing reference counting and smart pointers to clean up memory allocation problems. You can create a class that maintains the reference count for any derived class. For example, given a class `Window`:

```
class Window
{ // details here
};

class RefCount
{
 friend class SmartPointer;
 protected:
   unsigned int  _rc;
};
```

```
class RefCountWin : public Window,
                    private RefCount
{ // duplicate Window class constructors here
};
```

Now, objects of the SmartPointer class can increment and decrement the reference count _rc for a given RefCountWin object as necessary. In addition, you could keep a list of RefCount objects (possibly as a static member of the RefCount class) and perform debugging or reporting operations on all of the reference counted objects in the program at a given time. In this situation, it doesn't really matter whether you created the Window class or if it's part of an off-the-shelf class library. As long as there aren't any naming conflicts between the single member _rc and members of the other base classes (more on naming conflicts later), you won't have any problems.

Mixin Classes

If you're developing a relatively small class hierarchy where you know the full set of services the derived classes will need to provide, creating a *mixin* hierarchy may be acceptable. For example, examine the following classes:

```
class ThreeCourseMeal
{
 public:
  virtual const char*
  GetFirstCourse() = 0;

  virtual const char*
  GetSecondCourse() = 0;

  virtual const char*
  GetThirdCourse() = 0;

  void
  Eat()
  { cout << GetFirstCourse() << endl;
    cout << GetSecondCourse() << endl;
    cout << GetThirdCourse() << endl;
  }
};

class MexicanAppetizer : virtual public ThreeCourseMeal
{
 public:
  const char* GetFirstCourse()
```

```
      { return "Nachos"; }
 };

 class MexicanMainDish : virtual public ThreeCourseMeal
 {
  public:
   const char* GetSecondCourse()
   { return "Burrito"; }
 };

 class MexicanDesert : virtual public ThreeCourseMeal
 {
  public:
   const char* GetThirdCourse()
   { return "Fried Ice Cream"; }
 };

 class MexicanThreeCourseMeal : public MexicanAppetizer,
                                public MexicanMainDish,
                                public MexicanDesert
 {
 };
```

By specifying the full set of members in the base class `ThreeCourseMeal`, you've communicated what derived classes have to do. It doesn't matter which classes implement the different functions, as long as you implement them somewhere before you try to create an object of that type. When you're designing one of the "mixed-in" classes (one of the three courses), you'll know what members the other classes are going to have to define. Figure 4.2 shows the inheritance hierarchy along with a diagram that depicts which classes implement which functions.

If you like, you can specify that you can call the public functions of the mixin base class only from a pointer of the mixin base type. To do this, you'd simply declare the overriding functions in the intermediate classes protected sections. A mixin base class pointer will be able to call these functions since they're public in that class. However, the virtual function mechanism will ensure that the compiler calls the correct version of the functions at run-time.

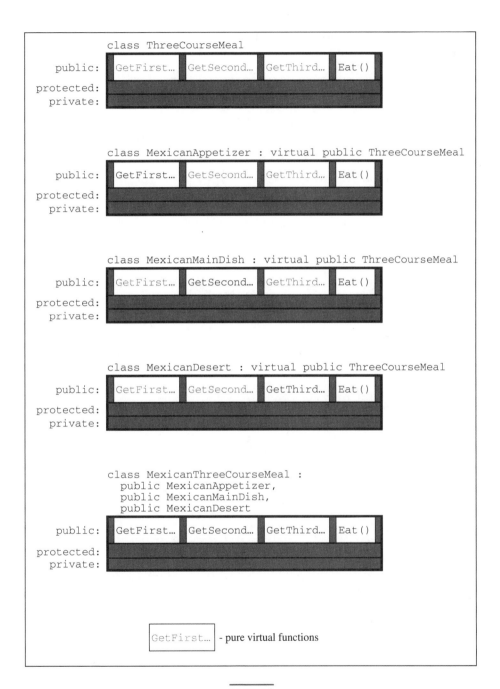

FIGURE 4.2

However, a mixin hierarchy will also usually define or predict how you'll combine definitions of the base class members in the intermediate classes. In the previous example, you should always define an intermediate class that defines just one course of the meal. Limiting the intermediate classes this way will allow you to confidently combine ChineseAppetizer, FrenchMainDish, and ItalianDesert classes into a brand new PotpouriThreeCourseMeal class without worrying about one class implementing the same functions as another class.

A variation on this form involves implementing a default version of each function in the base class, for example, if we changed the base class declaration to

```
class ThreeCourseMeal
{
 public:
  virtual const char*
  GetFirstCourse() { return "Water"; }

  virtual const char*
  GetSecondCourse() { return "Water"; }

  virtual const char*
  GetThirdCourse() { return "After-dinner Mint"; }

  void Eat() { // same as before }
};
```

we could then define a class like this

```
class MexicanFastFood : public MexicanMainDish,
                        public MexicanDesert
{
};
```

If you think about it, there are now two paths in the inheritance hierarchy for each of the GetSecondCourse() and GetThirdCourse() functions (the base class versions and derived class version of each). Graphically, you can see the paths for the GetSecondCourse() function in the MexicanFastFood class below in Figure 4.3.

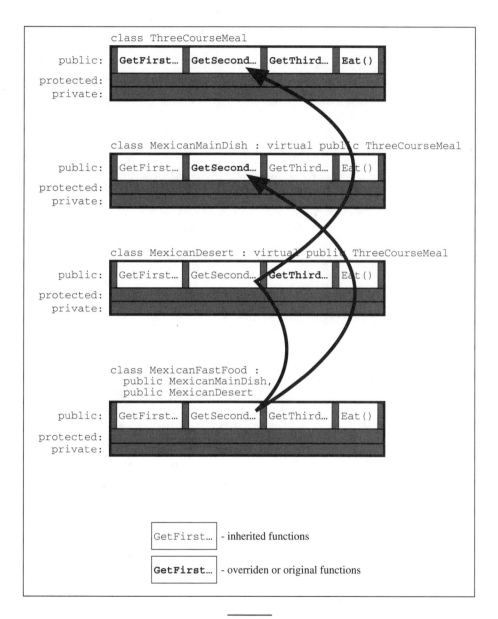

FIGURE 4.3

In C++, the dominance rule resolves this problem (if you're using virtual base classes). Because the MexicanMainDish class "knowingly" provides a new version of the GetSecondCourse() function (the author of the class should know they are either hiding a nonvirtual function of the same name, or overriding a virtual function from the base class), that's the one the compiler will call. Since the compiler assumes you defined the function this way intentionally, it assumes that this is the version you'll want to call instead of the base class version that's available via an alternate path.

Mixin/Addin Hybrids

If you're careful, you can create hybrid mixin/addin hierarchies. However, you may want to use protected or private inheritance for the addin classes. This is because pointers to the base class or sibling classes in the mixin hierarchy won't be able to call any of the addin class's member functions directly. In all likelihood, you'll call the addin class's member functions from inside the derived class versions of virtual functions from the base class.

Multiple Personality Classes and Virtual Bases

In the previous example, if you specified ThreeCourseMeal as a nonvirtual base class for the intermediate classes, a number of things happen. First, you'll have to perform an explicit cast if you want to use a pointer to a MexicanThreeCourseMeal object where the compiler expects a pointer to a ThreeCourseMeal object. This is because the compiler has no way of knowing which of the ThreeCourseMeal sub-objects (there would be three inside each MexicanThreeCourseMeal object) you want to use.

In addition, calling the Eat() function from an intermediate class pointer won't necessarily call the correct function anymore. This is because the VTABLE for any one of the ThreeCourseMeal objects will only contain the addresses of functions that you override in their derivation path to the MexicanThreeCourseMeal class. For example, the VTABLE for the ThreeCourseMeal sub-object that's inside the MexicanAppetizer sub-object will contain the addresses of the MexicanAppetizer::GetFirstCourse() function and the addresses of the ThreeCourseMeal::GetSecondCourse() and ThreeCourseMeal::GetThirdCourse() functions. (The VTABLE for the MexicanAppetizer sub-object will look the same.) Since the behavior of the object is different depending on what type of pointer you use to access it, we'll call this a multiple personality class. For some situations, this may be what you want—but it's not likely.

However, since we specified the `ThreeCourseMeal` class as a virtual base, given a `MexicanThreeCourseMeal` object, you can manipulate it via a pointer of any of the five types (`ThreeCourseMeal`, `Mexican-Appetizer`, `MexicanMainDish`, `MexicanDesert`, `MexicanThreeCourseMeal`). This works because each intermediate class adds its function addresses to the VTABLE that the common `ThreeCourseMeal` sub-object uses. No matter what the pointer type is, calling any of the three member functions will always work. This form of sibling class communication is powerful, but it can become confusing very quickly.

Example—Extending the Bank Services

Back at the bank, we've been told that our application will need to implement Negotiable Order of Withdrawal (NOW) accounts (often referred to as a checking account that pays interest). Let's look at three approaches to this problem.

Solution 1: Apply Multiple Inheritance

Since this is a chapter on multiple inheritance, you might expect to see the following:

```
class NowAccount : public CheckingAccount,
                   public SavingsAccount
{
};
```

Unfortunately, since we didn't specify `BaseAccount` as a virtual base class for the `CheckingAccount` class or the `SavingsAccount` class, this type of derivation would yield a multiple personality class. Even if we did go back and change this derivation, the current group of `BaseAccount`, `SavingsAccount`, and `CheckingAccount` classes don't qualify as a mixin hierarchy. This means that it's possible that these two classes could interact in some strange ways if we derive from both of them.

Solution 2: Create an InterestAccount Class

A second solution is to look at reorganizing our classes at the top of the hierarchy.

```
class InterestAccount : public BaseAccount
{};

class SavingsAccount : public InterestAccount
{};

class CheckingAccount : public InterestAccount
{};
```

To provide a CheckingAccount object that doesn't pay interest, we may be able to specify an interest rate of 0%. However, a list of all InterestAccount objects could contain checking accounts that aren't NOW accounts. To detect them we'd need to check the interest rate at run-time (a very non-C++ thing to do). If a NOW account differs in other ways, we may want to use the following:

```
class CheckingAccount : public BaseAccount
{};

class NowAccount : public InterestAccount
{};
```

Now, the compiler won't allow us to add a CheckingAccount object to a list of InterestAccount objects, but this design will require that we reimplement the CheckingAccount functions. We could do this by duplicating the code (bad idea), using layering with a CheckingAccount member object (better, but you still need to reimplement the CheckingAccount functions to pass them through to the member object), or using multiple inheritance to derive the NowAccount class from the InterestAccount class and the CheckingAccount class (similar problems as in Solution 1).

Solution 3: Use addin Classes and Multiple Inheritance

So far, we've looked at some typical solutions to this problem. If you think about it you'll realize that primarily what we want from the SavingsAccount class is its ability to calculate interest. By placing that code in either the SavingsAccount class or the InterestAccount class, we've used parasitic inheritance (we can't use the interest behavior without creating one of these objects). Since the interest calculating behavior and attributes probably won't change the behavior of the BaseAccount class, let's look at creating an addin class for calculating interest.

```
class InterestCalculator
{
 public:
  void
  CalculateInterest();

  void
  ApplyInterest() = 0; // call BaseAccount::deposit()
                       // or BaseAccount::withdraw()?

 protected:
  double
  GetInterest();
  double
  GetPrincipal() = 0; // call BaseAccount::balance()
};
```

Now, we can create a new SavingsAccount class by writing

```
class SavingsAccount : public BaseAccount,
                       public InterestCalculator
{
 public:
  ApplyInterest() { deposit(GetInterest()); }
                    // from BaseAccount

 protected:
  double
  GetPrincipal() { return 0; }
};
```

In addition, we've added some flexibility for the future. By using this same class we could create a LoanAccount class:

```
class LoanAccount : public LoanBase,
                    public InterestCalculator
{
 public:
  ApplyInterest() { AccrueInterest(GetInterest()); }

 protected:
  double
  GetPrincipal() { return GetLoanBalance(); }
};
```

Without too much trouble, we could now implement an ArmAccount (Adjustable Rate Mortgage) class, a HomeEquityLoan class, a CDAccount class, or others. For a different application, you might be able to use this class to derive an `AmortizationCalc` class for calculating amortization rates and tables. By looking for a possible addin class, we've created a true software building block.

APPLYING MULTIPLE INHERITANCE

In this last section, we'll examine a few of the issues that can complicate multiple inheritance in real projects. It's important to remember that these issues won't come into play very often if you primarily use multiple inheritance in the ways we discussed in the last section.

Name Clashes

One of the first complaints you'll hear when discussing multiple inheritance is "what if two of the base classes have members with the same name?" While this tends to be overrated, there are situations where you'll want to inherit from two or more classes that use the same name for a class member (either a member function or a data member). There are really two problems here: simple name clashes (nonvirtual member functions or data members that have the same name) and virtual function name clashes.

Simple Name Clashes

If the conflict involves a nonvirtual member function or a data member, you can use the fully qualified name of the member to access the correct element. For example, consider again using the `RefCount` addin class to create the `RefCountWin` class (a reference counted window object). Internally, the `RefCount` class keeps track of the number of smart pointers that are referring to it (the reference count) with the data member `_rc`. In the unlikely event that the `Window` class contains a member named `_rc`, all the member functions of the `Window` class that refer to `_rc` will automatically use `Window::_rc` instead of `RefCount::_rc`. unless you call them explicitly from a member function in the `RefCountWin` class. (Since the only reason for creating the `RefCountWin` class is to attach a reference count to each `Window` object, you shouldn't be overriding functions or adding members directly in this class anyway.)

Second, since all of the smart pointer member functions that will change the value of _rc will expect a pointer or reference to a RefCount object, the compiler will implicitly convert a pointer or reference to a RefCountWin object to one for a RefCount object. Once again, since these functions don't know about the surrounding RefCountWin object, any member function that uses the name _rc will automatically use RefCount::_rc instead of Window::_rc.

If you need to override some of the virtual functions from base classes that use the same name for class members, you'll need to use the full name of the data member or member function name. For example, if you override a virtual function from the Window class in the RefCountWin class, you'll need to use the name Window::_rc to access this member. By the way, making the _rc member private or using private derivation won't help eliminate the name clash. The compilers will check for a naming conflict before checking for accessibility.

NOTE

Remember that for any member function that exists in both classes, the function names and argument list types must match exactly for there to be a name clash. If they don't match, the derived class will contain both functions, they will overload each other based on the arguments you use when you call them, and no clash will exist.

If the name in question is part of the public section of either class (which means it's likely that other functions or classes will try to call it directly), all bets are off, and you have a name clash. However, once again, you'll usually be able to use the fully qualified name of the data member or member function to call the correct version. The only time you won't want to do this is if the name clash involves a virtual member function.

Virtual Function Name Clashes

If you use virtual functions very much, it might surprise you to realize that most naming conflicts you might expect to occur with data members and nonvirtual functions won't occur in the base class's member functions. This might surprise you because the virtual function mechanism makes sure that the sub-objects in a derived class object "know" about the virtual functions that the derived class overrides. However, if the derived class doesn't override any of the base class functions, there typically won't be a problem because each sub-object's VTABLE will only contain the addresses of functions that it inherits, functions it defines, or functions that the derived class overrides and defines.

In the last paragraph, "typically" means when you're not using virtual bases. As we saw in the section on mixin class hierarchies, using a virtual base can create a clash because the vtables on either side of the inheritance diagram will "know" about the functions defined on the other side.

As was the case with data members and nonvirtual member functions, you can use the fully qualified name of a virtual function to call the correct one. The down side of this is that the call is no longer virtual. (No matter whether or not any further derived classes override it, the code that uses the fully qualified name will call that version of the function.) The question becomes "how can you call one virtual function instead of the other when they both have the same name and argument list types without defeating the virtual function mechanism?"

The solution is to create an intermediate class for each base class that contains the name that clashes. In the intermediate classes, you'll simply override the clashing virtual function to call one of two new non-clashing pure virtual functions that replace the old function. In the derived class that brings together these intermediate classes, you'll define the new behavior that you want for the clashing virtual functions by overriding the new pure virtual functions, as shown in Figure 4.4.

Now, any call to the original function (vote()) will eventually call the newly named virtual function (vote_D() or vote_R()). It doesn't matter where the call comes from as long as you don't try to call it from the new derived class (once again, you'd have a name clash). Even member functions from a base class many derivations up the inheritance hierarchy will call the new version indirectly via the old name. In this way, further derivations of the class that contains the clashing virtual function names can continue to extend and enhance the behavior of the clashing virtual functions.

Addin Functions versus Parasitic Virtual Functions

It's not uncommon for an overriding virtual function to call the base class version of the same function. If you're deriving a new class from two or more classes that come from a common base class, you might be inclined to call the two different versions of the function to make sure that each part of the object has its turn to respond to the function call. This can cause problems when you're using virtual base classes.

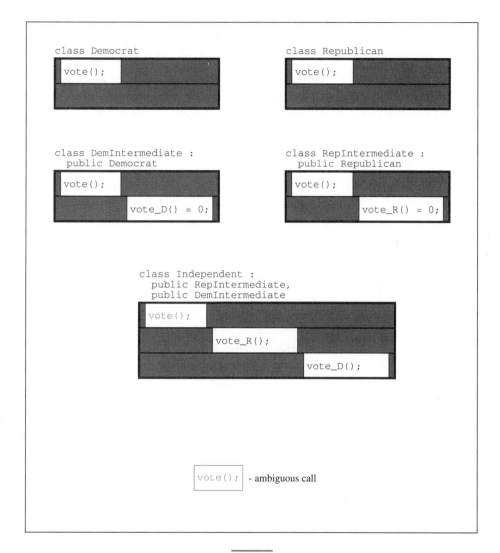

FIGURE 4.4

Consider again the CheckingAccount, SavingsAccount example. Instead of changing the hierarchy, we'll go ahead and derive the NowAccount class from the CheckingAccount and SavingsAccount classes, and make the BankAccount class a virtual base class of those classes. Now, consider what happens if we've defined a PrintAccount-Summary() virtual function in each class. The BaseAccount version of this function would probably print the account number and the balance. The CheckingAccount version would call the BaseAccount version of the function first, and then print a list of checks written from the account during the past month. Finally, the SavingsAccount version would call the BaseAccount version, and then display the accounts current interest rate and the interest credited to the account during the past month.

```
void BaseAccount::PrintAccountSummary()
{ cout << "Account #" << accountNum << endl;
  cout << "Balance - $" << balance() << endl; }


void CheckingAccount::PrintAccountSummary()
{ BaseAccount::PrintAccountSummary();
                    // call base class version
  for(checkCount = 0;
      checkCount < numChecks;
      ++checkCount)
      { cout << "#" << checks[checkCount].number;
        cout << " - $" << check[checkCount].amount << endl;
      }
}

void BaseAccount::PrintAccountSummary()
{ BaseAccount::PrintAccountSummary();
                    // call base class version

  cout << "Interest Rate - %" << interestRate << endl;
  cout << "Interest Paid - $" << InterestCredited() <<
endl; }
```

Now, when we create the NowAccount class, we'll want to provide a version of the PrintAccountSummary() virtual function that will correctly display all of the same data that the base class versions display. However, if we write

```
void NowAccount::PrintAccountSummary()
{ CheckingAccount::PrintAccountSummary();
                       // base class versions
  SavingsAccount::PrintAccountSummary(); }
                  //    "      "        "
```

we'll see the following output

```
Account #1234567
Balance - $266.19
```

```
Account #1234567
Balance - $266.19
Checks for this month:
#2330 -  $13.02

Interest Rate - %3.2
Interest Paid - $1.92
```

Why did the function call the `BaseAccount::PrintAccountSummary()` function twice? Because each of the intermediate account classes calls the base version of the function at the beginning of their versions.

Once again, if you look closely at the `PrintAccountSummary()` functions in `CheckingAccount` and `SavingsAccount` classes, you'll find that they do something useful in addition to calling the base class version of the function. Because these functions don't allow you to separate these useful actions from the action of the `BaseAccount` version, we'll call these a parasitic virtual functions.

In much the same way that we moved the members from a parasitic class and placed them into an addin class, you can introduce class specific implementation functions called *addin functions* (since the concept is similar to addin classes). To create an addin function, just take the code that the derived class function would have added, and place it into into a separate nonvirtual protected function, just as we placed behavior or attributes that a parasitic class added into an addin class. Once you've created the addin function, you'll change the companion virtual function to call the base class and then call the companion function.

In our example, you'd add the following protected nonvirtual function to the `CheckingAccount` class.

```
void CheckingAccount::_PrintAccountSummary()
{ for(checkCount = 0;
     checkCount < numChecks;
     ++checkCount)
   { cout << "#" << checks[checkCount].number;
     cout << " - $" << check[checkCount].amount << end;
   }
}
```

Then, we'd write a similar version for the `SavingsAccount` class to print the interest data. Now, we can rewrite the `NowAccount` class's version of the `PrintAccountSummary()` function.

```
void NowAccount::PrintAccountSummary()
{ BaseAccount::PrintAccountSummary();
                                   // call base class version
  CheckingAccount::_PrintAccountSummary();
  SavingsAccount::_PrintAccountSummary(); }
```

After you make this change, a NowAccount object will only print the BaseAccount data once when you call the PrintAccountSummary() function. Interestingly, this technique still works if you're not using virtual bases. However, the two BaseAccount sub-objects may not contain the same data (you may be making deposits to and writing checks from one BaseAccount sub-object, and crediting interest in the other), and this can cause some unexpected behavior.

Most Derived Class

In the previous section, we looked at how you can avoid calling a virtual function in a virtual base class multiple times. Now, consider what happens during construction time of a NowAccount object (BaseAccount is a virtual base class). If the constructors for the CheckingAccount class and the SavingsAccount class initialize the BaseAccount class, you might wonder why the constructor for the NowAccount class needs to initialize the BaseAccount class, and why the compiler doesn't initialize it multiple times.

First, when a class contains one or more virtual base classes, the compiler will always initialize those classes first. Second, the compiler will require the outermost enclosing object or *most derived* class, to initialize the virtual base. By requiring the most derived class to initialize virtual base classes and then ignoring all other initializers the compiler can guarantee that it will build the virtual base sub-object only once.

CONCLUSION

Most C++ programmers haven't spent the time to really understand the full implications of using single inheritance. Once they do, the mechanics of using multiple inheritance become fairly straightforward. However, once you have a solid foundation in inheritance fundamentals, you'll need to examine your class hierarchies regularly to spot potential uses for multiple inheritance. At that point, you'll only need to remember a few simple implementation issues to begin using multiple inheritance effectively.

COMPILATION FIREWALLS

Dan Saks

INTRODUCTION

In many ways, C++ classes provide solid support for data abstraction. A class gathers the representation of a data type (the data members) along with the operations on that type (the member and friend functions) into a single, clearly-defined program unit. Access specifiers (the keywords `public`, `protected`, and `private`) clearly distinguish those parts of the class that clients (users of the class) can access from those parts that only the class supplier can access. A well-written class defines an abstract type with complete and consistent behavior that you can use with little or no concern for how it works.

Many classes provide behavior that you can implement in more than one way. For example, you can implement the abstract behavior of a symbol dictionary using any number of concrete structures, like a binary tree, a b-tree or a hash table. Depending on the anticipated volume of data and the application's speed and memory requirements, you might store the entire dictionary in dynamic memory, or keep only the retrieval keys in memory and store the rest on disk.

No one implementation of a particular abstraction is right for all applications. Estimating system performance during analysis and design can guide you in selecting a good implementation. But you won't really know if you made the right choice until you measure the assembled application using real-live data. The measurements may indicate that another implementation yields better performance. If the class is well written, you simply slip a different implementation behind a given class interface and rebuild the application without modifying any client source code.

This is adapted from a two-part article that originally appeared in *The C Users Journal*, April and May 1994 (Volume 12, Numbers 4 and 5). Copyright (©) 1994 by Dan Saks.

C++ lets you do all this, except there's one hitch. Almost invariably, when you change the class implementation, you change the declarations for one or more private members. And those declarations are in the header that defines the class. If you use a make system (or the project system that comes with many development systems), rebuilding the application will recompile every source file that directly or indirectly includes the header for the revised class. (If you don't use make or its equivalent, you may get some real surprises when you test the application.) When your application is large, the lengthy build times can really reduce your productivity.

Actually, providing alternative implementations is a special case of a more general problem, namely, that any change to the private part of a class forces you to recompile source code that appears unaffected by the change. The root of the problem is that C++ syntax does not physically separate all the implementation details for a class from the client interface for that class. Another way to look at this is that the compilation interface of a class typically is wider than the public interface for that class.

The *compilation interface* of a class is what a compiler needs to know about that class to compile source code that uses the class. The compilation interface is the entire class definition—the member declarations (private and protected as well as public), the friend declarations, and the inline function definitions. The *public interface* is what a client programmer needs to know (yea verily, is allowed to access) about a class when writing code that uses that class. The public interface consists only of the all the public member declarations and friend declarations of the class.

Why was C++ designed with this apparent flaw? As with any language, C++ has its share of design trade-offs. C++ places space and time efficiency of generated code at a higher premium than the speed and convenience of the translation process. And the lack of physical separation between class interface and implementation offers real benefits in both storage efficiency and run-time performance of the resulting object code.

Morever, if you really need to physically separate a class interface from its implementation, C++ offers you a choice of programming conventions that will do this. By following these conventions, you can write any class so that its compilation interface is essentially the same as its public interface. Booch (1991) calls this building "compilation firewalls," so that changes in the implementation of one class don't trigger a massive recompilation.

The two most common techniques for building compilation firewalls in C++ are:

◆ "Cheshire Cat" classes

◆ Protocol-based classes

I'll begin by presenting a sample application that has a class with two distinct implementations for the same public interface. Like many complete C++ programming examples, it requires quite a bit of explanation, including a few side trips. So bear with me, and I'll to get to the point as quickly as possible.

A CROSS-REFERENCE PROGRAM

xr is a simple cross-reference generator inspired by exercise 6-3 from Kernighan & Ritchie (1988) that I've used as an example in earlier *C Users Journal* columns [Saks (1991a), (1991b) and (1991c)]. xr writes to standard output an alphabetized list of words appearing in a document read from standard input. The program views its input as a sequence of words (where a word is a sequence of letters and digits starting with a letter) separated by nonwords (such as spaces, punctuation, and digits). xr prints each word on a separate line followed by the sequence of line numbers on which that word appears in the document.

For example, if the word object appears in the input once on lines 3, 19, and 100, and twice on line 81, then the output entry for object is

```
object          3  19  81 100
```

The program makes the simplifying assumption that all line numbers will fit on a output line. That is, it doesn't include any logic to break overly long output lines at a nice, neat place.

The program spans several source and header files. The main function (Listing 1) uses the getword function to scan the input and pick out each word that goes in the cross-reference. main delegates the work of collecting and printing cross-reference entries to a single local object x of type xrt.

xrt is the cross-reference table class. The xrt class definition appears in xrt.h (Listing 2), and its implementation appears in xrt.cpp (Listing 3). This particular implementation uses a binary tree to store the cross-reference entries in alphabetical order.

xrt is a *handle* class. That is, xrt consists merely of a pointer (a handle) to an associated data structure (the body) that does the real work. That pointer is the private data member root, which is a pointer to a treenode.

xrt.h declares, but does not define, class treenode. The declaration

```
class treenode;
```

declares treenode as an *incomplete type*. You cannot declare objects of an incomplete type, because the type declaration doesn't specify any object size or layout. However, you can declare pointers and references to objects of an incomplete type, just like xrt::root in Listing 2.

Why did I declare treenode as an incomplete type? Why didn't I define the class at time I declared it? xrt and treenode are mutually referential types. That is, the definition for xrt refers to treenode, and the definition for treenode refers to xrt. As in C, the only way you can do this in C++ is by using pointers to incomplete types. You declare one class (in this case, treenode) as an incomplete type, then define the second class (xrt) with members that are pointers to the incomplete type. Then you complete the incomplete type (treenode) by defining it.

xrt.h does not complete treenode, because it doesn't have to. Only xrt.cpp uses treenode, so only xrt.cpp completes treenode before using it. Client code, like main, that includes xrt.h should not be aware that treenodes even exist. Therefore, it shouldn't matter to client code that the type remains incomplete.

Leaving treenode incomplete in xrt.h has the added advantage of removing implementation details from the header. Changes in the structure of a treenode don't induce changes in the header. The incomplete type acts as a compilation firewall. This mechanism is the foundation of the Cheshire Cat technique. As you will see shortly, the Cheshire Cat technique is a set of uniform stylistic conventions for building compilation firewalls from handle classes and incomplete types.

You could argue that leaving treenode incomplete in xrt.h also adds a little more security to the interface. xrt.h declares treenode at file scope, so any compilation that includes xrt.h adds treenode to its global namespace. But treenodes should be invisible to client code. If you can't make it invisible, the next best thing you can do is render it unusable. Leaving treenode incomplete seems to do just that. The compiler will reject any client code that tries to create an object of incomplete type treenode.

Unfortunately, nothing prevents client code from inadvertantly completing the incomplete type. Client code that completes type `treenode` may be in for some real surprises if it uses a definition for `treenode` that differs from the one in `xrt.cpp`. If the code makes it past the linker, the program may exhibit very subtle run-time errors.

The completed class `treenode` in `xrt.cpp` specifies the layout for each node in the binary tree. It pairs a word with a sequence of line numbers on which that word occurs in the input. It also contains left and right subtrees, implemented as `xrt` objects.

`treenode` uses a pointer to a dynamically allocated null-terminated character string that holds the spelling of a word. It uses an object of class type `lns` (line number sequence) to hold the set of line numbers associated with that word.

ALTERNATIVE IMPLEMENTATIONS FOR LNS

`lns` has a simple interface with only four member functions:

◆ the constructor, `lns(unsigned)`, initializes an `lns` object to hold a single line number.

◆ the destructor, `~lns()`, releases all the resources used by an `lns`.

◆ `add(unsigned)` adds a line number to the end of a sequence.

◆ `print()` writes an `lns` to `stdout`.

I will present two slightly different lns implementations

1. A "small" version, in which an `lns` consists of a single pointer to the first element in a singly-linked list of line numbers.

2. A "fast" version, in which an `lns` consists of a pair of pointers: one to the first element in a singly linked list of line numbers, and another to the last element.

The "small" version uses less memory (one pointer's worth) for each `lns` object, but it's relatively slow because it searches the entire list to find the last node every time it adds a line number. The "fast" version avoids that search by using a second pointer pointing directly to the tail of the list.

Indeed, there are other possible implementations, including "small" implementations that perform more-or-less as fast as the "fast" implementation. But in general, you might not hit upon the optimal implementation until the rest of the application is up and running. This article describes, by example, general techniques for packaging a class to dramatically reduce the cost of altering the implementation.

The definition for the "small" `lns` class appears in `lnsls.h` (Listing 4), and the corresponding member function definitions appear in `lnsls.cpp` (Listing 5). Like `xrt`, `lns` is a handle class; the handle is a pointer to the first node in the linked list. Unlike `xrt`, which uses an incomplete global type as its body class, `lns` uses a private nested type `node`.

A nested class is in the scope of its enclosing class. Therefore, I didn't bother adding a prefix to the name `node` (such as `lns_`), because the fully qualified name of the node class is `lns::node`. Since `lns::node` is private, it's inaccessible to client code.

Rather than define `lns::node` *in situ* (at the point of its declaration inside class `lns`), I prefer to use the new C++ feature that allows forward declaration of nested classes. The declaration

```
class node;
```

inside class `lns` declares `lns::node` as an incomplete type. The subsequent declaration

```
node *first;
```

declares `first` as a pointer to the nested node type. Since that is the only use of `node` inside the `lns` class definition, I delayed defining `lns::node` until after completing the `lns` class definition.

As of this writing (Spring 1994), few compilers support forward declaration of nested classes, but I've grown fond of this feature very quickly. Nested classes are great for name space and access control, but nested classes defined in situ can really clutter the enclosing class definition. I think forward declarations are much more readable. Granted, there are times when you must complete the nested class inside the enclosing class, but those times are fairly uncommon.

If your compiler does not yet support forward declaration of nested classes, then move the `node` definition back inside the `lns` definition.

Specifically, delete the forward declaration for node that appears inside class lns. Then move the complete definition for lns::node into lns in place of the deleted declaration. Be sure to delete lns:: from the heading of the nested class.

lnsls.h in Listing 4 contains two inline member function definitions. I prefer to place inline member function definitions outside their class definitions for the same reason I prefer forward class declarations. It's a little more verbose, but a lot more orderly.

Outside the scope of class lns, you must refer to the lns::node constructor as lns::node::node. The body of the lns constructor is in the scope of class lns, so it can refer to lns::node as just node.

lns::add always adds a new line number at the end of the list. Therefore, the "small" implementation (using a single pointer to the head of the list) must scan the list every time to find the last element just to tack the new number on the end. As an alternative, lns can maintain a separate pointer to the last element in the list. This eliminates the need to scan the list each time and greatly simplifies the logic of lns::add, at the cost of one additional pointer per cross-reference entry. The header for this "fast" implementation is lnslf.h (Listing 6). The corresponding member function definitions are in lnslf.cpp (Listing 7).

Listing 8 shows a makefile that will build the entire cross-reference program. It refers to the lns header and source file as lns.h and lns.cpp, respectively. To build the program using the "small" lns implementation, copy lnsls.* to lns.*, and then run make.

To use the "fast" lns implementation, copy lnslf.* to lns.*, and run make. You should see make rebuild the entire program, because all of the source files depend on lns.h, which just changed. (Some systems, notably MS-DOS, don't update the time stamp on the file that's the target of a copy. When you run make after copying the lns files, nothing happens because make thinks all of the files are up to date. If that happens, you should use a utility like touch to update the time stamps on the lns.* files. Then make will know that the files have changed.)

Both versions of the lns class are in "uninsulated" form, where the class definition contains private data members that reflect a particular implementation. When you change the implementation, you typically change the header as well as the source file. Changing the header can trigger a massive recompilation.

To avoid recompilation whenever you change the lns implementation, you must design a single lns header that works with both implementations, as well as with any others as yet unwritten. The Cheshire Cat technique helps you do just that.

CHESHIRE CAT CLASSES

Carolan (1989) coined the term "Cheshire Cat" to describe his technique for separating the implementation details for a class from its public interface using handle classes and incomplete types. You can transform a class X from its uninsulated form to its insulated (Cheshire Cat) form by following these steps:

1. Move X's private members to a separate implementation details class outside X's header file.
2. Declare the implementations details class as an incomplete type in X's header.
3. Replace X's private members with a single pointer to the implementation details class.
4. Rewrite X's public members as non-inline functions that manage and operate on an implementation details object.

Listing 9 shows lns2.h containing a new definition for class lns as a Cheshire Cat class. The public members are the same as before (in Listing 4 and 6), but the private data is now just a single pointer dp to an object of incomplete type lns::details. This one header now serves both implementations for class lns.

Listing 10 shows lns2s.cpp, the "small" lns implementation (using a single pointer). The completed definition for nested type lns::details looks almost identical to the lns class in uninsulated form that appears in Listing 4. The only difference is the class name, and hence, the names appearing in the declarations for the constructor and destructor (details instead of lns). By the same token, the nested class lns::details::node is identical to class lns::node in Listing 4, except for its name. The fully qualified name lns::details::node indicates that node is a nested class within a nested class.

The constructor for `lns::details::node` is the same as the constructor for `lns::node` in Listing 4. Similarly, all the member functions for `lns::details` are the same as the corresponding functions in Listing 4. Again, all I've done is push the functionality of the original uninsulated `lns` class down into the `lns::details` class.

At the end of Listing 10 are the new public member function definitions of `lns` itself. The constructor creates the `details` object. The destructor destroys it. And each of the other member functions does what it always did, except now it invokes the corresponding member function of the `details` class to do the real work.

I wrote `lns2s.cpp` (Listing 10) to make it easier for you to recognize the similarities with `lns1s.cpp` (Listing 5). In practice, you need not maintain such a rigorous separation between the handle object (in this case, `lns`) and the `details` object. After all, what's the point of hiding `details`' data members from `lns`; they're all part of the same implementation. You can safely make the data members of `lns::details` public because `details` itself is private to `lns`. I don't think this compromises the design at all.

For example, if the `lns::details` data members are public, you can rewrite the `lns` constructor as

```
lns::lns(unsigned n)
    {
    dp = new details;
    dp->first = new node(n);
    }
```

and simply eliminate the `lns::details` constructor altogether.

Listing 11 shows `lns2f.cpp`, the "fast" `lns` implementation (using two pointers). In this implementation, the `lns::details` data members are public. `lns::details` has no member functions, and all the work they would have done is in the `lns` member functions. If you compare this Cheshire Cat class with its uninsulated form (Listings 6 and 7), you should still recognize the common functionality.

LNS AS AN ABSTRACT BASE CLASS

Protocol-based classes offer an interesting variation on the Cheshire Cat technique. A protocol-based class uses an abstract base class instead of an incomplete type.

Listing 12 shows a header that defines Ins as an abstract base class (ABC). An ABC is a class with at least one pure virtual function. A pure virtual function is a virtual function with a pure virtual specifier (= 0) at the end of its declaration.

A virtual function declared in a base class specifies an abstract operation that may have a different implementation in a class derived from that base. An ordinary ("impure") virtual function has a definition (a function body) that accompanies the declaration, so that derived classes inherit a default implementation for that function. A derived class can override that default as appropriate.

A pure virtual function specifies an abstract operation without a default implementation. You cannot create objects of an ABC. However, you can declare pointers and references to an ABC that will refer at runtime to objects of types derived from the ABC. (Such pointers and references refer to objects whose *static* type is ABC, but whose *dynamic* type is some class derived from that ABC.) Thus, an ABC specifies a common interface for a variety of derived types, rather than the exact type of any real-live objects.

A class derived from an ABC can override any inherited pure virtual function with an "impure" virtual function declaration and corresponding function definition. Derived classes inherit pure virtual functions as pure virtual functions. Thus, if a derived class does not override every inherited pure virtual function with an impure virtual function, then that derived class is also an ABC. On the other hand, a derived class that overrides all its inherited pure virtual functions becomes a "concrete" (as opposed to "abstract") class, so that you can create objects of that type.

Class Ins in Listing 12 is an ABC that consists entirely of public members that are pure virtual functions. It specifies an inheritable interface with absolutely no implementation details. That interface is the same as the public interface in both the small and fast Ins classes (Listings 4 and 6), except that ABC Ins doesn't have a constructor. ABC Ins has no base classes or data members, so there's nothing for the constructor to initialize. Each concrete class derived from Ins will have its own constructor.

Why didn't I declare a pure virtual constructor in Ins? Because constructors cannot be virtual, and for good reason: A virtual function lets a client ask an object known only by its static type to perform a particular abstract operation in whatever way is appropriate for that object's dynamic type. How then does a client ask an object that doesn't yet exist to initialize itself in a way that's appropriate for whatever dynamic type it will have after it initializes itself? No way.

Destructors can be pure virtual. The 1ns destructor in Listing 12 is pure virtual. But, unlike other pure virtual functions, you must provide a definition for the destructor, however trivial. Why do you need this definition? Even though you can't create objects of type 1ns, you can derive concrete classes from 1ns and create objects of the concrete derived types. The destructor for a derived class automatically invokes the destructors for its base classes and members, even for a base that's an ABC.

Although ABC 1ns has no data members, in general an ABC can have data members. These data members provide a common partial implementation for all classes derived from the ABC. The destructor for such a derived class automatically calls the ABC's destructor to destroy resources used by inherited data members. The derived class destructor insists on calling the ABC's destructor even if the ABC's destructor is completely empty. If you don't supply a definition for the 1ns destructor, the linker complains when it can't find a definition.

ABCs as Protocols

ABC 1ns defines a protocol that all derived classes must observe. The 1ns header (1ns.h) contains only this class definition and no implementation details. Thus, the header completely insulates client sources, such as xr.cpp and xrt.cpp in Listings 1 and 3, from changes in the 1ns implementation.

You can create a concrete 1ns object by deriving it from the 1ns protocol, adding the appropriate data members, and overriding all the inherited pure virtual functions to provide the desired behavior. Placing the derived class in the source file (1ns.cpp) keeps the implementation details out of the header.

Listing 13 shows a class definition for 1ns_fast, a concrete "fast" 1ns class derived from ABC 1ns. Notice that this 1ns_fast is nearly identical to the "fast" 1ns class in Listing 6: both have a constructor as well as private data. But all the member functions in Listing 13 are virtual because they override inherited virtual functions. The bodies for the 1ns_fast member functions (omitted from Listing 13 for brevity) are identical to the corresponding function bodies in Listing 7.

This scheme for building a compilation firewall seems simple enough. It appears that all you need to do is define an ABC that specifies a protocol (abstract behavior) for all implementations, and then derive one or more concrete implementation classes from the ABC. However, it's just a little too simple and fails to insulate clients from changes to the implementation. Here's why.

Somewhere in the client source code (in this case, xrt.cpp in Listing 3), there must be declarations or statements that create concrete lns objects. For example, class treenode in Listing 3 has a member, lines, of type lns:

```
class treenode
    {
    ...
    lns lines;
    ...
    };
```

initialized by a member initializer in the treenode constructor:

```
treenode::treenode(const char *w, unsigned n)
    : lines(n)
    {
    ...
    }
```

Thus, creating a treenode object creates an lns as a member object.

Unfortunately, when you change lns to an ABC, xrt.cpp can no longer create concrete objects of type lns, only pointers or references to lns objects. Therefore, you must change the lines member to a pointer, as in

```
class treenode
    {
    ...
    lns *lines;
    ...
    };
```

and rewrite the constructor to dynamically allocate a concrete lns object. But even that dynamic allocation is a problem.

Rewriting the member initializer as

```
: lines(new lns(n))
```

is still an error because you can't create objects of an ABC using a new-expression either. You can create objects of concrete types derived from lns, such as lns_fast. However, if you change the initializer to

```
: lines(new lns_fast(n))
```

you must move the class definition for lns_fast into lns.h, which breaks through the insulation provided by the header.

An alternative to defining the derived class in the header is to add a static member function to the ABC called create as shown in Listing 14. The create function is a pseudoconstructor that dynamically allocates an object of a concrete type derived from the ABC. The corresponding definition for lns::create looks something like this:

```
lns *lns::create(n)
    {
    return new lns_fast(n);
    }
```

If you place this definition in lns.cpp, you need not move the definition for lns_fast into lns.h. Then you can rewrite the member initializer in the treenode constructor as

```
: lines(lns::create(n))
```

This create function effectively restores the compilation firewall.

RESTORING CONCRETE BEHAVIOR

Defining lns as an ABC has a serious drawback: clients can't manipulate lns objects as concrete objects. They must deal with lns objects only through pointers and references to dynamically allocated lns objects.

You can restore the concrete appearance of class lns using a handle class similar to that used in the Cheshire Cat technique. The key insight comes from recognizing that the ABC lns should be a protocol for lns implementation objects, not for lns objects themselves. Thus, lns should be a handle (a concrete class implemented as a single pointer) for an implementation object of a class derived from a protocol class, as shown in

Listing 15. As in the Cheshire Cat technique, each member function in the handle class delegates the bulk of its work to the corresponding member function of the implementation class.

You transform a class from its concrete, uninsulated form (lns as in either Listing 4 or 6) to its protocol-based insulated form (Listing 15) by following these steps:

1. Add a public member `protocol` as a forward-declared nested class.
2. Delete the private members and replace them with a single pointer to a `protocol` object.
3. Define the nested `protocol` class as an ABC with:
   - ◆ No constructor.
   - ◆ A public virtual destructor with an empty function body.
   - ◆ A public pure virtual function corresponding to each public member function in the handle class (other than the constructors and destructor).

If your compiler does not support forward-declared nested classes, change Listing 15 as follows:

- ◆ Delete the nested declaration for `protocol` inside class `lns`.
- ◆ Change all occurrences of either `lns::protocol` or just `protocol` to `lns_protocol`.
- ◆ Move the definition for class `lns_protocol` above the definition for class `lns`.

The `protocol` pointer `pp` points to an implementation object, much like the `details` pointer `dp` in a Cheshire Cat class. In a Cheshire Cat class, the pointer points to a `details` object of incomplete type. In a protocol-based class, the pointer points to an object of some concrete type derived from an ABC. Thus, the member function definitions for a concrete protocol-based class are nearly identical to their Cheshire Cat counterparts, with one key difference: You can define the protocol-based class members (except the constructor) as inline functions in the header, as in Listing 15.

Listing 16 shows an implementation for the `lns` class defined in Listing 15. `lns_fast` derives from `lns::protocol` and implements the "fast" line number sequence (using two pointers as in Listings 6 and 7).

The lns constructor appears at the end of Listing 16. It cannot be defined inline because it creates the implementation object of type lns_fast. lns_fast must not appear outside this source file in order to preserve the compilation firewall.

DIFFERENT IMPLEMENTATIONS SIMULTANEOUSLY

As we've seen, protocol-based classes bear many similarities to Cheshire Cat classes, but they have one powerful advantage: Protocol-based classes can support different implementations for the same class at the same time in a single program. For example, you can implement both the "fast" and "small" lns classes, and expand the lns interface to let users select either implementation at runtime. In fact, users can create both "fast" and "small" lns objects in the same program.

A simple way to let users select the implementation is to add an argument to the constructor. That is, declare the lns constructor (in the header) as

```
lns(unsigned n, style s = SMALL);
```

where style is an enumeration defined as

```
enum style { FAST, SMALL };
```

The style parameter in the constructor has a default argument value, so a user who doesn't care gets the "small" implementation by default. A user who wants the "fast" implementation simply asks for it by name, as in

```
treenode::treenode(const char *w, unsigned n)
    : lines(n, FAST)
    {
    ...
    }
```

The corresponding definition for the constructor looks like:

```
lns::lns(unsigned n, style s)
    {
    if (s == SMALL)
        pp = new lns_small(n);
```

```
    else // if (s == FAST)
        pp = new lns_fast(n);
}
```

You can even use protocol-based classes to build objects that monitor themselves and automatically switch to the most efficient implementation. For example, when an lns contains only a few elements, searching the list takes little time, so you might as well save memory and use the "small" implementation. But for longer lists, you probably prefer using the "fast" implementation.

Most of the work in implementing this self-adjusting lns is in changing the add function. The lns constructor always initializes lns objects as lns_small objects. The add function simply computes the length of the list each time it searches the list. If the length ever grows beyond a certain threshold, add creates a new lns_fast object that holds the list and then deletes the lns_small object.

The header for this self-adjusting lns is the same as the header in Listing 15, except that

1. protocol::add returns a pointer to a protocol object instead of void, as in

    ```
    virtual protocol *add(unsigned n) = 0;
    ```

2. The definition for lns::add appears in the source file (it cannot be an inline).

protocol::add returns a pointer to the protocol object. lns::add applies protocol's virtual add function to its protocol object and compares the returned pointer with the previous protocol pointer. If the values ever differ, it means the protocol object mutated. In that case, lns::add discards the old protocol objects and saves the new one.

lns_small objects can change into lns_fast objects, but not vice versa. Therefore, the lns_small::add does all the work to monitor the length of the list and decide when to mutate. The mutation does not create an entirely new copy of the linked list. Rather, it creates a new lns_fast object that shares the same list. Then it disconnects the lns_small object (by storing null in the pointer to the first element in the linked list).

Listing 17 also shows how to use an intermediate ABC to provide a partial implementation for further derived classes. The `lns_fast` and `lns_small` classes have very similar implementations, including the same destructor and `print` functions (see Listings 5 and 7). The self-adjusting `lns` class in Listing 17 uses class `lns_list` to capture that commonality.

`lns_list` is derived from `lns::protocol`. It declares the `node` type and a single pointer as private members, along with constructors, a destructor, and `print`. Though none of these functions is pure virtual, `lns_list` is still an ABC because it does not override the inherited `add` function. Classes `lns_fast` and `lns_small` derive from `lns_list`, and they each override `add` so that they are concrete classes.

`lns_fast` and `lns_small` also override `print`, but only for demonstration purposes. Each function adds a letter ('f' for fast and 's' for small) to the output so you can verify that the smaller lists are indeed `lns_small` lists, and the longer lists are `lns_fast` lists.

So What Does This Cost?

Both Cheshire Cat and protocol-based classes add considerable flexibility to class designs. Of course, this flexibility comes with a small price. Compared to an uninsulated implementation, a Cheshire Cat class

- ◆ Occupies a little more storage (one pointer's worth).
- ◆ Requires an extra level of indirection to access data members.
- ◆ Requires an extra call to `new` (during construction) and `delete` (during destruction) for the implementation object.

A protocol-based class is even a little more expensive. In addition to the cost for a Cheshire Cat class, a protocol-based class

- ◆ Occupies more storage. (Each implementation object has a pointer to a virtual table).
- ◆ Uses virtual function calls, which are typically a couple of instructions longer than nonvirtual calls.

Furthermore, neither Cheshire Cat classes nor protocol-based classes can do much inlining.

These techniques are typically inappropriate for small classes. But for larger class with many possible implementations, the productivity gains from greater abstraction typically outweigh the performance costs.

REFERENCES

Booch (1991). Grady Booch, *Software Development '91 Conference Keynote Address* "Object-Oriented Technology: An Engineering Perspective."

Carolan (1989). Jon Carolan, "Constructing Bullet-Proof Classes," *C++ at Work '89 Proceedings*. SIGS Publications.

Kernighan & Ritchie (1988). Brian W. Kernighan and Dennis M. Ritchie, *The C Programming Language*. Prentice Hall.

Saks (1991a). Dan Saks, "Writing Your First Class," *The C Users Journal*, March 1991, Vol. 9, No. 3.

Saks (1991b). Dan Saks, "Your First Class," *The C Users Journal*, May 1991, Vol. 9, No. 5.

Saks (1991c). Dan Saks, "Rewriting Modules as Classes," *The C Users Journal*, July 1991, Vol. 9, No. 7.

Listing 1 - The main module for the cross-reference program

```
//
// xr.cpp - a cross-reference generator
//
#include <assert.h>
#include <ctype.h>
#include <stdio.h>

#include "xrt.h"

int getword(char *word, size_t lim)
    {
    int c;
    char *w = word;

    assert(lim > 2);
    while (isspace(c = fgetc(stdin)) && c != '\n')
        ;
    if (c != EOF)
        *w++ = c;
    if (!isalpha(c))
```

```
        {
        *w = '\0';
        return c;
        }
    for ( ; lim- > 0; ++w)
        if (!isalnum(*w = fgetc(stdin)))
            {
            ungetc(*w, stdin);
            break;
            }
    *w = '\0';
    return *word;
    }

int main()
    {
    const size_t MAXWORD = 100;
    char word[MAXWORD];
    unsigned lineno = 1;
    xrt x;
    while (getword(word, MAXWORD) != EOF)
        if (isalpha(word[0]))
            x.add(word, lineno);
        else if (word[0] == '\n')
            ++lineno;
    x.print();
    return 0;
    }
```

Listing 2 - xrt class definition

```
//
// xrt.h - cross-reference table interface
//
#ifndef XRT_H_INCLUDED
#define XRT_H_INCLUDED

#include "lns.h"

class treenode;

class xrt
    {
public:
    xrt();
    ~xrt();
    void add(const char *w, unsigned n);
    void print();
private:
    treenode *root;
    };
```

```
inline xrt::xrt() : root(0)
    {
    }

#endif
```

Listing 3 - xrt member function definitions

```
//
// xrt.cpp - cross-reference table
//
#include <stdio.h>
#include <string.h>

#include "xrt.h"

class treenode
    {
public:
    treenode(const char *w, unsigned n);
    ~treenode();
    char *word;
    lns lines;
    xrt left, right;
    };

treenode::treenode(const char *w, unsigned n) : lines(n)
    {
    word = strcpy(new char[strlen(w) + 1], w);
    }

treenode::~treenode()
    {
    delete [] word;
    }

xrt::~xrt()
    {
    delete root;
    }

void xrt::add(const char *w, unsigned n)
    {
    int cond;

    if (root == 0)
        root = new treenode(w, n);
    else if ((cond = strcmp(w, root->word)) == 0)
        root->lines.add(n);
    else if (cond < 0)
```

```
            root->left.add(w, n);
        else
            root->right.add(w, n);
        }

void xrt::print()
    {
    if (root != 0)
        {
        root->left.print();
        printf("%12s: ", root->word);
        root->lines.print();
        printf("\n");
        root->right.print();
        }
    }
```

Listing 4 - Class definition for "small" lns (using a single pointer)

```
//
// lns1s.h - "small" line number sequence interface
//
#ifndef LNS_H_INCLUDED
#define LNS_H_INCLUDED

class lns
    {
public:
    lns(unsigned n);
    ~lns();
    void add(unsigned n);
    void print();
private:
    class node;
    node *first;
    };

class lns::node
    {
public:
    node(unsigned n);
    unsigned number;
    node *next;
    };

inline lns::node::node(unsigned n)
    : number(n), next(0)
    {
    }

inline lns::lns(unsigned n)
```

```
        {
        first = new node(n);
        }

    #endif
```

Listing 5 - Member function definitions for "small" lns

```
    //
    // lns1s.cpp - "small" line number sequence implementation
    //
    #include <stdio.h>

    #include "lns.h"

    lns::~lns()
        {
        node *p;
        while ((p = first) != 0)
            {
            first = first->next;
            delete p;
            }
        }

    void lns::add(unsigned n)
        {
        node *p = first;
        while (p->next != 0 && p->number != n)
            p = p->next;
        if (p->number != n)
            p = p->next = new node(n);
        }

    void lns::print()
        {
        node *p;
        for (p = first; p != 0; p = p->next)
            printf("%4d ", p->number);
        }
```

Listing 6 - Class definition for "fast" lns (using a pair of pointers)

```
    //
    // lns1f.h - "fast" line number sequence interface
    //
    #ifndef LNS_H_INCLUDED
    #define LNS_H_INCLUDED

    class lns
        {
```

```
public:
    lns(unsigned n);
    ~lns();
    void add(unsigned n);
    void print();
private:
    class node;
    node *first, *last;
    };

class lns::node
    {
public:
    node(unsigned n);
    unsigned number;
    node *next;
    };

inline lns::node::node(unsigned n)
    : number(n), next(0)
    {
    }

#endif
```

Listing 7 - Member function definitions for "fast" lns

```
//
// lns1f.cpp - "fast" line number sequence implementation
//
#include <stdio.h>

#include "lns.h"

lns::lns(unsigned n)
    {
    first = last = new node(n);
    }

lns::~lns()
    {
    node *p;
    while ((p = first) != 0)
        {
        first = first->next;
        delete p;
        }
    }

void lns::add(unsigned n)
    {
```

```
        if (last->number != n)
            last = last->next = new node(n);
        }

void lns::print()
    {
    node *p;
    for (p = first; p != 0; p = p->next)
        printf("%4d ", p->number);
    }
```

Listing 8 - A makefile for the cross-reference program

```
# modify these symbols as appropriate for your compiler

CC=cc
CFLAGS=-c

# make xr

xr: xr.exe

xr.exe: xr.obj xrt.obj lns.obj
    $(CC) xr.obj xrt.obj lns.obj

xr.obj: xr.cpp xrt.h lns.h
    $(CC) $(CFLAGS) xr.cpp

xrt.obj: xrt.cpp xrt.h lns.h
    $(CC) $(CFLAGS) xrt.cpp

lns.obj: lns.cpp lns.h
    $(CC) $(CFLAGS) lns.cpp
```

Listing 9 - The Cheshire Cat class definition for lns

```
//
// lns2.h - line number sequence interface
//
#ifndef LNS_H_INCLUDED
#define LNS_H_INCLUDED

class lns
    {
public:
    lns(unsigned n);
    ~lns();
    void add(unsigned n);
    void print();
private:
    class details;
```

```
    details *dp;
    };

#endif
```

Listing 10 - The Cheshire Cat implementation for "small" lns

```
//
// lns2s.cpp - "small" line number sequence implementation
//
#include <stdio.h>

#include "lns.h"

class lns::details
    {
public:
    details(unsigned n);
    ~details();
    void add(unsigned n);
    void print();
private:
    class node;
    node *first;
    };

class lns::details::node
    {
public:
    node(unsigned n);
    unsigned number;
    node *next;
    };

inline lns::details::node::node(unsigned n)
    : number(n), next(0)
    {
    }

inline lns::details::details(unsigned n)
    {
    first = new node(n);
    }

lns::details::~details()
    {
    node *p;
    while ((p = first) != 0)
        {
        first = first->next;
        delete p;
```

```
        }
    }

void lns::details::add(unsigned n)
    {
    node *p = first;
    while (p->next != 0 && p->number != n)
        p = p->next;
    if (p->number != n)
        p = p->next = new node(n);
    }

void lns::details::print()
    {
    node *p;
    for (p = first; p != 0; p = p->next)
        printf("%4d ", p->number);
    }

lns::lns(unsigned n)
    {
    dp = new details(n);
    }

lns::~lns()
    {
    delete dp;
    }

void lns::add(unsigned n)
    {
    dp->add(n);
    }

void lns::print()
    {
    dp->print();
    }
```

Listing 11 - The Cheshire Cat implementation for "fast" lns

```
//
// lns2f.cpp - "fast" line number sequence implementation
//
#include <stdio.h>

#include "lns.h"

class lns::details
    {
public:
```

```
        class node;
        node *first, *last;
        };

    class lns::details::node
        {
    public:
        node(unsigned n);
        unsigned number;
        node *next;
        };

    inline lns::details::node::node(unsigned n)
        : number(n), next(0)
        {
        }

    lns::lns(unsigned n)
        {
        dp = new details;
        dp->first = dp->last = new node(n);
        }

    lns::~lns()
        {
        node *first = dp->first;
        node *p;
        while ((p = first) != 0)
            {
            first = first->next;
            delete p;
            }
        }

    void lns::add(unsigned n)
        {
        if (dp->last->number != n)
            dp->last = dp->last->next = new node(n);
        }

    void lns::print()
        {
        node *p;
        for (p = dp->first; p != 0; p = p->next)
            printf("%4d ", p->number);
        }
```

Listing 12 - An lns header with lns as an abstract base class

```
    //
    // lns3.h - line number sequence interface
```

```
//
#ifndef LNS_H_INCLUDED
#define LNS_H_INCLUDED

class lns
    {
public:
    virtual ~lns() = 0;
    virtual void add(unsigned n) = 0;
    virtual void print() = 0;
    };

inline lns::~lns()
    {
    }

#endif
```

Listing 13 - A concrete lns class derived from the lns protocol class

```
//
// lns3f.cpp - a "fast" line number sequence implementation
//
#include <stdio.h>

#include "lns.h"

class lns_fast : public lns
    {
public:
    lns_fast(unsigned n);
    ~lns_fast();
    void add(unsigned n);
    void print();
private:
    struct node;
    node *first, *last;
    };

struct lns_fast::node
    {
    node(unsigned n);
    unsigned number;
    node *next;
    };

//
// plus the member function definitions
// for lns_fast and lns_fast::node ...
//
```

Listing 14 - An lns header with lns as an abstract base class and a static create function

```
//
// lns3.h - line number sequence interface
//
#ifndef LNS_H_INCLUDED
#define LNS_H_INCLUDED

class lns
    {
public:
    static lns *create(unsigned n);
    virtual ~lns() { }
    virtual void add(unsigned n) = 0;
    virtual void print() = 0;
    };

#endif
```

Listing 15 - lns as a concrete class with a single private pointer to a protocol-based implementation object

```
//
// lns4.h - line number sequence interface
//
#ifndef LNS_H_INCLUDED
#define LNS_H_INCLUDED

class lns
    {
public:
    lns(unsigned n);
    ~lns();
    void add(unsigned n);
    void print();
    struct protocol;
private:
    protocol *pp;
    };

struct lns::protocol
    {
    virtual ~protocol() { }
    virtual void add(unsigned n) = 0;
    virtual void print() = 0;
    };

inline lns::~lns()
    {
```

```
    delete pp;
    }

inline void lns::add(unsigned n)
    {
    pp->add(n);
    }

inline void lns::print()
    {
    pp->print();
    }

#endif
```

Listing 16 - A "fast" implementation for the protocol-based lns defined in Listing 11

```
//
// lns4f.cpp - line number sequence implementation
//
#include <stdio.h>

#include "lns.h"

class lns_fast : public lns::protocol
    {
public:
    lns_fast(unsigned n);
    ~lns_fast();
    void add(unsigned n);
    void print();
private:
    struct node;
    node *first, *last;
    };

struct lns_fast::node
    {
    node(unsigned n);
    unsigned number;
    node *next;
    };

inline lns_fast::node::node(unsigned n)
    : number(n), next(0)
    {
    }

inline lns_fast::lns_fast(unsigned n)
    {
```

```
    first = last = new node(n);
    }

lns_fast::~lns_fast()
    {
    node *p;
    while ((p = first) != 0)
        {
        first = first->next;
        delete p;
        }
    }

void lns_fast::add(unsigned n)
    {
    if (last->number != n)
        last = last->next = new node(n);
    }

void lns_fast::print()
    {
    node *p;
    for (p = first; p != 0; p = p->next)
        printf(" %4d", p->number);
    }

lns::lns(unsigned n)
    {
    pp = new lns_fast(n);
    }
```

Listing 17 - Implementation for a self-adjusting lns class

```
//
// lns5.cpp - line number sequence implementation
//
#include <stdio.h>

#include "lns.h"

//
// lns_list
//
class lns_list : public lns::protocol
    {
public:
    lns_list();
    lns_list(unsigned n);
    ~lns_list();
    void print();
protected:
```

```
    struct node;
    node *first;
    };

struct lns_list::node
    {
    node(unsigned n);
    unsigned number;
    node *next;
    };

inline lns_list::node::node(unsigned n)
    : number(n), next(0)
    {
    }

//
// lns_list member definitions
//
inline lns_list::lns_list()
    {
    }

inline lns_list::lns_list(unsigned n)
    : first(new node(n))
    {
    }

lns_list::~lns_list()
    {
    node *p;
    while ((p = first) != 0)
        {
        first = first->next;
        delete p;
        }
    }

void lns_list::print()
    {
    node *p;
    for (p = first; p != 0; p = p->next)
        printf(" %4d", p->number);
    }

//
// lns_small
//
class lns_small : public lns_list
    {
public:
```

```
        lns_small(unsigned n);
        protocol *add(unsigned n);
        void print();
    private:
        enum { THRESHOLD = 5 };
        };

//
// lns_fast
//
class lns_fast : public lns_list
    {
public:
    lns_fast(node *fn, node *ln);
    lns_fast(unsigned n);
    protocol *add(unsigned n);
    void print();
private:
    node *last;
    };

//
// lns_fast member definitions
//
inline lns_fast::lns_fast(node *fn, node *ln)
    {
    first = fn;
    last = ln;
    }

inline lns_fast::lns_fast(unsigned n)
    : lns_list(n)
    {
    last = first;
    }

lns::protocol *lns_fast::add(unsigned n)
    {
    if (last->number != n)
        last = last->next = new node(n);
    return this;
    }

void lns_fast::print()
    {
    printf("  (f)");
    lns_list::print();
    }

//
// lns_small member definitions
```

```
//
inline lns_small::lns_small(unsigned n)
    : lns_list(n)
    {
    }

lns::protocol *lns_small::add(unsigned n)
    {
    int len = 1;
    node *p;
    for (p = first; p->next != 0; p = p->next)
        ++len;
    if (p->number != n)
        {
        p = p->next = new node(n);
        if (++len > THRESHOLD)
            {
            lns_fast *q = new lns_fast(first, p);
            first = 0;
            return q;
            }
        }
    return this;
    }

void lns_small::print()
    {
    printf(" (s)");
    lns_list::print();
    }

//
// lns constructor
//
lns::lns(unsigned n)
    {
    pp = new lns_small(n);
    }

void lns::add(unsigned n)
    {
    protocol *np = pp->add(n);
    if (np != pp)
        {
        delete pp;
        pp = np;
        }
    }
```

SPECIAL MEMBER FUNCTIONS AND PROGRAMMING TECHNIQUES

Bruce Eckel

INTRODUCTION

There are certain member functions in C++ that go beyond the ordinary and need special understanding in order to properly build them into your classes. These include overloading the operators `new` and `delete` (and changing the behavior of the new-handler, which is called when `new` runs out of memory), the so-called *smart pointer*, automatic type conversion operations, pointers to members, the function call operator, and the issue of when to use member operators versus when to use friend operators. First, however, the concept of containers and iterators will be introduced in a template called `xbag`, which supports some of the examples in this chapter.

The second part of this chapter covers some potentially useful programming techniques in C++ that you may not have seen before, including the idea of a *wrapper* used with a C `struct`, the memory management technique called *reference counting* (also known as *counted pointers*), concepts and techniques to simulate *virtual constructors*, and some tips and techniques that may help during debugging.

This chapter was adapted from Borland's *Beyond the World of C++* video training course. The author gratefully acknowledges Borland's permission to use it here.

THE XBAG CONTAINER TEMPLATE

A *container* is a type of object whose sole purpose in life is to hold objects or pointers to objects. This is very much like an array, except it has the intelligence of a true C++ object. For example, most containers keep you from going out of bounds. An iterator is like an intelligent pointer, which moves within the container. Containers and iterators find very common use in object-oriented programming.

The following container and iterator class templates support a number of examples in this chapter:

```
//: XBAGT.H -- XBAG as a template with iterator
#ifndef XBAGT_H_
#define XBAGT_H_
#include <stdlib.h>
#include <string.h>
#include <assert.h>

template<class T>
class xbag {
  T ** v;
  int sz, next;
  enum { increment = 10 };
  int owns; // does it own what it contains?
public:
  // Default to ownership:
  xbag(int Owns = 1)
    : v(0), sz(0), next(0), owns(Owns) {}
  void add(T* P) {
    if(next >= sz) {
      sz += increment;
      v = (T**)realloc(v, sz * sizeof(T*));
      assert(v); // 0 means heap exhausted
      // zero the new memory:
      memset(&v[next], 0,
             increment * sizeof(T*));
    }
    v[next++] = P;
  }
  void flush(int destroy = 0) {
    if(destroy)
      for(int i = 0; i < next; i++)
        delete v[i]; // proper deletion
    free(v);
    v = 0;
    sz = next = 0;
  }
```

```
    ~xbag() { flush(owns); }
    const int size() { return next; }
    T& operator[](int i) {   // reference
      assert(i >= 0 && i < size());
      return *v[i];
    }
    friend class xbagIterator<T>;
};

template<class T>
class xbagIterator {
  xbag<T> & bag;
  int i;
public:
  xbagIterator(xbag<T>& B) : bag(B), i(0) {}
  T * operator->() {
    assert(i >= 0 && i < bag.size());
    return bag.v[i];
  }
  T * top() { return bag.v[i=0]; }
  T * end() { return bag.v[i = bag.size()-1]; }
  int size() { return bag.size(); }
  T * operator++() {   // prefix
    assert(i >= 0);
    i++;
    if(i < bag.size()) return bag.v[i];
    return 0;
  }
  T * operator++(int) {   // postfix
    assert(i >= 0);
    if(i < bag.size()) return bag.v[i++];
    return 0;
  }
  T * operator--() { // prefix
    assert(i >= 0);
    if(i > 0) return bag.v[--i];
    return 0;
  }
  T * operator--(int) { // postfix
    assert(i >= 0);
    if(i == 0) return 0;
    T * tmp = bag.v[i];
    i--;
    return tmp;
  }
};

#endif // XBAGT_H_
```

The constructor simply initializes everything to zero, but when you try to add something to the bag and it has no place to put your pointer (as is the case with a new xbag object), the bag is expanded using the ANSI C library function realloc(). If you call this function for a 0 pointer, it acts the same as malloc(), otherwise it allocates an additional amount of memory (which may entail moving the entire block). If it successfully allocates more memory, it returns the pointer to that new memory. If it fails, it returns zero.

The return value is tested with the ANSI C assert() macro. The argument must resolve to something true or false; you are asserting that it is true. If it is false, the program stops and prints a message. assert() is a quick and portable way to do simple error checking and is used frequently in this chapter. It's convenient because it makes a statement without a lot of distracting code, but any asserts that make it through into your final program should be replaced with friendlier messages for the end-user. Note that you can set a preprocessor flag to disable the effect of assert().

The bag is expanded by an amount called increment, which is an *untagged enumeration*. Its only use is to play the part of a const inside the class. If you used const instead, you would end up with storage that must be initialized in the constructor and not changed throughout the life of the object. You can get constant folding inside a class by using an untagged enumeration.

In any container, there must always be a way to put things in (the add() member, here) and to get things out. In xbag, you pull things out using the overloaded operator[]. Notice that you are responsible for ensuring that the index you use is between zero and size().

Because a template is used in the xbag class, the exact type of pointer that you want to hold can be specified in the template argument list. This means that when the xbag object is destroyed, it may optionally destroy all of the objects it points to. This is sometimes referred to as *ownership* since an object that destroys all of the objects it points to would seem to own them. Whether the container owns the objects it points to is controlled by the owns flag.

Iterators

An iterator is like a pointer or index, which is bound to a particular container for the lifetime of the iterator object; generally, iterators also have friend status with their associated container. While an ordinary pointer or index doesn't know enough to prevent itself from running off the end of an array, an iterator does. In addition, an iterator can generally provide access to the elements inside the container. In fact, the iterator is often the primary means of manipulating a container.

If the container is a class that is analogous to an array in C (although much smarter and safer), the iterator is a class that is analogous to the array index. Of course, the container could have its own idea of where its "next" element is, but it's more powerful to abstract the idea of control away from the idea of containment. For one thing, it allows you to remember more than one place in the container. In addition, iterators can make programming easier and clearer, and sometimes they can be more efficient.

This iterator also has a *smart pointer*, a feature described later in this chapter.

OVERLOADING NEW AND DELETE, AND CHANGING THE NEW-HANDLER

Sometimes you want to do your own storage allocation when objects are created dynamically with new and destroyed with delete. You can overload the global operator new and delete.

NOTE

If you do this, you lose the ability to call the original global operator new **and** delete.

You can also create an operator new and delete for a class, which will only be called when objects of that class are created and destroyed. Creating your own new and delete is very helpful when you want to control where the storage is located (as in an embedded system) or if you want to speed up storage allocation for a particular class.

In addition, C++ allows you to modify what happens when new runs out of storage. When this occurs, a special function called the *new-handler* is called (more modern implementations will throw an exception). Normally, the new-handler does nothing, but you can install your own new-handler with a call to set_new_handler() (declared in NEW.H). This function takes a pointer to your new-handler (which must take no arguments and return `void`) and returns a pointer to the previous new-handler (in case you want to restore it later).

A Trivial Garbage Collector

The following example demonstrates overloading `new` and `delete` and changing the new-handler by creating a rudimentary garbage collector. An xbag is created to hold pointers of type `garbage`. The overloaded opera-tor new for `garbage` stores the address of the new object in the xbag.

NOTE   This is just the *memory* for the object—inside `new`, the constructor hasn't been called yet.

The new-handler cleans up the memory by calling `flush()` with an argument of 1 to cause deletion of all the stored objects.

```cpp
//: GARBAGE.CPP -- New, delete & the new-handler
#include <iostream.h>
#include <new.h>
#include "xbagt.h"

class garbage {
  enum { garbage_chunk = 1024 };
  char memory[garbage_chunk];
public:
  // global declarations look the same:
  void* operator new(size_t sz);
  void operator delete(void* dp);
};

xbag<garbage> memtable;

void* garbage::operator new(size_t sz) {
  void * g = ::new unsigned char[sz];
  memtable.add((garbage*)g);
  return g;
}

void garbage::operator delete(void* dp) {
  cout.put('~');
  ::delete(dp);
}

void garbage_collector() {
```

```
    cout << "Garbage Collecting ";
    cout << memtable.size() << " items ... ";
    memtable.flush(1);
    cout << "done." << endl;
}

void main() {
  set_new_handler(garbage_collector);
  while(1)
    new garbage;  // exhaust free store
}
```

Since each object is 1K long, you can see how much heap space there is for each memory model (in machines that use segmented architectures). In new, the size_t argument, which is the number of bytes necessary to store that object, is determined and passed by the compiler. You are responsible for allocating a chunk of storage of at least that size, and returning the address of that storage from operator new. When creating an object on the heap, the compiler first calls operator new and then takes the resulting memory and applies the constructor to it. If you don't create at least enough storage to hold the object, the results will be unpredictable.

NEW AND DELETE FOR ARRAYS

C++ allows you to define an overloaded operator new and operator delete on a class-by-class basis. Thus, if you use new to create an object of that type, the class' new is called. However, in the past, if you created an *array* of objects of that type, the *global* new was still called to allocate storage. You can redefine the global operator new, but until now you haven't had any way to control storage allocation for arrays of specific types.

You can create an operator new and operator delete for arrays, both globally and on a class-by-class basis. Here's an example:

```
//: ARRAYNEW.CPP -- new & delete for arrays
#include <stdlib.h> // malloc() & free()
#include <stdio.h>
#include <assert.h>
#include <string.h>

class Tracefile {
  FILE * f;
public:
```

```
  Tracefile(char * filename = "trace.txt") {
    f = fopen(filename, "w");
    assert(f);
  }
  ~Tracefile() { fclose(f); }
  operator FILE*() { return f; }
} trace; // global object

// Overload ordinary global new & delete.
// Cannot use iostreams to print from global
// operator new:
void* operator new(size_t size) {
  fprintf(trace,
    "::operator new() size=%x, ", size);
  void * p = malloc(size);
  fprintf(trace,"address=%x\n", p);
  return p;
}

void operator delete(void * mem) {
  fprintf(trace,
    "::operator delete() address=%x\n", mem);
  free(mem);
}

// Overload array global new & delete:
void* operator new[](size_t size) {
  fprintf(trace,
    "::operator new[]() size=%x, ", size);
  void * p = malloc(size);
  fprintf(trace,"address=%x\n", p);
  return p;
}

void operator delete[](void * mem) {
  fprintf(trace,
    "::operator delete[]() address=%x\n", mem);
  free(mem);
}

class alloc {
  enum { sz = 0x100 };
  char message[sz];
  static int i; // array counter
public:
  alloc(char * ID = "") {
    if(*ID)
      sprintf(message, "%s", ID);
    else
      sprintf(message, "array element %d ", i++);
    fprintf(trace,
```

```
      "alloc::alloc() for %s, this = %x\n",
      message, this);
  }
  ~alloc() {
    fprintf(trace,
      "alloc::~alloc() for %s, this = %x\n",
      message, this);
  }
  // For a single object:
  void* operator new(size_t size) {
    fprintf(trace,
      "alloc::operator new() size=%x, ", size);
    void * p = malloc(size);
    fprintf(trace,
      "address=%x\n", p);
    return p;
  }
  void operator delete(void * mem) {
    fprintf(trace,
      "alloc::operator delete()"
      " address=%x\n", mem);
    free(mem);
  }
  // For an array of objects:
  void* operator new[](size_t size) {
    fprintf(trace,
      "alloc::operator new[]()"
      " size=%x, ", size);
    void * p = malloc(size);
    fprintf(trace,
      "address=%x\n", p);
    return p;
  }
  void operator delete[](void * mem) {
    fprintf(trace,
      "alloc::operator delete[]()"
      " address=%x\n", mem);
    free(mem);
  }
};

int alloc::i = 0; // static member definition

class object {
  enum { sz = 0x100 };
  char message[sz];
  static int i; // array counter
public:
  object(char * ID = "") {
    if(*ID)
      sprintf(message,"%s", ID);
```

```
      else
        sprintf(message,"array element %d", i++);
      fprintf(trace,
        "object::object() for %s, this = %x\n",
        message, this);
    }
    ~object() {
      fprintf(trace,
        "object::~object() for %s, this = %x\n",
        message, this);
    }
  };

  int object::i = 0; // static member definition

  int main() {
    fprintf(trace, "creating new object\n");
    object * ap = new object("single 'object'");
    fprintf(trace, "deleting object\n");
    delete ap;
    fprintf(trace, "creating array of objects\n");
    object * aa = new object[3];
    fprintf(trace, "deleting array of objects\n");
    delete []aa;
    fprintf(trace, "creating new alloc\n");
    alloc * Ap = new alloc("single 'alloc'");
    fprintf(trace, "deleting alloc\n");
    delete Ap;
    fprintf(trace, "creating array of allocs\n");
    alloc * AA = new alloc[2];
    fprintf(trace, "deleting array of allocs\n");
    delete []AA;
    return 0;
  }
```

The class Tracefile encapsulates a FILE* to ensure proper initialization and cleanup. The operator FILE*() means that you can use a Tracefile object anywhere you'd normally use a FILE*, and the compiler will perform the automatic type conversion.

The reason stdio.h is used instead of iostreams is that the global operator new is being overloaded, and this is used by the ostream constructor. If you use iostreams then when the ostream constructor called the global operator new, the first write to output inside that function also tries to call the global operator new, and the program crashes.

Here, both the ordinary global operator new() and operator delete() are overloaded, along with the global array versions operator new[]() and operator delete[]().

The function signatures are identical, except that the array versions have the additional **[]**.

Inside class `alloc`, you can see that creating a class version of the array `operator new[]()` and `operator delete[]()` has the identical signature as the global versions. All these versions use `malloc()` and `free()` to allocate their memory so the output trace will be clear.

The class `object` does not overload the storage allocation operators. If a class doesn't overload these operators, the `global new()` and `delete()` is used to allocate a single object on the heap, and the `global new[]()` and `delete[]()` is used to allocate an array of objects on the heap.

Both the `alloc` and `object` classes carry an internal character array to hold printable information about their objects. Notice that the size of the character array is 0x100, since all the information is printed out in hex and it's easier to see the array objects being constructed that way. In the constructor, if the default argument is used it is assumed (for the pedagogical purposes of this example) that an array object is being created, so an appropriate message, along with an object number created using a `static` data member, is generated. All of the information is sent to the trace file TRACE.TXT.

In `main()`, all the different possibilities are exercised by creating and destroying a single instance of type object (which uses the global `operator new()` and `operator delete()`) and an array of type object (which uses the global `operator new[]()` and `operator delete[]()`), as well as a single instance of `alloc` (which uses `alloc::operator new()` and `alloc::operator delete()`) and an array of objects of `alloc` (which uses `alloc::operator new[]()` and `alloc::operator delete[]()`).

It's important to remember that the overloaded versions of `operator new` are only called to *allocate* storage before the constructor is called. Your only responsibility is to return the address of a piece of storage of the size that was requested. Construction hasn't occurred yet, nor will it occur until after this function finishes. With the overloaded `operator delete`, the address you get is that of the destructed object (the destructor is called, then the storage is freed). Your only responsibility is to free that storage.

By looking at the output of this program, you can see the way the overloaded `new` and `delete` are called, and in what order. Remember that some global calls to `new` and `delete` may be made at the beginning and end of the output by the start-up code, to perform initialization of certain objects; you can ignore these for the purposes of this example

ISSUES IN OPERATOR OVERLOADING

Smart Pointers

A *smart pointer* is the overloaded `operator->()`. It is treated specially by the compiler, even for an operator. It seems most useful in classes like iterators, because the compiler performs several levels of indirection for you. What this means is you can set up an iterator to call a member function of an object it is pointing to. For example, if you have an iterator I pointing to a bag of objects with a `print()` function, a smart pointer will allow you to say `I->print()` for the current object.

The following example shows several levels of indirection with smart pointers:

```
//: SMARTP.CPP -- convoluted smart pointers
#include <iostream.h>
struct bob {
  virtual void foo() = 0;
};

struct ralph : bob {
  void foo() { cout << "ralph::foo()" << endl; }
};

struct fred {
  virtual bob* operator->() = 0;
};

struct joe : fred {
  bob* operator->() { return new ralph; }
};

struct base {
  virtual fred& operator->() = 0;
};

struct derived : base {
```

```
    fred& operator->() { return *new joe; }
};

class holder {
  base* b;
public:
  holder(base* B) : b(B) {}
  // reference essential here:
  base& operator->() { return *b; }
  // must return object or pointer, and
  // you can't return *b as an object!
};

void main() {
  holder H(new derived);
  H->foo();
}
```

The rule for using smart pointers is this: A smart pointer function must return either (A) an *object* of a class that has a smart pointer, or (B) a pointer to an object that has the member function the arrow is selecting. You can see that the smart pointer for fred, since it returns a bob*, could be used to call bob::foo. But fred is also pure abstract, so it's just the interface. joe redefines it to return a ralph*, which is derived from bob (so the upcast is implicit).

base doesn't return a pointer, but an object (the compiler is also satisfied with a reference, when using smart pointers). As the rule states, this object has a smart pointer defined for it. Again, it is a pure abstract base class, which is inherited into derived.

Finally, holder contains a base* and also has a smart pointer, which returns a reference to what it holds.

N O T E   For polymorphism to work, holder must contain a pointer to a base (which is abstract). If you tried to return a base object instead of a base reference, you would run into two problems. First, the object would be "sliced"—anything larger than base would be trimmed off. But that can't even happen, because base is abstract, so the compiler can't create an instance of it. The only way things work is by returning a reference.

main() seems fairly simple, but a lot is going on. A holder is created, and its b pointer is initialized with a new derived object. Then foo() is called with the smart pointer. First, the compiler calls operator->() for holder. This produces a base&, and the compiler calls operator->() for that (which is virtual, notice). The call produces a fred&, and fred's `operator->()` produces a `bob*`, and (finally) `bob` has a `foo()` function, which is called. All the calls are established at compile-time, so the compiler can see you're making a legitimate call and will generate an error message otherwise.

> The `xbag` template also contains a smart pointer; the use of smart pointers with iterators is particularly common.
>
> N O T E

Automatic Type Conversion

Automatic type conversion operations in C++ allow you to teach the compiler to perform the same kinds of tricks with your classes that it does with built-in data types (for example, the automatic conversion of an `int` to a `float`). Automatic type conversion operations can greatly simplify your programming and cut the amount of code you must write. It can also get you into trouble.

There are two ways to perform automatic type conversion. The first is by overloading `operator type()`, where type is what you want to automatically convert to. This is an unusual overloaded operator, since it has no return type specified in the usual way—the return type is the name of the operator!

The second way is in the *destination* type—if the type you want to convert *to* has a constructor that takes a single argument of the type you want to convert *from*, the compiler will use that constructor to perform automatic type conversion.

Some "interesting" problems occur with automatic type conversion, because you can easily introduce ambiguity into your type system. For example, what happens if both types "own" the conversion from one type to another? If `class X` has an `operator Y()`, and `class Y` has a constructor `Y(X)`, the compiler cannot know which one to use for a conversion. However, this is not such a bad problem, because you find out soon after you create your classes and can fix it.

A more insidious problem occurs when there is more than one automatic conversion *from* a single type. This introduces a potential for multiple conversion paths, which can bite you later. The following examples show these problems:

```
//: CONVERT.CPP -- Automatic conversion pitfalls

struct B; // name declaration

struct A {
  operator B();  // make a B from an A
};

struct B {
  B(A);  // make a B from an A
};

void f(B);

void test1() {
  A a;
  f(a);  // which one to use?
}

// More insidious -- ambiguous type structure:

struct X;
struct Y;

struct Z {
  operator X();
  operator Y();
};

void g(X);
void g(Y);

void test2() {
  Z z;
  g(z); // which conversion to use?
}

// Later introduction of new type breaks things:

struct U {};

struct V {
  V(U);  // convert from U
};

void h(V);

void test3() {
  U u;
  h(u); // converts from U to V
}
```

```
// works fine, but what if you later include:

struct W {
  W(U);
};

void h(W);

// then the above code suddenly breaks.
// (move this before test3() to see the effect)
```

You can see you need to be careful when introducing automatic type conversion. Use it when you have to, and when you know the exact situations where your types are used.

NOTE

Don't have more than one automatic type conversion operator from a type.

Pointers to Members

The standard C offsetof() macro allows you to find the offset of any member in a struct. This allows you to select a member at run-time by indexing into the struct. The concept of selecting a member at run-time is really a pointer idea, but pointers are complicated by the fact that they must point to a specific address, and the exact address of a class member isn't known until you have the object's address. To embody this concept, C++ has *pointers* to *members*, which are sort of pointers, and sort of offsets. They are pointers into objects, but the pointers don't become "live" until they are connected to a particular object.

Defining a pointer to member is a straightforward extension to ordinary definitions. A pointer to an ordinary int looks like this:

```
int *foo;
```

If it is a pointer to member, you simply add the class name and scope-resolution operator before the pointer:

```
int classname::*foo;
```

To dereference a pointer to member, you must have an object of the correct type, and you must be selecting a member of the correct type. For a `classname` object called F

```
F.*foo = 47;
```

and for a pointer FP

```
FP->*foo = 47;
```

It's just like selecting an ordinary member, but you must dereference the pointer as well.

The common example given for pointers to members is a container member function to "apply" a member function to all of the objects in a collection. The `xbag` class can be extended this way:

```
//: PMEM.CPP -- Pointer-to-member demonstration
#include <iostream.h>
#include "xbagt.h"

class wompus {
  char * name;
public:
  wompus(char * Name) : name(Name) {}
  void jump() {cout << name << " jump" << endl;}
  void sit() {cout << name << " sit" << endl; }
  void beg() {cout << name << " beg" << endl; }
  ~wompus() { cout << "bye " << name << endl; }
};

class wompusbag : public xbag<wompus> {
public:
  void apply(void(wompus::*f)()) {
    for(int i = 0; i < size(); i++)
      (operator[](i).*f)();
  }
};

void main() {
  wompusbag W;
  W.add(new wompus("bob"));
  W.add(new wompus("bill"));
  W.add(new wompus("fred"));
  W.add(new wompus("roscoe"));
  W.apply(&wompus::jump);
  W.apply(&wompus::beg);
}
```

Function Call Operator

The function call operator()() is unique among operators in that you can have any number of arguments (actually, the placement syntax for operator new allows multiple arguments, as you will see later, but that's much less general). This can be handy in some situations.

Member versus Friend Operators

When overloading operators, many people get confused about whether to use member functions or friend functions. There is a difference—the compiler can do conversion for *both* operands of a friend function, whereas it can only convert the right-hand argument of a member function. The left-hand argument of a member function must always be an object of the class type.

This means you can control the use of the operator by choosing a friend or member function. In the following example, you can *only* add apples to oranges, but because operator+() is a member function of apple, you can't add oranges to apples. On the other hand, operator-() is a friend function so it is reflexive, and since there is a way to convert from an orange to an apple (the conversion constructor in apple) you can subtract apples and oranges in any combination.

```
//: APPLES.CPP -- Adding apples to oranges
//. Member vs. friend operators

struct orange {};

struct apple {
  void operator+(orange) {}
  friend void operator-(apple, apple) {}
  apple(orange) {}  // make apple from orange
  apple() {} // must create a default
};

void main() {
  apple a;
  orange o;
  a + o;  // this works
//  o + a;  // this doesn't
  a - a;  // this works
```

```
a - o;  // this works
o - a;  // this works too
o - o;  // this even works!
}
```

The last statement is a little surprising. You can even subtract an `orange` from an `orange`, even though there's no `operator-()` defined for `orange`! Automatic type conversion is happening for *both* arguments. This is another situation that points out that automatic type conversion can cause tricky things to happen.

> NOTE
>
> `Struct`s are used here where normally the kind of information necessary to create an `apple` from an `orange` would be `private`. In that case, `orange` would have to grant the `apple` constructor `friend` status. This connects the two classes a little more closely and gives the reader a cue.

PROGRAMMING TECHNIQUES

The following techniques may prove useful:

A *wrapper* is a way to package an existing C `struct` and associated functions so that it has the convenience and safety of a C++ class. It's a way to quickly make an existing C library easier to use.

Reference counting is important when you have a class containing pointers pointing to memory or other resources. You may not want to duplicate these resources (the data in a very big matrix, for example) every time you copy an object, especially when passing and returning it by value. If you end up with more than one object pointing to the same resources, you need a way to make sure that the resources don't get destroyed along with the first object that goes out of scope. The common technique, described here, is reference counting.

The *virtual constructor* is only an illusion. Since the constructor is responsible for setting the exact type of the object, *including* the information that will be used by virtual functions, you can't use the virtual mechanism to select which constructor to call. That is, you can't say: "Make me an object of an exact type, except I don't know what that type is." However, sometimes it's convenient to provide a bunch of information to a constructor or constructor-like function and have it return an object of the correct type. This section shows some simple techniques to produce this effect.

Finally, some tips and techniques are presented which may help during debugging. These include the use of the Standard C library assert() macro, using the preprocessor to create trace macros, trace files with iostreams, abstract base classes for debugging, and a system for tracking dynamic memory allocations and dynamic object creations so you can detect problems and memory leaks.

Wrappers and Inheriting from C structs

A *wrapper* is a class that encapsulates the functionality of a group of C functions, possibly with associated C structs. You use wrappers so you can benefit by all the work that was done in a C library, but in an object-oriented framework.

You should especially be on the lookout for uses of wrappers when a group of functions all act upon a particular structure. Here you can see that if this programmer had been using C++, they would have created a class instead. All you have to do is reform the existing code into a class.

However, just because someone created a struct in C doesn't mean that you have to treat it that way when you're creating a wrapper. Since it's a struct, you can inherit from it! This gives you all the benefits C++ has built in, like automatic creation of constructors.

As an example, consider the findfirst() and findnext() functions for finding DOS file information in Borland C. These act upon a struct called ffblk that contains all the information about the file (name, data, size, etc.). In the following example, notice the definition of the copy-constructor for dfile, which inherits ffblk. If there were no explicit definition of the copy-constructor, one would have been created by the compiler. The one defined here forces the file name to lower case as it performs the copy. But notice, before it does this, it calls the base-class copy constructor. The base class is ffblk, and it was created by a C programmer who knew nothing about copy-constructors, so it can't exist, right? What is being called is the copy-constructor the compiler synthesizes for ffblk.

```
//: DLIST.CPP -- simple directory lister
#include <dir.h>
#include <conio.h>
#include <string.h>
#include <iostream.h>
#include <iomanip.h>
```

```cpp
#include "xbagt.h"
#include "str.h"
const screensize = 24;

class dfile : public ffblk {
public:
  dfile(dfile& df) : ffblk(df) {
    strlwr(ff_name);  // force to lower case
  }
  dfile() {} // must provide default constructor
  friend ostream&
  operator<<(ostream& os, dfile& df) {
    os << setiosflags(ios::left) << setw(15)
       << df.ff_name << " "
       << df.ff_fsize << " bytes";
    return os;
  }
};

class filelist : public xbag<dfile> {
public:
  void add(char * fd) {
    dfile file;
    int done =
      findfirst(fd, &file, 0);  // upcast
    while(!done) {
      // copy-constructor:
      xbag<dfile>::add(new dfile(file));
      done = findnext(&file);
    }
  }
};

void main(int argc, char * argv[]) {
  filelist flist;
  if(argc == 1)
    flist.add("*.*");
  else
    for(int i = 1; i < argc; i++)
      flist.add(argv[i]);
  long total = 0;
  for(int j = 0; j < flist.size(); j++) {
    // struct elements still accessible:
    total += flist[j].ff_fsize;
    cout << flist[j] << endl;
    if(j % screensize == screensize - 1)
      if(getch() == 27) return;
  }
  cout << total << " total bytes in "
       << flist.size() << " files " << endl;
}
```

The functions findfirst() and findnext() have been "wrapped" inside filelist.

Notice this also localizes system-specific and/or compiler-specific function calls inside a class. In main(), all the code is generic.

Reference Counting

If your class contains pointers to data, you have two choices when copying objects of that class, and when building new objects of the class from existing objects (as in passing and returning by value). You can make a new copy of the data for every object (the safe and easy approach, but not the most efficient), or you can alias more than one object to the same piece of data. This requires a fair amount of bookkeeping, especially to prevent the data from being deallocated while objects are still using it. To accomplish this, the most common and (relatively) simple technique is called *reference counting*. The data you point to must be a structure containing a *reference count*, which is incremented every time a new object is attached to it, and decremented every time an object is detached. When the reference count goes to zero, the data is destroyed. Here's a very simple example:

```
//: REFCOUNT.CPP -- Reference counting demo
class block {
  struct data {
    int refcount;  // reference counter
    enum { size = 100 };
    int i[size];
  } * Data;
public:
  block() {
    Data = new data;
    Data->refcount = 1; // one object using it
  }
  block(block& rv) {
    // point to the same data chunk:
    Data = rv.Data;
    // additional object using it:
    Data->refcount++;
  }
  block& operator=(block& rv) {
    if(!--(Data->refcount)) delete Data;
    Data = rv.Data;
    Data->refcount++;
    return *this;
```

```
  }
  ~block() {
    if(!--Data->refcount) delete Data;
  }
};

// pass-by-value (copy-constructor):
void f(block) {}

void main() {
  block A, B;
  f(B);
  A = B;
  block C = A;
}
```

The Data pointer inside class block points to a chunk of data which has attached to it a reference counter. The counter is incremented and decremented according to how many objects are using that data chunk. The most important situations occur with creation, copy-construction, assignment, and destruction. When a data chunk is originally created, only the creating object is using it so refcount is one. In copy-construction, a brand new (uninitialized) object is attached to an existing data chunk, so the reference count is incremented. However, with assignment the object on the left side of the = sign is already pointing to its own data chunk, so it must detach itself from that first. The process of detachment means the reference count must be decremented, and if the count goes to zero that data chunk must be destroyed. Only then can the Data pointer be attached to the data chunk of the object on the right-hand side of the = (and the reference count incremented, just like in the copy constructor).

The destructor detaches this particular object from the data chunk, by again decrementing the reference count and destroying the data chunk if it goes to zero.

Of course, reference counting doesn't take care of all of the problems that occur when you alias more than one object to the same piece of data. You also have the following conundrum: What happens when you have several objects aliased to the same piece of data, and one of the objects wants to change the data? What does this mean? In some cases, you need to check the reference count, and if more than one object is using the data it must be cloned before the data is changed. This is called *copy-on-write*.

Virtual Constructors

The constructor is the only function that cannot be virtual. That's because the virtual mechanism works with a pointer to a base type; run-time binding determines the exact type of the object. The problem is that the *compiler* must know the exact type of the object when it creates it, so it can set the VPTR to the proper VTABLE. Therefore, there can be no late binding inside a constructor. You can think of a constructor as being different from all other functions, since it brings the object into existence.

You may want to implement a virtual constructor scheme for two reasons. First, you may want to use late binding inside a constructor. Second, if you have many types your coding may be simplified if you can determine the exact type of the object at run-time instead of compile-time.

There are numerous schemes to implement virtual constructors. See, for example, James Coplien's *Advanced C++ Programming Styles and Idioms* (Addison-Wesley, 1992). However, sometimes a very simple approach will suffice.

Most virtual constructor schemes rely on a pointer inside the class with the virtual constructor, which points to the "important parts." These are the parts where you need run-time binding inside the virtual constructor, or which represent the differences between the "many types" mentioned above. Sometimes the easiest way to handle the problem is for the virtual constructor to take an address as its argument, and simply assign that address to its "special" pointer. Then all function calls can be made through that pointer and the right thing will happen, even in the constructor. Here's a simple example:

```
//: VIRCONS.CPP -- Simple virtual constructors
#include <iostream.h>

struct shape_ {
  virtual void draw() = 0;
  virtual void erase() = 0;
  virtual ~shape_() {}
};

#define SHAPE(arg) \
struct arg : shape_ { \
  void draw() { \
    cout << #arg "::draw" << endl; \
  } \
  void erase() { \
```

```
      cout << #arg "::erase" << endl; \
    } \
};
SHAPE(circle)
SHAPE(square)
SHAPE(triangle)
SHAPE(line)

class Shape {
  shape_ * s;
public:
  Shape(shape_* S) : s(S) {
    s->draw(); // late binding
  }
  void draw() { s->draw(); }
  void erase() { s->erase(); }
  ~Shape() {
    s->erase(); // late binding
    delete s;
  }
  void Transmogrify(shape_* S) {
    s->erase();
    delete s;
    s = S; // "pluggable pointer composition"
    s->draw();
  }
};

void main() {
  Shape s[] = {
    Shape(new circle),
    Shape(new square),
    Shape(new triangle),
    Shape(new line)
  };
  for(int i = 0; i < sizeof s / sizeof *s; i++)
    s[i].draw();
  s[0].Transmogrify(new line);
};
```

The constructor for Shape simply assigns its shape_ address argument to s, then calls draw() for that pointer. Since the shape_ constructor completes before the Shape constructor is entered, the proper late binding occurs.

The draw() and erase() functions are simply reinvoked through the pointer s.

In the destructor, the call to s->erase() will work properly with late binding since s hasn't been destroyed yet. delete s will call the virtual destructor.

A potentially beneficial side effect to this approach is all Shape objects are the same size (they don't even have a vptr, since none of the calls need to be virtual).

The approach of using a base-class pointer inside another object is sometimes called *pluggable pointer composition*. As seen in the Transmogrify() function, not only does it allow virtual constructors, but it also allows you to change the behavior of an object in midlife. This can be very useful in some designs.

Debugging

This section contains some tips and techniques that may help during debugging.

Assert

The ANSI C library assert() macro has been used regularly through this chapter. It's brief, to the point, and portable. In addition, when you're finished debugging you can remove all the code by defining NDEBUG, either on the command-line or in code.

Also, assert() can be used while roughing out the code. Later, the calls to assert() that are actually providing information to the end user can be replaced with more civilized messages.

Trace Macros

Sometimes it's very helpful to print the code of each statement before it is executed, either to cout or to a trace file. Here's a preprocessor macro to accomplish this:

```
#define TRACE(arg) cout << #arg << endl; arg
```

Now you can go through and surround the statements that you trace with this macro. Of course, it can introduce problems. For example, if you take the statement

```
for(int i = 0; i < 100; i++)
  cout << i << endl;
```

and put both lines inside TRACE() macros, you get this:

```
TRACE(for(int i = 0; i < 100; i++))
TRACE(  cout << i << endl;)
```

which expands to this:

```
cout << "for(int i = 0; i < 100; i++)" << endl;
for(int i = 0; i < 100; i++)
  cout << "cout << i << endl;" << endl;
cout << i << endl;
```

Which isn't what you want. Thus, this technique must be used carefully.

Trace File

This code allows you to easily create a trace file and send all the output that would normally go to cout into the file. All you have to do is #define TRACEON and include the header file (of course, it's fairly easy just to write the following two key lines right into your file):

```
//: TRACE.H -- Creating a trace file
#ifndef TRACE_H_
#define TRACE_H_
#include <fstream.h>

#ifdef TRACEON
ofstream TRACEFILE__("TRACE.OUT");
#define cout TRACEFILE__
#endif

#endif // TRACE_H_
```

Here's a simple test of the previous file:

```
//: TRACETST.CPP -- Test of trace.h
#include <iostream.h>
#include <fstream.h>
#include <assert.h>
#define TRACEON
#include "trace.h"

void main() {
  ifstream f("tracetst.cpp");
  assert(f);
  cout << f.rdbuf();
}
```

Abstract Base Class for Debugging

In the Smalltalk tradition, you can create your own object-based hierarchy and install pure virtual functions to perform debugging. Then everyone on the team must inherit from this class and redefine the debugging functions. All objects in the system will then have debugging functions available.

Of course, this suffers from the usual inconveniences of an object-based hierarchy.

Tracking new/delete and malloc/free

Common problems with memory allocation include calling delete for things you have malloced, calling free for things you allocated with new, forgetting to release objects from the free store, and releasing them more than once. This section provides a system to help you track these kinds of problems down.

To use the memory checking system, you simply link the obj file in and all the calls to malloc(), realloc(), calloc(), free(), new and delete are intercepted. However, if you also include the following file (which is optional), all the calls to new will store information about the file and line where they were called. This is accomplished with a use of the *placement syntax* for operator new (this trick was suggested by Reg Charney of the ANSI/ISO C++ committee). The placement syntax is intended for situations where you need to place objects at a specific point in memory. However, it allows you to create an operator new with any number of arguments. This is used to advantage here to store the results of the __FILE__ and __LINE__ macros whenever new is called:

```
//: MEMCHECK.H -- Memory testing system
//. This file is only included if you want to
//. use the special placement syntax to find
//. out the line number where "new" was called.
#ifndef MEMCHECK_H_
#define MEMCHECK_H_
#include <stdlib.h>  // size_t

// From an idea by Reg Charney:
// Use placement syntax to pass extra arguments.
void *
operator new(size_t sz, char * file, int line);
#define new new(__FILE__, __LINE__)

#endif // MEMCHECK_H_
```

In the following file containing the function definitions, you will note that everything is done with standard IO rather than iostreams. This is because, for example, the cout constructor allocates memory. Standard IO ensures against cyclical conditions that can lock up the system.

```
//: MEMCHECK.CPP -- Memory allocation tester
#include <stdlib.h>
#include <string.h>
#include <stdio.h>
// MEMCHECK.H must not be included here

// output file object using stdio.h.
// (cout constructor calls malloc() )
class ofile {
  FILE* f;
public:
  ofile(char * name) : f(fopen(name, "w")) {}
  ~ofile() { fclose(f); }
  operator FILE*() { return f; }
};
extern ofile memtrace;
// comment out the following to send all the
// information to the trace file:
#define memtrace stdout

const unsigned long _pool_sz = 50000L;
static unsigned char _memory_pool[_pool_sz];
static unsigned char* _pool_ptr = _memory_pool;

void* getmem(size_t sz) {
  if(_memory_pool + _pool_sz - _pool_ptr < sz) {
    fprintf(stderr,
            "out of memory. Use bigger model\n");
    exit(1);
  }
  void* p = _pool_ptr;
  _pool_ptr += sz;
  return p;
}

// holds information about allocated pointers:
class membag { // similar to xbag
public:
  enum type { Malloc, New };
private:
  char * typestr(type t) {
    switch(t) {
      case Malloc: return "malloc";
      case New: return "new";
      default: return "?unknown?";
```

```
    }
  }
  struct m {
    void * mp;   // memory pointer
    type t;      // allocation type
    char * file; // file name where allocated
    int line;  // line number where allocated
    m(void * v, type T, char* F, int L)
      : mp(v), t(T), file(F), line(L) {}
  } * v;
  int sz, next;
  enum { increment = 50 };
public:
  membag() : v(0), sz(0), next(0) {}
  void* add(void * P, type T = Malloc,
            char* S = "library", int L = 0) {
    if(next >= sz) {
      sz += increment;
      // this memory is never freed, so it
      // doesn't "get involved" in the test:
      const memsize = sz * sizeof(m);
      // equivalent of realloc, no registration:
      void* p = getmem(memsize);
      if(v) memmove(p, v, memsize);
      v = (m*)p;
      memset(&v[next], 0,
             increment * sizeof(m));
    }
    v[next++] = m(P, T, S, L);
    return P;
  }
  // Print information about allocation:
  void allocation(int i) {
    fprintf(memtrace, "pointer %p"
      " allocated with %s",
      v[i].mp, typestr(v[i].t));
    if(v[i].t == New)
      fprintf(memtrace, " at %s: %d",
        v[i].file, v[i].line);
    fprintf(memtrace, "\n");
  }
  void validate(void * p, type T = Malloc) {
    for(int i = 0; i < next; i++)
      if(v[i].mp == p) {
        if(v[i].t != T) {
          allocation(i);
          fprintf(memtrace,
          "\t was released as if it were "
          "allocated with %s \n", typestr(T));
        }
        v[i].mp = 0;  // erase it
```

```
        return;
      }
    fprintf(memtrace,
    "pointer not in memory list: %p\n", p);
  }
  ~membag() {
    for(int i = 0; i < next; i++)
      if(v[i].mp != 0) {
        fprintf(memtrace,
        "pointer not released: ");
        allocation(i);
      }
  }
};
extern membag MEMBAG_;

void* malloc(size_t sz) {
  void* p = getmem(sz);
  return MEMBAG_.add(p, membag::Malloc);
}

void* calloc(size_t num_elems, size_t elem_sz) {
  void* p = getmem(num_elems * elem_sz);
  memset(p, 0, num_elems * elem_sz);
  return MEMBAG_.add(p, membag::Malloc);
}

void* realloc(void *block, size_t sz) {
  void* p = getmem(sz);
  if(block) memmove(p, block, sz);
  return MEMBAG_.add(p, membag::Malloc);
}

void free(void* v) {
  MEMBAG_.validate(v, membag::Malloc);
}

void * operator new(size_t sz) {
  void* p = getmem(sz);
  return MEMBAG_.add(p, membag::New);
}

void *
operator new(size_t sz, char * file, int line) {
  void * p = getmem(sz);
  return MEMBAG_.add(p, membag::New, file,line);
}

void operator delete(void * v) {
  MEMBAG_.validate(v, membag::New);
}
```

```
membag MEMBAG_;
// Placed here so the constructor is called
// AFTER that of MEMBAG_ :
#ifdef memtrace
#undef memtrace
#endif
ofile memtrace("memtrace.out");
// Causes 1 "pointer not in memory list" message
```

ofile is a simple wrapper around a FILE*; the constructor opens the file, and the destructor closes it. The operator FILE*() allows you to simply use the ofile object anyplace you would ordinarily use a FILE* (in the fprintf() statements in this example). The #define that follows simply sends everything to standard output, but if you need to put it in a trace file you simply comment out that line.

Memory is allocated from an array called _memory_pool. The _pool_ptr is moved forward every time storage is allocated. For simplicity, the storage is never reclaimed, and realloc() doesn't try to resize the storage in the same place.

All the storage allocation functions call getmem(), which ensures that there is enough space left and moves the _pool_ptr to allocate your storage. Then they store the pointer in a special container of class membag called MEMBAG_, along with pertinent information (notice the two versions of operator new; one which just stores the pointer and the other which stores the file and line number). The membag class is the heart of the system.

You will see many similarities to xbag in membag. A distinct difference is that realloc() is replaced by a call to getmem() and memmove(), so that storage allocated for the membag is not registered. In addition, the type enum allows you to store the way the memory was allocated; the typestr() function takes a type and produces a string for use with printing.

The nested struct m holds the pointer, the type, a pointer to the file name (which is assumed to be statically allocated), and the line where the allocation occurred. v is a pointer to an array of m objects—this is the array which is dynamically sized.

The allocation() function prints out a different message depending on whether the storage was allocated with new (where it has line and file information) or malloc() (where it doesn't). This function is used inside validate(), which is called by free() and delete() to ensure that everything is OK, and in the destructor, to ensure that the pointer was cleaned up.

In `validate()` the pointer value `v[i].mp` is set to zero, to indicate that it has been cleaned up.

The following is a simple test using the memcheck facility. The MEMCHECK.OBJ file must be linked in for it to work:

```
//: MEMTEST.CPP -- test of memcheck system
#include "memcheck.h"

void main() {
  void * v = malloc(100);
  delete v;
  int * x = new int;
  free(x);
  new double;
}
```

The trace file created in MEMCHECK.CPP causes the generation of one extra "pointer not in memory list" message, apparently from the creation of the file pointer on the heap.

DESIGNING C++ CLASS LIBRARIES

Thomas Keffer

INTRODUCTION

Imagine a world where housing contractors, obsessed with energy "efficiency" and convinced that no one else could do it better than the old "meister" himself, built their own doors and windows. Every French door, every sash, and every threshold would be lovingly crafted. Special attention would be paid to the hinges for this was a skill that every self-respecting contractor was taught in detail in school and was expected to have mastered.

Romantic, yes. But imagine the expense! And imagine the variations in quality—some builders would consistently turn out smoothly swinging doors while others would never get it right.

This is the software world we live in. Every programmer is expected to master not only their problem domain, but also fundamental data structures, user interfaces, mathematical algorithms, etc. Every piece of every application is crafted from scratch.

But this world is undergoing a revolution. We are learning how to package algorithms and structures into *objects*, greatly improving their reusability. Languages have been designed to support this reusability.

This chapter is about the elements of reuse, specifically the design and implementation of C++ *libraries*. It is a specialized kind of design problem, different from the more usual *application* design problem, in that the overriding design goal is code reusability. How do we design and implement classes that encourage *reusability*? What are the elements of reusability? What motivates a user to use a library rather than write their own?

ONCE IS NOT ENOUGH!

The major reasons why a user chooses to use a library instead of writing custom code are:

Portability

Write once, port many. The goal of portability can be a major reason why a user chooses to use a library instead of writing custom code. A library can mask differences across compilers, operating systems, and hardware platforms through abstraction. This means finding the essential data model that is common among different environments. This becomes the applications programmer's user interface (the library API).

Adaptability

The library should be able to react to unforseen situations gracefully. For example, low memory restrictions, hardware failures, etc. It should not demand that the architecture of an application revolve around it by taking over global resources.

Performance

Good performance is essential so the user will not be tempted to write custom code. An even higher goal is a library that can improve performance over what a user could typically achieve, perhaps by using sophisticated algorithms too complex for the average user to handle.

Understandability

The library should have a simple interface that does not intimidate the user.

CLASS ARCHITECTURES

Let's look first at the overall "look and feel" of a library. What sorts of patterns might we find?[1] How does this affect reusability?

In practice, seldom does a library adhere to a single architecture. More likely, it consists of many different sets of classes, each with a different kind of architecture. Hence, it is probably more accurate to refer to "Class Architectures" rather than "Library Architectures."

Interface Classes

The distinguishing feature of interface classes is that they supply an *interface*, not an implementation. That is, they consist mostly of abstract base classes with (possibly) a few instantiable specializing classes. There are many pure virtual functions and few, if any, nonpure virtual functions.

To actually *use* such a set of classes, you must derive off one of the abstract base classes and supply an implementation. This may be the user's job, or the library vendor may have supplied a few such classes, either for common tasks or as an example to the user of how to do so. Because of the need to subclass, these class architectures have a tree-like structure.

Interface classes:

◆ Supply interfaces, but not implementation

◆ Have nodes that are generally not instantiable

◆ Have many pure virtual functions.

Tree-Like

The distinguishing feature of a tree-like class architecture is that all objects are rooted in a single object or, possibly, a few objects. Tree-like architectures are similar to interface classes (see above) in that they tend to rely

---

[1]To my knowledge, Mike Vilot was the first to attempt to classify library structures in such a manner.

heavily on base classes to supply an interface, but they differ in that the base classes also supply implementation. That is, the abstract base classes have many nonpure virtuals in addition to any pure virtual functions.

An example is the Microsoft Foundation Classes (MFC). Much (but not all) of the library inherits from object `CObject`, which provides facilities for serialization (persistence) and classification. The entire windowing and messaging facility is rooted in `CCmdTarget` which not only provides the interface for messaging, but also its implementation in that it encapsulates the Windows message loop. This is convenient because all such logic can be put in one spot, making it easy to subclass and reuse this machinery.

However, this convenience comes at a cost: The message loop is a global resource in that there is only one in an application. Hence, if two such libraries meet each other, the user will be unable to use them both.

Typically, tree-like architectures support many abstractions within the tree. For example, MFC not only provides support for persistence, but also window messaging within the same hierarchy.

Tree-like architectures:

◆ Rely heavily on base classes to supply implementation, as well as the interface

◆ Support many abstractions within a single tree hierarchy

◆ Have nodes that are instantiable

◆ Make heavy use of virtual functions

◆ Have considerable code reuse within the library

◆ Allow simpler sharing of global (or, at least, library-wide) resources.

Forest-Like

Forest-like class architectures tend to take the trees and break them up into many separate, smaller, hierarchies, each representing a single abstraction. The resultant root nodes tend to be smaller, simpler, and more focused, making them easier to combine with other libraries.

The classes are frequently intended to be used as a "mix-in," that is, combined with a user class via multiple inheritance to provide the func-tionality needed. For example, suppose a user wanted to make his or her class persistent. With a "tree architecture," the user would be required to inherit from the root class, possibly bringing along unwanted functionality. With a "forest-like" approach, the user would "mix-in" persistence ability by multiply inheriting from his or her class and a class providing "persistence" ability.

To summarize forest-like architectures:

◆ Each tree describes a single abstraction

◆ Each tree can exist in isolation

◆ Instantiation happens via specialization or templates

◆ Clients frequently use multiple inheritance via "mix ins."

Concrete Data Types

Concrete data types typically appear to the user as an extension to the language. That is, their semantics are similar to built in types such as `int` or `double`. They follow value semantics and are not designed for inheritance. Examples of concrete data types are the `string` and `bitstring` classes found in the ISO/ANSI C++ Draft Standard.

Because such classes appear to be little different from familiar built-in types, users find them easy to use and understand. They can stand in isolation, so using one or two such classes is easy without pulling in lots of ancillary classes. But it is hard to specialize such classes with inheritance. Why is this? Here's an example. Class `string` allows two strings to be concatenated via an overloaded '+' operator:

```
string operator+(const string&, const string&);
```

If you created a class (call it `MyString`) that inherited from `string`, then using `operator+` on it would would return the wrong type! You would have to replace `operator+`, as well as all other operators, to make sure they return the correct type. It is this sort of heavily value oriented semantics that makes it difficult to derive from concrete data types.

To summarize concrete data types:

◆ Classes act like extensions to the language

- ◆ Highly dependent on an implementation
- ◆ Used to specialize Abstract Data Types, perhaps as a template parameter
- ◆ Not designed for inheritance
- ◆ Superior efficiency.

Layered

Layered class architectures rely more on "using" relationships between objects rather than inheritance or specialization via templates. Typically, the classes will offer a simplified "outer" interface with easy-to-use semantics. However, the more savvy user can reach into the inner machinery to replace parts to achieve alternative semantics.

An example is iostreams. On the outside are classes `istream` and `ostream`. But on the inside is class `streambuf`, the ultimate sink and source of the bytes that `istream` and `ostream` format and consume.

Most users are content to simply shift values in and out of streams:

```
cout << "Hello world";
```

The more sophisticated user might want to use the internal streambuf directly, or replace it with another streambuf:

```
char buf[100];
cout.rdbuf()->sgetn(buf, sizeof(buf));
```

In summary, the properties of layered class architectures are

- ◆ Classes are instantiable
- ◆ The architecture injects policy as well as interface and implementation
- ◆ Several independent types work in concert
- ◆ The user can replace parts for different functionality (but classes come with a default configuration).

Design Issues

In this section we will visit a number of design issues that arise when writing a class library.

Designing a New Class

When it comes time to design a new class, there are two golden rules:

1. Use an existing class rather than write a new one.
2. If you can't use an existing class, then see rule number 1.

Introducing a new class means that your users will have to become familiar with a whole new object. If this is because whole new functionality is being introduced, that's OK. But even then you should strive to use old tools to build new tools.

Very frequently, new functionality is *not* being introduced. It's just old functionality looked at in new ways. For example, if you need an array of graphical objects, then do *not* do this:

```
class Composite {
  .
  .
  .
private:
  Graphic* vec_;        // Vector of graphical objects
  unsigned N_;          // Number of objects in vec
  unsigned capac_;      // Capacity of vec
};
```

This is a perfect opportunity for an ordered collection. This will allow new objects to be inserted into the composite without worrying about growing the vector. Debugging becomes easier, the class becomes smaller, and users will find the results easier to understand without extraneous functionality cluttering their vision.

Push Policy Up, Implementation Down

In general, you should try to avoid making policy, deferring it to higher classes. What is policy? Examples include:

- What an interface might look like (particularly an issue with template parameters).
- Whether an exception will be thrown.
- Which stream to print to (e.g., you should print to `ostream`, rather than `cout`).
- Whether searches should be case-sensitive or case-insensitive.

By constrast, how to implement something should be pushed into lower classes. For example:

- Use a collection class rather than roll-your-own.
- Draw to an abstract canvas rather than X11 or Windows.
- Use `strcmp()` instead of writing your own loop.

Value versus Reference Semantics

An important design decision is whether to chose value or reference semantics for your class design. Here are two examples, designed to show the difference:

Value semantics:

```
String a("abc");
String b = a;
b[0] = 'A';
assert(b=="Abc");    // True
assert(a=="abc");    // True
```

Reference semantics:

```
String a("abc");
String b = a;
b[0] = 'A';
assert(b=="Abc");    // True
assert(a=="Abc");    // Also true!
```

In general, value semantics is easier to understand, adhering to the "Principle of Least Astonishment." On the other hand, it is much harder to program efficiently. Copy On Write (COW) is a nice technique for achieving both goals.

A pragmatic approach is to use value semantics throughout, relying on COW where necessary. But if efficiency is really critical, then drop back to reference semantics (an example is mathematical classes).

Global Resources

For maximum reusability and adaptability, it is important that your library not take over global resources. Examples of global resources are

- Memory allocations (`new`, `delete`, etc.)
- Message loops
- Global error handlers.

Information Flow

Your users will find it easier to understand your classes if they can conceptually think of information as flowing into a function via its arguments, and then back out through its return value.

Function Arguments

Generally, a function should not change its arguments. Hence, they should either all be passed by value, or as a constant reference.

An exception to this rule is a collection class or other class that must maintain a relationship with another object. In this case, a pointer to the other object should be passed, *never a reference*. This is to remind the user that an interrelationship has been established. Hence, you should use:

```
OrderedCollection::insert(Object*);
Model::addDependent(ModelClient* client);
```

and not

```
OrderedCollection::insert(Object&);
Model::addDependent(ModelClient&);
```

With the latter, it is all too easy to think that the argument is being passed in by value, forgetting that a reference to the argument will be retained.

Furthermore, using a pointer as a formal argument discourages passing in a stack-based argument, because the address of the argument would have to be taken:

```
OrderedCollection collect;

// Insert stack-based variable:
String s("a string");
collect.insert(&s);      // Looks weird; should ring bells

// Proper idiom:
collect.insert(new String("a string"));
```

Objects that must be initialized with another object in order to work are an important exception. In C++, a reference represents a real object. It cannot be nil. Hence, it can be useful in the constructor of an object that requires a "partner" object in order to function. Iterators are an example:

```
OrderedCollectionIterator(OrderedCollection& ord);
```

Return Values

As stated, a function should return its results through the return value, never through an argument. This means that only one "thing" can be returned per function call. This is much easier for the user to understand. If you find that you must return two pieces of information, then you are probably discovering the basis for a new class. These disparate pieces should be packaged together into a single object, then returned.

Or, rethink your problem.

"const" Correct

The const qualifier should be used whenever possible. *This is particularly true of low-level libraries.* If the low-level routines are not const correct, then it will be impossible for higher-level clients to be const correct.

The C++ language defines a "const" object in a strict bitwise sense. That is, a const function is one that does not change the struct to which the `this` pointer points. In practice, this makes nearly every function `const`, even those for which this may seem counterintuitive. The reason why is that this definition allows pointed-to objects to change, while the object itself remains `const`. For many classes, this means that even the assignment operator could be declared `const`, so long as a level of indirection is adhered to!

Hence, to make "constness" useful in practice, this definition must be broadened to include pointed-to objects as well in *a logical sense*. If a member function is to be considered `const`, then

♦ The object pointed to by `this` should not change in a strict bitwise sense

♦ Any pointed-to objects cannot change in a logical sense.

Note that this is a rather severe definition of "constness" and will mean that many fewer member functions can be declared `const`. It will require considerable work on your part or it will limit which member functions can be considered `const`. This is as it should be.

Note, however, that it *does* allow the caching of data. If an accessor function does an expensive calculation and caches the result, then that function can be declared const *if it will return identical results if called again.* Even in this case, it is not permitted to change the struct pointed to by `this`. The caching must occur through a level of indirection. This is to protect against aggressive optimizing compilers.

Protected Data

Protected data should be considered part of the public interface. By making data or functions protected, you are signaling that you expect someone to subclass off the class. Hence, changes should not be taken lightly and should be avoided.

Beware of Public Virtual Functions

Because virtual functions can be overridden in a derived class, a subclass may inadvertently miss implementing some functionality necessary for correct semantics. For example, suppose a class requires a lock to be set and unset:

```
class Writer
{
public:
  virtual void putData(ostream&);
};

void Writer::putData(ostream& str)
{
  setLock();              // Set a lock, perhaps for a multi-
                          // threading environment
  str << 22;              // Write some data.
  releaseLock();          // Release lock.
}
```

If a user derives from this class, perhaps intending to write a double instead of an int, but forgets to set the lock, incorrect semantics can result:

```
class MyWriter:public Writer
{
public:
  virtual void putData(ostream&);
};

void MyWriter::putData(ostream& str)
{
  str << 5.2;    // Oops.  Lock not set.
}
```

A better choice is to use a public nonvirtual function to set the lock, then a protected virtual function to manipulate the data:

```
class BetterWriter
{
public:
  void putData(ostream&);        // Public non-virtual
protected:
  virtual void doPutData(ostream&);  // Protected virtual
};

void BetterWriter::putData(ostream& str)
{
  setLock();
  doPutData(str);
  releaseLock();
}

// Can be safely overridden:
void BetterWriter::doPutData(ostream& str)
```

```
{
    str << 22;
}
```

Because the user of this class has access only to the public nonvirtual `putData()`, you guarantee that the lock will always be set.

IMPLEMENTATION ISSUES

Compile Goals

You should strive for short compiler command lines. This means that you should not rely on the user defining preprocessor flags on the command line.

You should also strive for compilations that emit no warnings. Even though *you* know that the warnings are harmless, your users do not. It is amazing the number of technical support calls that get generated from people who are concerned about innocuous "possible unintended assignment" warnings from while loops that do an assignment in their conditional.

Unfortunately, the goal of "compiling with no warnings" means that `#pragma`s cannot be used because they usually generate warnings from compilers that do not understand them.

Copy On Write (COW)

Copy on Write is a technique that should be in every programmer's bag of tricks. It allows you to support the simple-to-understand semantics of value-based classes, without their normal overhead. Here's how it works.

There are two parts of an object supporting COW: a reference counted *reference* class and a *wrapper* class. Let's look first at the reference class, using a `string` class as an example. Many features, such as support for embedded nulls, multi-threading, memory pools, etc. have been omitted in the interest of clarity:

```
struct StringRef
{
```

```
   unsigned refs_;        // Reference count
   char* str_;            // Data array

   // Copy constructor does a deep copy:
   StringRef(const StringRef& s)
   {
     str_ = new char[strlen(s.str_)+1];
     strcpy(str_, s.str_);
   }

   // ...
};
```

Note that the copy constructor of this class does a *deep copy*. That is, the entire data structure is copied into the new instance. Naturally, this is expensive, necessitating the existence of the wrapper to minimize the number of times this happens:

```
class String
{
   StringRef* pref_;
public:
   String(const char*);

   // Copy constructor does reference counted,
   // shallow copy:
   String(const String& st)
   {
     pref_ = st.pref_;
     pref_->refs_++;
   }

   char  operator[](unsigned) const;
   char& operator[](unsigned);
};
```

Note that the copy constructor of the wrapper merely increments a reference count, thus deferring the actual copy. This makes the copy constructor extremely cheap: it just needs to initialize a pointer, and increment a count. This makes it attractive to return Strings by value from a function:

```
String sayHello()
{
   return String("hello");
}
```

But what happens when two strings share the same reference and one of them changes? To honor the value semantics, we have to make sure that we make a copy just before changing the string:

```
String a("xyz");
String b(a);            // Both a and b share the same
                        // reference
b[2] = 'd';             // Copy made: "xyd"
assert(b=="xyd");       // OK
assert(a=="xyz");       // OK
```

How do we do this? Let's look at the indexing operator:

```
inline char& String::operator[](unsigned i)
{
  if (pref_->refs_ > 1)
  {
    // More than one string using the reference.
    --pref_->refs;
    // Now do the deep copy:
    pref_ = new StringRef(*pref_);
  }
  return pref_->str_[i];
}
```

Note that it returns the indexed element *by reference*, thus allowing it to be used as an lvalue (that is, on the left hand side of an assignment). Because it can be used as an lvalue, it is possible that the user might change it. Hence, the function checks to make sure that no other String is sharing the StringRef pointed to by pref_; if another String is, it makes a copy. Then the element is returned.

As you might imagine, the conditional in this operator can exact a runtime penalty—not only does the if statement take time to execute, but it can clog pipes in superscalar machines. If you know that this operator will never be used as an lvalue then the test can be avoided. Such is the case with the const version of the indexing operator:

```
inline char String::operator[](unsigned i) const
{
  return pref_->str_[i];
}
```

Because this is a *const* function, it will not and should not modify the object. Note that this function returns a char *by value*. That is, the return argument is actually a copy of the indexed element. The user will be unable to modify the string using this function, thus honoring its constness. There is no need to check the reference count, thus retaining efficiency.

Inlines

Inlined functions should be used for only the simplest of functions. Accessor functions that return a simple type are good candidates for inlining. Mutator functions that simply reset member data are also good candidates (although beware of inlined assignment operators which could generate a lot of code).

Beware in particular of inlines containing the new operator. They can generate an amazing amount of code:

```
class Link
{
  Link* next_;
  void* data_;
public:
  Link(Link* n, void* d) : next_(n), data_(d) {;}
};

class List
{
  Link* head_;

public:
  void append(void* v) {head_ = new Link(head_, v);}
};

void foo(List& list, void* a)
{
  list.append(a);
}
```

The function foo() becomes (cfront V2.1):

```
char foo__FR4ListPv (__0list, __0a)
    struct List * __0list;
    char * __0a;
{
    struct Link * __0__this;
    struct Link * __0__a;
```

```
  ((__Olist -> head___4List = ((__0__this = 0),
    ((__0__a=__Olist -> head___4List),
    (((__0__this ||
    (__0__this = (struct Link*) __nw__FUi (sizeof (struct
Link))))
    ? (((__0__this -> next___4Link = __0__a),
    (__0__this ->    data___4Link = __0a)), 0) : 0),
    ((__0__this)))))), (((char) 0)));

}
```

Operator new

You should not check the return value of operator new to see if it's nil. Instead, assume than an exception inheriting from bad_alloc will be thrown . Not all compilers have implemented this feature, but as exception handling becomes commonplace, this will be the norm.

Copy Avoidance

Copies of large objects are expensive. You should strive to avoid copies wherever possible.

Large objects (anything larger than a pointer) and small objects with a nontrivial copy constructor should generally be passed into a function by const reference, thus avoiding the copy. Also note that there is no point in adding const when a parameter is passed by value:

```
void foo(const string s);     // Redundant
void foo(const int i);        // Redundant
```

Doing so tends to confuse the reader and leave him or her wondering if the ampersand ('&') was accidentally left off.

To get an object back out of a function, it is usually cheaper to construct the object in the return statement. Most compilers can then build the object right where it's going to go:

```
// Do this:
string name()
{
  return string("fred");      // Avoids copy constructor
```

```
}
// Not this:
string name()
{
  string myName("fred");
  return myName;
}
```

This works because most compilers return a complex object on the stack: Space is allocated for it right in the call frame. The compiler uses this address to build the object directly in the return statement, thus avoiding a copy.

Return by const Value

Note that there is a difference between returning an object by value and returning it by const value. This is a recent (November 1993) change in the language. "Constness" is no longer stripped from the return type. A return type that is a const value cannot be used as an lvalue:

```
const string operator+(const string&, const string&);
string a("a"), b("b");

a + b = "z";         // Compile time error
string c = a + b;    // OK
```

Use Initialization Rather Than Assignment

In constructors, be sure to use initialization rather than assignment when possible. For example, given the class

```
class Address
{
  string street_;
public:
  Address(const string& s);
  // ...
};
```

the constructor should be written like this

```
Address::Address(const string& s)
 : street_(s)
{;}
```

rather than like this:

```
Address::Address(const string& s)
{
  street_ = s;   // No.
}
```

The latter approach causes the default constructor to be called to initialize street_, then the assignment operator. This is much slower than simply initializing street_ with the appropriate constructor.

Static Initializers

Static initializers are objects that are at file scope and must be initialized:

```
string staticInit("a string");
string foo() {
  return string(staticInit);
}
```

Exactly when the initialization of staticInit occurs is not specified by the language. It is only guaranteed to be done before the function foo() is entered. In practice, all compilers do the initialization at program startup. This means that programs that make extensive use of static initializers can be very slow to start up.

Static initializers are a popular trick to insure that initialization of some subsystem happens before possible use.

SYSTEM.H

```
    // Classes declaring the subsystem.

struct Init {
  Init();
  ~Init();
};

static Init InitObj;
```

SYSTEM.CPP

```
static short initcount = 0;

Init::Init(){
  if( initcount++ == 0 ) {
        // Start up the subsystem
  }
}

Init::~Init(){
  if( --initcount == 0 ) {
        // Shut down the subsystem
  }
}
```

While this is a useful trick, care must be taken to keep the number of static initializers to a minimum. If you expect the header file declaring the static initializer to be used a lot (file system.h, in this example), you should probably require the user to explicitly start up and shut down the subsystem.

Linkage Dependencies

The junction of two different classes must be treated with care, lest the use of one class inadvertently drag in the code for the other class. An example is, say, conversion from Dates to Strings. If this conversion code was located in the file implementing dates, then if the user uses date-related code, the linker must pull in the string related code as well. A better choice is to locate such code in a separate module. This way it will only get pulled in if actually used.

THE ANSI/ISO ERROR MODEL

This section discusses the ANSI/ISO Error Model, adopted by the C++ Standarization Committee in San Jose in November 1993.

In the model, errors are divided into two broad categories: *logic* errors and *runtime* errors. The distinguishing characteristic of logic errors is that they are due to errors in the internal logic of the program. In theory, they are preventable. As you might expect, they can be difficult to recover from and, indeed, the default response is commonly to abort the program. By contrast, runtime errors are due to events beyond the scope of the program. They cannot be easily predicted.

Logic Errors

Logic errors are due to faulty logic or coding in the program. A large subclass of such errors (but not all) are violated preconditions or *domain errors*. Another large class is violated class invariants. Examples of logic errors are:

◆ Out of bounds errors

◆ Attempting to use a bad file descriptor

◆ Calling `acos` with an argument outside of the domain −1.0 to 1.0.

In theory, given enough diligence on the part of the programmer, these kinds of errors are preventable. In practice, of course, they will occur.

The treatment of logic errors can be divided into two general categories, depending on the cost of error detection and, hence, whether or not the system can afford to detect the error: nonrecoverable logic errors and recoverable logic errors.

Nonrecoverable Logic Errors

The performance characteristics of some code may be so stringent that the system cannot afford to check for violated preconditions. An example is indexing or bounds errors: The cost of checking that an index is in bounds may well exceed the cost of the array access itself. Hence, for good performance, it may be necessary to forgo error checking. However, as a debugging aid, it is useful to offer the programmer "debug" versions of the libraries, which, although slower and bulkier that the production version of the library, do check for such errors.

Recoverable Logic Errors

If the cost of error detection is relatively low, then it starts to make sense to detect an error in the production version of the library. An example is a bounds error in a linked list: The cost of walking the list will far exceed the cost of detecting whether the index is in bounds. Hence, you can afford to check for a bounds error on every access.

Recoverable or Not?

We have pointed out that, depending on the cost of error detection, a library may elect to forgo checking preconditions.

But there is another kind of cost, and that is the cost of the *consequences* of an undetected error. Unfortunately, this cost cannot be known by the sort of low-level classes found in the Standard C++ Library. This suggests that the library should assume the worse and check for all possible errors and, indeed, this is the approach of the Standard C++ Library. All possible logic errors are treated as potentially recoverable.

Runtime Errors

The distinguishing characteristic of *runtime errors* is that they cannot be reasonably predicted in advance without extraordinary efforts on the part of the programmer. They are frequently caused by either external conditions beyond the scope of the program, or by range errors (violated postconditions) such as arithmetic overflow from legal arguments. Examples of runtime errors are:

◆ Attempt to set a date object to a bad date (E.g., "31 June 1993")

◆ Attempt to invert a singular matrix

◆ Disk full error

◆ Out of memory.

Logic or Runtime?

The line between logic and runtime errors can sometimes be fuzzy. For example, the constructor for a date class could state a precondition: "don't give me an invalid date" and then the programmer would be responsible for detecting a bad date before invoking the constructor. To do otherwise would be a logic error. Of course, this is a lot of work and, in any case, the date object is probably in a better position to detect the bad date than its client. Hence, a better choice would be to treat such an error as a runtime error.

Very frequently a runtime error can be converted into a logic error. An example is IEEE arithmetic: Overflow is accounted for in the postcondition. It's not actually an error until the results are fed into another function at which point it becomes a violated precondition. Another example is the Standard C++ Library string class. It could be designed such that length errors are eliminated: It would not be an error to augment (append) a string beyond it's maximal theoretical capacity (NPOS less one), only to *use* such a string.

Finally, it is worth noting that while a good error model suggests a good exception class hierarchy, the two issues are not necessarily coupled. Having identified an error model, you could as easily design an error handling strategy around return values rather than exceptions.

THE ANSI/ISO EXCEPTION HIERARCHY

The Standard C++ Library uses the following, singly rooted, exception hiearchy:

```
exception
    logic_error
        domain_error
        invalid_argument
        length_error
        out_of_range
        bad_cast
        bad_typeid
    runtime_error
        range_error
        overflow_error
        bad_alloc
```

Class exception

The class exception is the root class of the exception hierarchy. All exceptions thrown by the Standard C++ library are rooted in this class. Hence, if the user does nothing else, she or he can write a handler catching class exception and be sure to catch all exceptions thrown by the Standard C++ library. Many commercial library vendors (for example, Borland and Rogue Wave) also root their exception hierarchy in exception, and so exceptions thrown by these libraries can also be caught.

Class `exception` contains a message, retrievable via member function `what()`, that summarizes what happens.

```
class exception
{
public:
  exception(const string& what);
  exception(const exception&);
  exception& operator=(const exception&);
  virtual ~exception();
  virtual string what() const;
protected:
  exception();
};
```

Class logic_error

Classes inheriting from class `logic_error` are thrown in response to a *logic error*; that is, an error in the logic of the program, usually in response to a violated precondition. Under these circumstances, recovery is doubtful. An important subclass of class `logic_error` is class `domain`, representing exceptions thrown in response to domain errors, or violated preconditions.

Here's an example, as it might look in class `dyn_array`, a class that is part of the Standard C++ Library:

```
T dyn_array<T>::operator[](size_t i) const
{
  if (i>=maxLength_)
    throw domain("Subscript out of domain");
  return vec_[i];
}
```

Class runtime_error

Classes inheriting from class `runtime_error` are thrown in response to a *runtime error*; that is, errors outside the scope of the program. Recovery is highly likely as the basic integrity of the program has not been compromised. Recovery might be as simple as a retry. An important subclass of class `runtime_error` is class `bad_alloc`, representing exceptions thrown in response to being out of heap memory.

Here's an example, using the standard `string` class to illustrate:

```
string&
string::append(const string& s, size_t pos, size_t n)
{
 if (len >= NPOS - n)
    throw range_error("Out of range");
 return *this;
}
```

Canonical Handler

The division of the exception hierarchy into logic and runtime errors allows a very simple handler to be written:

```
while (1)
{
  try {
    something_tricky();
  }
  catch (logic_error x) {
    cerr << "Internal failure\n";
    emergency_exit();
  }
  catch (runtime_error x) {
    cerr << "Something went wrong: ";
    cerr << x.what() << endl;
    cerr << "Retry.\n";
  }
}
```

SUMMARY

Reuse is not automatic. And just coding in C++ will not make your code more likely to be reused.

Reuse is encouraged by making your interface robust and unambiguous, your implementation adaptable, and your algorithms world class.

C++ Under the Hood

Jan Gray

INTRODUCTION

It is important to understand how your programming language is implemented. Such knowledge dispels the fear and wonder of "what on earth is the compiler doing here?," imparts confidence to use the new features, and provides insight when debugging and when learning other language features. It also gives a feel for the relative costs of different coding choices that is necessary to write the most efficient code day to day.

This paper looks "under the hood" of C++, explaining "runtime" C++ implementation details such as class layout techniques and the virtual function call mechanism. Questions to be answered include:

- How are classes laid out?
- How are data members accessed?
- How are member functions called?
- What is an adjuster thunk?
- What are the costs of
  - Single, multiple, virtual inheritance?
  - Virtual functions and virtual function calls?
  - Casts to bases, to virtual bases?
  - Exception handling?

First, you'll review struct layout, of C-like structs, single inheritance, multiple inheritance, and virtual inheritance, then consider data member access, and member functions, virtual and not. You will examine the workings of constructors, destructors, and assignment operator special member functions, and dynamic construction and destruction of arrays. Finally, you will briefly consider the impact of exception handling support.

For each language feature topic, I very briefly present motivation and semantics for the language feature (although "Introduction to C++" this is not) and examine how the language feature was implemented in Microsoft Visual C++. Note the distinction between abstract language semantics and a particular concrete implementation. Other vendors have sometimes made different implementation choices for whatever reasons. In a few cases, we contrast the Visual C++ implementation with others.

CLASS LAYOUT

In this section you will consider the storage layouts required for different kinds of inheritance.

C-like Structs

As C++ is based upon C, it is "mostly" upwards compatible with C. In particular, the working papers specify the same simple `struct` layout rules that C has: members are laid out in their declaration order, subject to implementation defined alignment padding. All C/C++ vendors ensure that valid C structs are stored identically by their C and C++ compilers. Here A is a simple C `struct` with the obvious expected member layout and padding.

```
struct A {                A*->  ┌─────────┐
    char c;                     │A::c     │
    int i;                      │A::i     │
};                              └─────────┘
```

C-like Structs with C++ Features

Of course, C++ is an object-oriented programming language: It provides inheritance, encapsulation, and polymorphism by extending the mundane C struct into the wondrous C++ class. Besides data members, C++ classes can also encapsulate member functions and many other things. However, except for hidden data members introduced to implement virtual functions and virtual inheritance, the instance size is solely determined by a class's data members and base classes.

Here B is a C-like struct with some C++ features: There are `public/protected/private` access control declarations, member functions, `static` members, and nested type declarations. Only the nonvirtual data members occupy space in each instance. Note that the standards committee working papers permit implementations to reorder data members separated by an access declarator, so these three members could have been laid out in any order. (In Visual C++, members are always laid out in declaration order, just as if they were members of a C struct)

```
struct B {                              B*->    ┌─────────┐
public:                                         │ B::bm1  │
    int bm1;                                    ├─────────┤
protected:                                      │ B::bm2  │
    int bm2;                                    ├─────────┤
private:                                        │ B::bm3  │
    int bm3;                                    └─────────┘
    static int bsm;
    void bf();
    static void bsf();
    typedef void* bpv;
    struct N { };
};
```

Single Inheritance

C++ provides inheritance to factor out and share common aspects of different types. A good example of a classes-with-inheritance data type organization is biology's classification of living things into kingdoms, phyla, orders, families, genera, species, and so on. This organization makes it possible to specify attributes, such as "mammals bear live young" at the most appropriate level of classification; these attributes are then *inherited* by other classes, so we can conclude without further specification that whales, squirrels, and people bear live young. Exceptional cases, such as platypi (a mammal, yet lays eggs), will require that we *override* the inherited attribute or behavior with one more appropriate for the derived class. More on that later.

In C++, inheritance is specified by using the : base syntax when defining the derived class. Here D is derived from its base class C.

```
struct C {                      C*->    ┌─────────┐
    int c1;                             │ C::c1   │
    void cf();                          └─────────┘
};
struct D : C {                  C*,D*-> ┌─────────┐
    int d1;                             │ C::c1   │
    void df();                          ├─────────┤
};                                      │ D::d1   │
                                        └─────────┘
```

Since a derived class inherits all of the properties and behavior of its base class, each instance of the derived class will contain a complete copy of the instance data of the base class. Within D, there is no requirement that C's instance data precede D's. But by laying D out this way, you ensure that the address of the C object within D corresponds to the address of the first byte of the D object. As we shall see, this eliminates adding a displacement to a D* when you need to obtain the address of its embedded C. This layout is used by all known C++ implementations. Thus, in a single inheritance class hierarchy, new instance data introduced in each derived class is simply appended to the layout of the base class. Note your layout diagram labels the "address points" of pointers to the C and D objects within a D.

Multiple Inheritance

Single inheritance is quite versatile and powerful, and generally adequate for expressing the (typically limited) degree of inheritance present in most design problems. Sometimes, however, we have two or more sets of behavior that we wish our derived class to acquire. C++ provides multiple inheritance to combine them.

For instance, say we have a model for an organization which has a class Manager (who delegates) and class Worker (who actually does the work). Now how can we model a class MiddleManager, who, like a Worker, accepts work assignments from his or her manager and who, like a Manager, delegates this work to his or her employees? This is awkward to express using single inheritance: for MiddleManager to inherit behavior from both Manager and Worker, both must be base classes. If this is arranged so that MiddleManager inherits from Manager which inherits from Worker, it erroneously ascribes Worker behavior to Managers. (Vice versa, the same problem.) Of course, MiddleManager could inherit from just one (or neither) of Worker or Manager, and instead, duplicate (redeclare) both interfaces, but that defeats polymorphism, fails to reuse the existing interface, and leads to maintenance woes as interfaces evolve over time.

Instead, C++ allows a class to inherit from multiple base classes:

```
struct Manager ... { ... };
struct Worker ... { ... };
struct MiddleManager : Manager, Worker { ... };
```

How might this be represented? Continuing with our "classes of the alphabet" example,

```
struct E {                      E*->  ┌─────────────┐
    int e1;                           │ E::e1       │
    void ef();                        └─────────────┘
};

struct F : C, E {               C*,F*->  ┌─────────────┐
    int f1;                              │ C::c1       │
    void ff();                   E*->     ├─────────────┤
};                                        │ E::e1       │
                                          ├─────────────┤
                                          │ F::f1       │
                                          └─────────────┘
```

Struct F multiply inherits from C and E. As with single inheritance, F contains a copy of the instance data of each of its base classes. Unlike single inheritance, it is not possible to make the address point of each base's embedded instance correspond to the address of the derived class:

```
F f;
// (void*)&f == (void*)(C*)&f;
// (void*)&f <  (void*)(E*)&f;
```

Here, the address point of the embedded E within F is not at the address of the F itself. As we shall see when we consider casts and member functions, this displacement leads to a small overhead that single inheritance does not generally require.

An implementation is free to lay out the various embedded base instances and the new instance data in any order. Visual C++ is typical in laying out the base instances in declaration order, followed by the new data members, also in declaration order.

NOTE

As we shall see, this is not necessarily the case when some bases have virtual functions and others don't.

Virtual Inheritance

Returning to the MiddleManager example, which motivated multiple inheritance in the first place, we have a problem. What if both Manager and Worker are derived from Employee?

```
struct Employee { ... };
struct Manager : Employee { ... };
struct Worker : Employee { ... };
struct MiddleManager : Manager, Worker { ... };
```

Since both `Worker` and `Manager` inherit from `Employee`, they each contain a copy of the `Employee` instance data. Unless something is done, each `MiddleManager` will contain two instances of `Employee`, one from each base. If `Employee` is a large object, this duplication may represent an unacceptable storage overhead. More seriously, the two copies of the `Employee` instance might get modified separately or inconsistently. We need a way to declare that `Manager` and `Worker` are each willing to *share* a single embedded instance of their `Employee` base class, should `Manager` or `Worker` ever be inherited with some other class which also wishes to share the `Employee` base class.

In C++, this "sharing inheritance" is (unfortunately) called *virtual inheritance* and is indicated by specifying that a base class is `virtual`.

```
struct Employee { ... };
struct Manager : virtual Employee { ... };
struct Worker : virtual Employee { ... };
struct MiddleManager : Manager, Worker { ... };
```

Virtual inheritance is considerably more expensive to implement and use than single and multiple inheritance. Recall that for single (and multiply) inherited bases and derived classes, the embedded base instances and their derived classes either share a common address point (as with single inheritance and the leftmost base inherited via multiple inheritance), or have a simple constant displacement to the embedded base instance (as with multiply inherited nonleftmost bases, such as E). With virtual inheritance, on the other hand, there can (in general) be no fixed displacement from the address point of the derived class to its virtual base. If such a derived class is further derived from, the further deriving class may have to place the one shared copy of the virtual base at some other, different offset in the further derived class. Consider this example:

```
struct G : virtual C {
    int g1;
    void gf();
};
```

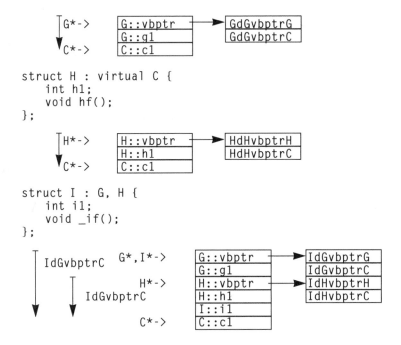

```
struct H : virtual C {
    int h1;
    void hf();
};
```

```
struct I : G, H {
    int i1;
    void _if();
};
```

Ignoring the vbptr members for a moment, notice that within a G object, the embedded C immediately follows the G data member, and similarly notice that within an H, the embedded C immediately follows the H data member. Now when we layout I we can't preserve both relationships. In the previous Visual C++ layout, the displacements from G to C in a G instance and in an I instance are different. Since classes are generally compiled without knowledge of what may be derived from them, each class with a virtual base must have a way to compute the location of the virtual base from the address point of its derived class.

In Visual C++, this is implemented by adding a hidden vbptr ("virtual base table pointer") field to each instance of a class with virtual bases. This field points to a shared, per-class table of displacements from the address point of the vbptr field to the class's virtual base(s).

Other implementations use embedded pointers from the derived class to its virtual bases, one per base. This other representation has the advantage of a smaller code sequence to address the virtual base, although an optimizing code generator can often common-subexpression-eliminate repeated virtual base access computations. However, it also has the disadvantages of larger instance sizes for classes with multiple virtual bases, of slower access to virtual bases of virtual bases (unless one incurs yet further hidden pointers), and of a less regular pointer to member dereference.

In Visual C++, G has a hidden `vbptr` which addresses a virtual base table whose second entry is `GdGvbptrC`. (This is our notation for "in G, the displacement from G's vbptr to C." (We omit the prefix to "d" if the quantity is constant in all derived classes.)) For example, on a 32-bit platform, `GdGvbptrC` would be 8 (bytes). Similarly, the embedded G instance within an I addresses a `vbtable` customized for G's within I's, and so `IdGvbptrC` would be 20.

As can be seen from the layouts of G, H, and I, Visual C++ lays out classes with virtual bases by:

◆ Placing embedded instances of the nonvirtually inherited bases first

◆ Adding a hidden `vbptr` unless a suitable one was inherited from one of the nonvirtual bases

◆ Placing the new data members declared in the derived class

◆ Placing a single instance of each of the virtually inherited bases at the end of the instance

This representation lets the virtually inherited bases "float" within the derived class (and its further derived classes) while keeping together and at constant relative displacements those parts of the object that are not virtually inherited.

DATA MEMBER ACCESS

Now that we have seen how classes are laid out, let's consider the cost to access data members of these classes.

No inheritance. In absence of inheritance, data member access is the same as in C: a dereference off some displacement from the pointer to the object.

```
C* pc;
pc->c1; // *(pc + dCc1);
```

Single inheritance. Since the displacement from the derived object to its embedded base instance is a constant 0, that constant 0 can be folded with the constant offset of the member within that base.

```
D* pd;
pd->c1; // *(pd + dDC + dCc1); // *(pd + dDCc1);
pd->d1; // *(pd + dDd1);
```

Multiple inheritance. Although the displacement to a given base, or to a base of a base, and so on, might be nonzero, it is still constant, and so any set of such displacements can be folded together into one constant displacement off the object pointer. Thus, even with multiple inheritance, access to any member is inexpensive.

```
F* pf;
pf->c1; // *(pf + dFC + dCc1); // *(pf + dFc1);
pf->e1; // *(pf + dFE + dEe1); // *(pf + dFe1);
pf->f1; // *(pf + dFf1);
```

Virtual inheritance. Within a class with virtual bases, access to a data member or nonvirtually inherited base class is again just a constant displacement off the object pointer. However, access to a data member of a virtual base is comparatively expensive, since it is necessary to fetch the vbptr, fetch a vbtable entry, and then add that displacement to the vbptr address point, just to compute the address of the data member. However, as shown for i.c1 which follows, if the type of the derived class is statically known, the layout is also known, and it is unnecessary to load a vbtable entry to find the displacement to the virtual base.

```
I* pi;
pi->c1; // *(pi + dIGvbptr + (*(pi+dIGvbptr))[1] + dCc1);
pi->g1; // *(pi + dIG + dGg1); // *(pi + dIg1);
pi->h1; // *(pi + dIH + dHh1); // *(pi + dIh1);
pi->i1; // *(pi + dIi1);
I i;
i.c1; // *(&i + IdIC + dCc1); // *(&i + IdIc1);
```

What about access to members of transitive virtual bases, for example, members of virtual bases of virtual bases (and so on)? Some implementations follow one embedded virtual base pointer to the intermediate virtual base, then follow its virtual base pointer to its virtual base, and so on. Visual C++ optimizes such access by using additional vbtable entries, which provide displacements from the derived class to any transitive virtual bases.

Casts

Except for classes with virtual bases, it is relatively inexpensive to explicitly cast a pointer into another pointer type. If there is a base-derived relationship between class pointers, the compiler simply adds or subtracts the displacement between the two (often 0).

```
F* pf;
(C*)pf; // (C*)(pf ? pf + dFC : 0); // (C*)pf;
(E*)pf; // (E*)(pf ? pf + dFE : 0);
```

In the C* cast, no computations are required, because dFC is 0. In the E* cast, we must add dFE, a nonzero constant, to the pointer. C++ requires that null pointers (0) remain null after a cast. Therefore, Visual C++ checks for null before performing the addition. This check occurs only when a pointer is implicitly or explicitly converted to a related pointer type, not when a derived* is implicitly converted to a base*const this pointer when a base member function is invoked on a derived object.

As you might expect, casting over a virtual inheritance path is relatively expensive: about the same cost as accessing a member of a virtual base:

```
I* pi;
(G*)pi; // (G*)pi;
(H*)pi; // (H*)(pi ? pi + dIH : 0);
(C*)pi; // (C*)(pi ? (pi+dIGvbptr + (*(pi+dIGvbptr))[1]) : 0);
```

In general, you can avoid a lot of expensive virtual base field accesses by replacing them with one cast to the virtual base and base relative accesses:

```
/* before: */          ... pi->c1 ... pi->c1 ...
/* faster: */ C* pc = pi; ... pc->c1 ... pc->c1 ...
```

MEMBER FUNCTIONS

A C++ member function is just another member in the scope of its class. Each (nonstatic) member function of a class X receives a special hidden `this` parameter of type X *const, which is implicitly initialized from the object the member function is applied to. Also, within the body of a member function, member access off the `this` pointer is implicit.

```
struct P {
    int p1;
    void pf(); // new
    virtual void pvf(); // new

};
        P*->    ┌────────────┐    ┌────────────┐
                │ P::vfptr   ├───►│ &P::pvf    │
                ├────────────┤    └────────────┘
                │ P::g1      │
                └────────────┘
```

P has a nonvirtual member function pf() and a virtual member function pvf(). It is apparent that virtual member functions incur an instance size hit, as they require a virtual function table pointer. More on that later. Notice there is no instance cost to declaring nonvirtual member functions. Now consider the definition of P::pf():

```
void P::pf() { // void P::pf([P *const this])
    ++p1; // ++(this->p1);
}
```

Here P::pf() receives a hidden `this` parameter, which the compiler has to pass each call.

NOTE

Also note that member access can be more expensive than it looks, because member accesses are `this` relative. On the other hand, compilers commonly enregister `this` so that member access cost is often no worse than accessing a local variable. On the other hand, compilers may not be able to enregister the instance data itself because of the possibility `this` is aliased with some other data.

Overriding Member Functions

Member functions are inherited just as data members are. Unlike data members, a derived class can override, or replace, the actual function definition to be used when an inherited member function is applied to a derived instance. Whether the override is static (determined at compile time by the static types involved in the member function call) or dynamic (determined at run time by the dynamic object addressed by the object pointer) depends upon whether the member function is declared virtual.

Class Q inherits P's data and function members. It declares pf(), overriding P::pf(). It also declares pvf(), a virtual function overriding P::pvf(), and declares a new nonvirtual member function qf(), and a new virtual function qvf().

```
struct Q : P {
    int q1;
    void pf();  // overrides P::pf
    void qf();  // new
    void pvf(); // overrides P::pvf
    virtual void qvf(); // new
};
```

```
P*<,*->     ┌─────────┐      ┌────────┐
            │P::vfptr ├─────►│&Q::pvf │
            │P::p1    │      │&Q::qvf │
            │Q::q1    │      └────────┘
            └─────────┘
```

For nonvirtual function calls, the member function to call is statically determined, at compile time, by the type of the pointer expression to the left of the -> operator. In particular, even though ppq points to an instance of Q, ppq->pf() calls P::pf(). (Also notice the pointer expression left of the -> is passed as the hidden this parameter.)

```
P p; P* pp = &p; Q q; P* ppq = &q; Q* pq = &q;
pp->pf();  // pp->P::pf();  // P::pf(pp);
ppq->pf(); // ppq->P::pf(); // P::pf(ppq);
pq->pf();  // pq->Q::pf();  // Q::pf((P*)pq);
pq->qf();  // pq->Q::qf();  // Q::qf(pq);
```

For virtual function calls, the member function to call is determined at run time. Regardless of the declared type of the pointer expression left of the -> operator, the virtual function to call is the one appropriate to the type of the actual instance addressed by the pointer. In particular, although ppq has type P*, it addresses a Q, and so Q::pvf() is called.

```
pp->pvf();  // pp->P::pvf();  // P::pvf(pp);
ppq->pvf(); // ppq->Q::pvf(); // Q::pvf((Q*)ppq);
pq->pvf();  // pq->Q::pvf();  // Q::pvf((P*)pq);
```

Hidden `vfptr` members are introduced to implement this mechanism. A `vfptr` is added to a class (if it doesn't already have one) to address that class's virtual function table (`vftable`). Each virtual function in a class has a corresponding entry in that class' `vftable`. Each entry holds the address of the virtual function override appropriate to that class. Therefore, calling a virtual function requires fetching the instance's `vfptr`, and indirectly calling through one of the `vftable` entries addressed by that pointer. This is in addition to the usual function call overhead of parameter passing, call, and return instructions. In the previous example, we fetch q's `vfptr`, which addresses Q's `vftable`, whose first entry is &Q::pvf. Thus Q::pvf() is called.

Looking back at the layouts of P and Q, we see that the Visual C++ compiler has placed the hidden `vfptr` member at the start of the P and Q instances. This helps ensure virtual function dispatch is as fast as possible. In fact, the Visual C++ implementation *ensures* that the first field in any class with virtual functions is always a `vfptr`. This can require inserting the new `vfptr` before base classes in the instance layout, or even require that a right base class which does begin with a `vfptr` be placed before a left base which does not have one.

Most C++ implementations will share or reuse an inherited base's `vfptr`. Here Q did not receive an additional `vfptr` to address a table for its new virtual function qvf(). Instead, a qvf entry is appended to the end of P's vftable layout. In this way, single inheritance remains inexpensive. Once an instance has a `vfptr` it doesn't need another one. New derived classes can introduce yet more virtual functions, and their `vftable` entries are simply appended to the end of their one per-class `vftable`.

Virtual Functions: Multiple Inheritance

It is possible for an instance to contain more than one `vfptr` if it inherits them from multiple bases, each with virtual functions. Consider R and S:

```
struct R {
    int r1;
    virtual void pvf(); // new
    virtual void rvf(); // new
};
```

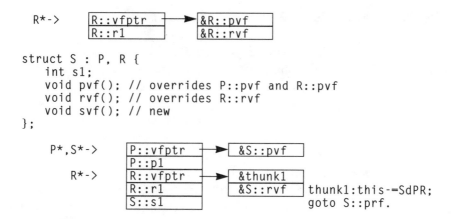

```
struct S : P, R {
    int s1;
    void pvf(); // overrides P::pvf and R::pvf
    void rvf(); // overrides R::rvf
    void svf(); // new
};
```

Here R is just another class with some virtual functions. Since S multiply inherits from P and R, it contains an embedded instance of each, plus its own instance data contribution, S::s1. Notice the right base R has a different address point than do P and S, as expected with multiple inheritance. S::pvf() overrides both P::pvf() and R::pvf(), and S::rvf() overrides R::rvf(). Here are the required semantics for the pvf override:

```
S s; S* ps = &s;
((P*)ps)->pvf(); // ((P*)ps)->P::vfptr[0])((S*)(P*)ps)
((R*)ps)->pvf(); // ((R*)ps)->R::vfptr[0])((S*)(R*)ps)
ps->pvf();       // one of the above; calls S::pvf()
```

Since S::pvf() overrides both P::pvf() and R::pvf(), it must replace their vftable entries in the S vftables. However, notice that it is possible to invoke pvf() both as a P and an R. The problem is that R's address point does not correspond to P's and S's. The expression (R*)ps does not point to the same part of the class as does (P*)ps. Since the function S::pvf() expects to receive an S* as its hidden this parameter, the virtual function call itself must automatically convert the R* at the call site into an S* at the callee. Therefore, S's copy of R's vftable's pvf slot takes the address of an adjuster thunk, which applies the address adjustment necessary to convert an R* pointer into an S* as desired.

In MSC++, for multiple inheritance with virtual functions, adjuster thunks are required only when a derived class virtual function overrides virtual functions of multiple base classes.

Address Points and "Logical this Adjustment"

Consider next S::rvf(), which overrides R::rvf(). Most implementations note that S::rvf() must have a hidden this parameter of type S*. Since R's rvf vftable slot may be used when this call occurs:

```
((R*)ps)->rvf(); // (*((R*)ps)->R::vfptr[1])((R*)ps)
```

most implementations add another thunk to convert the R* passed to rvf into an S*. Some also add an additional vftable entry to the end of S's vftable to provide a way to call ps->rvf() without first converting to an R*. MSC++ avoids this by intentionally compiling S::rvf() so as to expect a this pointer which addresses not the S object but rather the R embedded instance within the S. (We call this "giving overrides the same expected address point as in the class which first introduced this virtual function".) This is all done transparently, by applying a "logical this adjustment" to all member fetches, conversions from this, and so on that occur within the member function.

NOTE

Just as with multiple inheritance member access, this adjustment is constant-folded into other member displacement address arithmetic.

Of course, we have to compensate for this logical this adjustment in our debugger.

```
ps->rvf(); // ((R*)ps)->rvf(); // S::rvf((R*)ps)
```

Thus, MSC++ generally avoids creating a thunk and an additional extra vftable entry when overriding virtual functions of nonleftmost bases.

Adjuster Thunks

As described, an adjuster thunk is sometimes necessary, to adjust this (which is found just below the return address on the stack, or in a register) by some constant displacement en route to the called virtual function. Some implementations (especially cfront-based ones) do not employ adjuster thunks. Rather, they add additional displacement fields to each virtual function table entry. Whenever a virtual function is called, the displacement field, which is quite often 0, is added to the object address as it is passed in to become the this pointer:

```
ps->rvf();
// struct { void (*pfn)(void*); size_t disp; };
// (*ps->vfptr[i].pfn)(ps + ps->vfptr[i].disp);
```

The disadvantages of this approach include both larger vftables and larger code sequences to call virtual functions.

More modern PC-based implementations use adjust-and-jump techniques:

```
S::pvf-adjust: // MSC++
    this -= SdPR;
    goto S::pvf()
```

Of course, the following code sequence is even better (but no current implementation generates it):

```
S::pvf-adjust:
    this -= SdPR; // fall into S::pvf()
S::pvf() { ... }
```

Virtual Functions: Virtual Inheritance

Here T virtually inherits P and overrides some of its member functions. In Visual C++, to avoid costly conversions to the virtual base P when fetching a vftable entry, new virtual functions of T receive entries in a new vftable, requiring a new vfptr, introduced at the top of T.

```
struct T : virtual P {
    int t1;
    void pvf();        // overrides P::pvf
    virtual void tvf(); // new
};
```

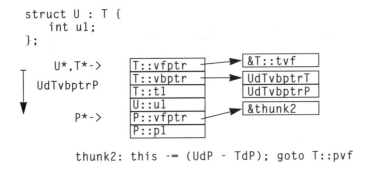

```
void T::pvf() {
    ++p1; // ((P*)this)->p1++; // vbtable lookup!
    ++t1; // this->t1++;
}
```

As previously shown above, even within the definition of a virtual function, access to data members of a virtual base must still use the `vbtable` to fetch a displacement to the virtual base. This is necessary because the virtual function can be subsequently inherited by a further derived class with different layout with respect to virtual base placement. And here is just such a class:

```
struct U : T {
    int u1;
};
```

Here U adds another data member, which changes the dP, the displacement to P. Since T::pvf expects to be called with a P* in a T, an adjuster thunk is necessary to adjust this so it arrives at the callee addressing just past T::t1 (the address point of a P* in a T). (Whew! That's about as complex as things get!)

SPECIAL MEMBER FUNCTIONS

This section examines hidden code compiled into (or around) your special member functions.

Constructors and Destructors

As we have seen, sometimes there are hidden members that need to be initialized during construction and destruction. Worst case, a constructor may perform these activities:

◆ If "most-derived," initialize `vbptr` field(s) and call constructors of virtual bases

◆ Call constructors of direct nonvirtual base classes

◆ Call constructors of data members

◆ Initialize `vfptr` field(s)

◆ Perform user-specified initialization code in body of constructor definition

A "most-derived" instance is an instance that is not an embedded base instance within some other derived class.

So, if you have a deep inheritance hierarchy, even a single inheritance one, construction of an object may require many successive initializations of a class's `vfptr`. (Where appropriate, Visual C++ will optimize away these redundant stores.)

Conversely, a destructor must tear down the object in the exact reverse order to how it was initialized:

◆ Initialize `vfptr` field(s)

◆ Perform user-specified destruction code in body of destructor definition

◆ Call destructors of data members (in reverse order)

◆ Call destructors of direct nonvirtual bases (in reverse order)

◆ If "most-derived," call destructors of virtual bases (in reverse order)

In Visual C++, constructors for classes with virtual bases receive a hidden "most-derived flag" to indicate whether or not virtual bases should be initialized. For destructors, we use a "layered destructor model," so that one (hidden) destructor function is synthesized and called to destroy a class *including* its virtual bases (a "most-derived" instance) and another to destroy a class *excluding* its virtual bases. The former calls the latter, then destroys virtual bases (in reverse order).

Virtual Destructors and Operator Delete

Consider structs V and W.

```
struct V {                V*->    V::vfptr  ───►  &V::~V
    virtual ~V();
};

struct W : V {            W*->    V::vfptr  ───►  &W::~W
    operator delete();
};
```

Destructors can be virtual. A class with a virtual destructor receives a hidden vfptr member, as usual, which addresses a vftable. The table contains an entry holding the address of the virtual destructor function appropriate for the class. What is special about virtual destructors is they are implicitly invoked when an instance of a class is deleted. The call site (delete site) does not know what the dynamic type being destroyed is, and yet it must invoke the appropriate operator delete for that type. For instance, when the following pv below addresses a W, after W::~W() is called, its storage must be destroyed using W::operator delete().

```
V* pv = new V;
delete pv;    // pv->~V::V(); // use ::operator delete()
pv = new W;
delete pv;    // pv->~W::W(); // use W::operator delete()
pv = new W;
::delete pv; // pv->~W::W(); // use ::operator delete()
```

To implement these semantics, Visual C++ extends its "layered destructor model" to automatically create another hidden destructor helper function, the "deleting destructor," whose address replaces that of the "real" virtual destructor in the virtual function table. This function calls the destructor appropriate for the class, then optionally invokes the appropriate operator delete for the class.

Arrays

Dynamic (heap allocated) arrays further complicate the responsibilities of a virtual destructor. There are two sources of complexity. First, the dynamic size of a heap allocated array must be stored along with the array itself, so dynamically allocated arrays automatically allocate extra storage to hold the number of array elements. The other complication occurs because a derived class may be larger than a base class, yet it is imperative that an array delete correctly destroy each array element, even in contexts where the array size is not evident:

```
struct WW : W { int w1; };
pv = new W[m];
delete [] pv; // delete m W's  (sizeof(W)  == sizeof(V))
pv = new WW[n];
delete [] pv; // delete n WW's (sizeof(WW) >  sizeof(V))
```

Although, strictly speaking, polymorphic array delete is undefined behavior, we had several customer requests to implement it anyway. Therefore, in MSC++, this is implemented by yet another synthesized virtual destructor helper function, the so-called "vector delete destructor," which (since it is customized for a particular class, such as WW) has no difficulty iterating through the array elements (in reverse order), calling the appropriate destructor for each.

EXCEPTION HANDLING

Briefly, the exception handling proposal in the C++ standards committee working papers provides a facility by which a function can notify its callers of an exceptional condition and select appropriate code to deal with the situation. This provides an alternative mechanism to the conventional method of checking error status return codes at every function call return site.

Since C++ is object-oriented, it should come as no surprise that objects are employed to represent the exception state, and that the appropriate exception handler is selected based upon the static or dynamic type of exception object "thrown." Also, since C++ always ensures that frame objects that are going out of scope are properly destroyed, implementations must ensure that in transferring control (unwinding the stack frame) from throw site to "catch" site, (automatic) frame objects are properly destroyed.

Consider this example:

```
struct X { X(); }; // exception object class
struct Z { Z(); ~Z(); }; // class with a destructor
extern void recover(const X&);
void f(int), g(int);

int main() {
    try {
            f(0);
    } catch (const X& rx) {
            recover(rx);
    }
    return 0;
}

void f(int i) {
    Z z1;
    g(i);
    Z z2;
    g(i-1);
}

void g(int j) {
    if (j < 0)
            throw X();
}
```

This program will throw an exception. main() establishes an exception handler context for its call to f(0), which in turn constructs z1, calls g(0), constructs z2, and calls g(-1). g() detects the negative argument condition and throws an X object exception to whatever caller can handle it. Since neither g() nor f() established an exception handler context, you will consider whether the exception handler established by main() can handle an X object exception. Indeed it can. Before control is transferred to the catch clause in main(), however, objects on the frame between the throw site in g() and the catch site in main() must be destroyed. In this case, z2 and z1 are therefore destroyed.

An exception handling implementation might employ tables at the throw site and the catch site to describe the set of types that might catch the thrown object (in general) and can catch the thrown object at this specific catch site, respectively, and generally, how the thrown object should initialize the catch clause "actual parameter." Reasonable encoding choices can ensure that these tables do not occupy too much space.

However, let us reconsider function f( ). It looks innocuous enough. Certainly it contains neither try, catch, nor throw keywords, so exception handling would not appear to have much of an impact on f( ). Wrong! The compiler must ensure that, once z1 is constructed, if any subsequently called function were to raise an exception ("throw") back to f( ), and therefore out of f( ), that the z1 object is properly destroyed. Similarly, once z2 is constructed, it must ensure that a subsequent throw is sure to destroy z2 and then z1.

To implement these "unwind semantics," an implementation must, behind the scenes, provide a mechanism to dynamically determine the context (site), in a caller function, of the call that is raising the exception. This can involve additional code in each function prolog and epilog, and, worse, updates of state variables between each set of object initializations. For instance, in the previous example, the context in which z1 should be destroyed is clearly distinct from the subsequent context in which z2 and then z1 should be destroyed, and therefore Visual C++ updates (stores) a new value in a state variable after construction of z1 and again after construction of z2.

All these tables, function prologs, epilogs, and state variable updates, can make exception handling functionality a significant space and speed expense. As you have seen, this expense is incurred even in functions that do not employ exception handling constructs.

Fortunately, some compilers provide a compilation switch and other mechanisms to disable exception handling and its overhead from code which does not require it.

SUMMARY

There, now go write your own compiler.

Seriously, you have considered many of the significant C++ runtime implementation issues. You see that some wonderful language features are almost free, and others can incur significant overhead. These implementation mechanisms are applied quietly for you, behind the curtains, so to speak, and it is often hard to tell what a piece of code costs when looking at it in isolation. The frugal coder is well advised to study the generated native code from time to time and question whether use of this or that particularly cool language feature is worth its overhead.

ACKNOWLEDGMENTS

The Microsoft C++ Object Model described herein was originally designed by Martin O'Riordan and David Jones.

MEMORY MANAGEMENT IN C++

Nathan C. Myers

INTRODUCTION

Many programs have little need for memory management; they use a fixed amount of memory, or they simply consume it until they exit. The best that can be done for such programs is to stay out of their way. Other programs, including most C++ programs, are much less deterministic, and their performance can be profoundly affected by the memory management policy they run under. Unfortunately, the memory management facilities provided by many system vendors have failed to keep pace with growth in program size and dynamic memory usage.

Because C++ code is naturally organized by class, a common response to this failure is to overload member operator `new` for individual classes. In addition to being tedious to implement and maintain, however, this piecemeal approach can actually hurt performance in large systems. For example, applied to a tree-node class, it forces nodes of each tree to share pages with nodes of other (probably unrelated) trees, rather than with related data. Furthermore, it tends to fragment memory by keeping large, mostly empty blocks dedicated to each class. The result can be a quick `new`/`delete` cycle that accidentally causes virtual memory thrashing. At best, the approach interferes with systemwide tuning efforts.

Thus, while detailed knowledge of the memory usage patterns of individual classes can be helpful, it is best applied by tuning memory usage for a whole program or major subsystem. The first half of this chapter describes an interface, which can ease such tuning in C++ programs.

NOTE

Before tuning a particular program, however, it pays to improve performance for all programs, by improving the global memory manager. The second half of this chapter covers the design of a global memory manager that is as fast and space-efficient as per-class allocators.

Raw speed and efficiency are only a beginning. A memory management library written in C++ can be an organizational tool in its own right. Even as we confront the traditional problems involving large data structures, progress in operating systems is yielding different *kinds* of memory—shared memory, memory-mapped files, persistent storage—which must be managed as well. With a common interface to all types of memory, most classes need not know the difference. This makes quite a contrast with systems of classes hard-wired to use only regular memory.

THE GLOBAL OPERATOR NEW

In C++, the only way to organize memory management on a larger scale than the class is by overloading the global operator new. To select a memory management policy requires adding a *placement argument*, in this case a reference to a class which implements the policy:

```
extern void* operator new(size_t, class Heap&);
```

When we overload the operator new in this way, we recognize that the regular operator new is implementing a policy of its own, and we would like to tune it as well. That is, it makes sense to offer the same choices for the regular operator new as for the placement version.

In fact, one cannot provide an interesting placement operator new without also replacing the regular operator new. The global operator delete can take no user parameters, so it must be able to tell what to do just by looking at the memory being freed. This means that the operator delete and all operators new must agree on a memory management architecture.

For example, if our global operators new were to be built on top of malloc(), we would need to store extra data in each block so that the global operator delete would know what to do with it.

SHORTCUT

> Adding a word of overhead for each object to malloc()'s own overhead (a total of 16 bytes, on most RISCs), would seem a crazy way to improve memory management. Fortunately, all this space overhead can be eliminated by bypassing malloc(), as will be seen later.

The need to replace the global operators new and delete when adding a placement operator new has profound effects on memory management system design. It means that it is impossible to integrate different memory management architectures. Therefore, the top-level memory management architecture must be totally general, so that it can support any policy we might want to apply. Total generality, in turn, requires absolute simplicity.

AN INTERFACE

How simple can we get? Consider some declarations. Heap is an abstract class:

```
class Heap {
 protected:
  virtual ~Heap();
 public:
  virtual void* allocate(size_t) = 0;
  static Heap& of(void*);
};
```

(The static member function of(void*) is discussed later.) Heap's abstract interface is simple enough. Given a global Heap pointer, the regular global operator new can use it:

```
extern Heap* __global_heap;

inline void*
operator new(size_t sz)
  { return ::__global_heap->allocate(sz); }
```

Inline dispatching makes it fast. It's general, too; we can use the Heap interface to implement the placement operator new, providing access to any private Heap:

```
inline void*
operator new(size_t size, Heap& heap)
  { return heap.allocate(size); }
```

What kind of implementations might we define for the Heap interface? Of course, the first must be a general purpose memory allocator, class HeapAny. (HeapAny is the memory manager described in detail in the second half of this chapter). The global Heap pointer, used by the regular operator new previously defined, is initialized to refer to an instance of class HeapAny:

```
extern class HeapAny __THE_global_heap;
Heap* __global_heap = &__THE_global_heap;
```

Users, too, can instantiate class HeapAny to make a private heap:

```
HeapAny& myheap = *new HeapAny;
```

and allocate storage from it, using the placement operator new:

```
MyType* mine = new(myheap) MyType;
```

As promised, deletion is the same as always:

```
delete mine;
```

Now we have the basis for a memory management architecture. It seems that all we need to do is provide an appropriate implementation of class Heap for any policy we might want. As usual, life is not so simple.

COMPLICATIONS

What happens if MyType's constructor itself needs to allocate memory? That memory should come from the same heap, too. We could pass a heap reference to the constructor:

```
mine = new(myheap) MyType(myheap);
```

and store it in the object for use later, if needed. However, in practice this approach leads to a massive proliferation of Heap& arguments—in constructors, in functions that call constructors, everywhere!—which penetrates from the top of the system (where the heaps are managed) to the bottom (where they are used). Ultimately, almost every function needs a Heap& argument. Applied earnestly, the result can be horrendous. Even at best, such an approach makes it difficult to integrate other libraries into a system.

One way to reduce the proliferation of heap arguments is to provide a function to call to discover what heap an object is on. That is the purpose of the Heap::of() static member function. For example, here's a MyType member function that allocates some buffer storage:

```
char*
MyType::make_buffer()
{
  Heap& aHeap = Heap::of(this);
  return new(aHeap) char[BUFSIZ];
}
```

(If this points into the stack or static space, Heap::of() returns a reference to the default global heap.)

Another way to reduce heap argument proliferation is to substitute a private heap to be used by the global operator new. Such a global resource must be handled gingerly. Class HeapStackTop's constructor replaces the default heap with its argument, but retains the old default so it can be restored by the destructor:

```
class HeapStackTop {
  Heap* old_;
 public:
  HeapStackTop(Heap& h);
  ~HeapStackTop();
};
```

We might use this as follows:

```
{
  HeapStackTop top = myheap;
  mine = new MyType;
}
```

Now space for the MyType object, and any secondary store allocated by its constructor, comes from myheap. At the closing bracket, the destructor ~HeapStackTop() restores the previous default global heap. If one of MyType's member functions might later want to allocate more space from the same heap, it can use Heap::of(); or the constructor can save a pointer to the current global heap before returning.

Creating a HeapStackTop object is a very clean way to install any global memory management mechanism: A HeapStackTop object created in main() quietly slips a new memory allocator under the whole program.

Some classes must allocate storage from the top-level global heap regardless of the current default. Any object can force itself to be allocated there by defining a member operator new, and can control where its secondary storage comes from by the same techniques described previously.

With HeapStackTop, many classes need not know about Heap at all; this can make a big difference when integrating libraries from various sources. On the other hand, the meaning of Heap::of() (or a Heap& member or argument) is easier to grasp; it is clearer, and therefore safer. While neither approach is wholly satisfactory, a careful mix of the two can reduce the proliferation of Heap& arguments to a reasonable level.

USES FOR PRIVATE HEAPS

But what can private heaps do for us? We have hinted that improved locality of reference leads to better performance in a virtual memory environment, and that a uniform interface helps when using special types of memory.

One obvious use for private heaps is as a sort of poor man's garbage collection:

```
Heap* myheap = new HeapTrash;
... // lots of calls to new(*myheap)
delete myheap;
```

Instead of deleting objects, we discard the whole data structure at one throw. This approach is sometimes called *lifetime management*.

WARNING

Since the destructors are never called, you must carefully control what kind of objects are put in the heap; it would be hazardous ever to install such a heap as the default (with HeapStack-Top) because many classes, including iostream, allocate space at unpredictable times. Dangling pointers to objects in the deleted heap must be prevented, which can be tricky if any objects secretly share storage among themselves. Objects whose destructors do more than just delete other objects require special handling; the heap may need to maintain a registry of objects that require *finalization*.

But private heaps have many other uses that don't violate C++ language semantics. Perhaps the quietest one is simply to get better performance than your vendor's malloc() offers. In many large systems, member operator new is defined for many classes just so that they may call the global operator new less often. When the global operator new is fast enough, such code can be deleted, yielding easier maintenance, often with a net gain in performance from better locality and reduced fragmentation.

An idea that strikes many people is that a private heap could be written that is optimized to work well with a particular algorithm. Because it need not field requests from the rest of the program, it can concentrate on the needs of that algorithm. The simplest example is a heap that allocates objects of only one size; as we will see later, however, the default heap can be made fast enough so that this is no great advantage. A mark/release mechanism is optimal in some contexts (such as parsing), if it can be used for only part of the associated data structure.

When shared memory is used for interprocess communication, it is usually allocated by the operating system in blocks larger than the objects that you want to share. For this case a heap that manages a shared memory region can offer the same benefits that regular operator new does for private memory. If the interface is the same as for non-shared memory, objects may not need to know that they are in shared memory. Similarly, if you are constrained to implement your system on an architecture with a tiny address space, you may need to swap memory segments in and out. If a private heap knows how to handle these segments, objects that don't even know about swapping can be allocated in them.

In general, whenever a chunk of memory is to be carved up and made into various objects, a heap-like interface is called for. If that interface is the same for the whole system, then other objects need not know where the chunk came from. As a result, objects written without the particular use in mind may safely be instantiated in very peculiar places.

In a multithreaded program, the global operator new must carefully exclude other threads while it operates on its data structures. The time spent just getting and releasing the lock can itself become a bottleneck in some systems. If each thread is given a private heap that maintains a cache of memory available without locking, the threads need not synchronize except when the cache becomes empty (or too full). Of course, the operator delete must be able to accept blocks allocated by any thread, but it need not synchronize if the block being freed came from the heap owned by the thread that is releasing it.

A heap that remembers details about how, or when, objects in it were created can be very useful when implementing an object-oriented database or remote procedure call mechanism. A heap that segregates small objects by type can allow them to simulate virtual function behavior without the overhead of a virtual function table pointer in each object. A heap that zero-fills blocks on allocation can simplify constructors.

Programs can be instrumented to collect statistics about memory usage (or leakage) by substituting a specialized heap at various places in a program. Use of private heaps allows much finer granularity than the traditional approach of shadowing malloc() at link time.

In the remainder of this chapter we will explore how to implement HeapAny efficiently, so that malloc(), the global operator new(size_t), the global operator new(size_t, Heap&), and Heap::of(void*) can be built on it.

A MEMORY MANAGER IN C++

An optimal memory manager has minimal overhead: Space used is but fractionally larger than the total requested, and the new/delete cycle time is small and constant. Many factors work against achieving this optimum.

In many vendor libraries, memory used by the memory manager itself, for bookkeeping, can double the total space used. Fragmentation, where blocks are free but unavailable, can also multiply the space used. Space matters, even today, because virtual memory page faults slow down your program (indeed, your entire computer), and swap space limits can be exceeded just as can real memory.

A memory manager can also waste time in many ways. On allocation, a block of the right size must be found or made. If made, the remainder of the split block must be placed where it can be found. On deallocation, the freed block may need to be coalesced with any neighboring blocks, and the result must be placed where it can be found again. System calls to obtain raw memory can take longer than any other single operation; a page fault that results when idle memory is touched is just a hidden system call. All these operations take time, time spent not computing results.

 WARNING The effects of wasteful memory management can be hard to see. Time spent thrashing the swap file doesn't show up on profiler output and is hard to attribute to the responsible code. Often, the problem is easily visible only when memory usage exceeds available swap space. Make no mistake: Poor memory management can multiply your program's running time, or so bog down a machine that little else can run.

Before buying (or making your customers buy) more memory, it makes sense to see what can be done with a little code.

PRINCIPLES

A memory manager project is an opportunity to apply principles of good design: Separate the common case from special cases; make the common case fast and cheap, and other cases tolerable; make the user of a feature bear the cost of its use; use hints; reuse good ideas.

Before delving into detailed design, we must be clear about our goals. We want a memory manager that satisfies the following:

◆ **Speed.** It must be much faster than existing memory managers, especially for small objects. Performance should not suffer under common usage patterns, such as repeatedly allocating and freeing the same block.

◆ **Low overhead.** The total size of headers and other wasted space must be a small percentage of total space used, even when all objects are tiny. Repeated allocation and deallocation of different sizes must not cause memory usage to grow without bound.

◆ **Small working set.** The number of pages touched by the memory manager in satisfying a request must be minimal, to avoid paging delays in virtual memory systems. Unused memory must be returned to the operating system periodically.

◆ **Robustness.** Erroneous programs must have difficulty corrupting the memory manager's data structures. Errors must be flagged as soon as possible; they should not be allowed to accumulate. Out-of-memory events must be handled gracefully.

◆ **Portability.** The memory manager must adapt easily to different machines.

◆ **Convenience.** Users mustn't need to change code to use it.

◆ **Flexibility.** It must be easily customized for unusual needs, without imposing any additional overhead.

TECHNIQUES

Optimal memory managers would be common if they were easily built. They are scarce, so you can expect that a variety of subtle techniques are needed even to approach the optimum.

One such technique is to treat different request sizes differently. In most programs, small blocks are requested overwhelmingly more often than large blocks, so both time and space overhead for them is felt disproportionately.

Another technique results from noting that there are only a few different sizes possible for very small blocks, so that each such size may be handled separately. We can even afford to keep a vector of free block lists for those few sizes.

A third is to avoid system call overhead by requesting memory from the operating system in big chunks, and by not touching unused (and possibly paged-out) blocks unnecessarily. This means data structures consulted to find a block to allocate should be stored compactly, apart from the unused blocks they describe.

The final, and most important, technique is to exploit address arithmetic, which, while not strictly portable according to language standards, works well on all modern flat-memory architectures. A pointer value can be treated as an integer, and bitwise logical operations may be used on it to yield a new pointer value. In particular, the low bits may be masked off to yield a pointer to a header structure that describes the block pointed to. In this way, a block need not contain a pointer to that information. Furthermore, many blocks can share the same header, amortizing its overhead across all. (This technique is familiar in the LISP community, where it is known as *page-tagging*.)

A Design

The first major feature of the design is suggested by the final two previous techniques. We request memory from the operating system in units of a large power of two (e.g., 64K bytes) in size, and place them so they are aligned on such a boundary. We call these units "segments." Any address within the segment may have its low bits masked off, yielding a pointer to the segment header. We can treat this header as an instance of the abstract class HeapSegment:

```
class HeapSegment {
 public:
   virtual void free(void*) = 0;
   virtual void* realloc(void*) = 0;
   virtual Heap& owned_by(void*) = 0;
};
```

The second major feature of the design takes advantage of the small number of small-block sizes possible. A segment (with a header of class HeapPageseg) is split up into pages, where each page contains blocks of only one size. A vector of free lists, with one element for each size, allows instant access to a free block of the right size. Deallocation is just as quick; no coalescing is needed. Each page has just one header to record the size of the blocks it contains, and the owning heap. The page header is found by address arithmetic, just like the segment header. In this way, space overhead is limited to a few percent, even for the smallest blocks, and the time to allocate and deallocate the page is amortized over all usage of the blocks in the page.

For larger blocks, there are too many sizes to give each a segment; but such blocks may be packed adjacent to one another within a segment, to be coalesced with neighboring free blocks when freed. (We will call such blocks "spans," with a segment header of type HeapSpanseg.)

Fragmentation, the proliferation of free blocks too small to use, is the chief danger in span segments, and there are several ways to limit it. Because the common case, small blocks, is handled separately, we have some breathing room: Spans may have a large granularity, and we can afford to spend more time managing them. A balanced tree of available sizes is fast enough that we can use several searches to avoid creating tiny, unusable spans. The tree can be stored compactly, apart from the free spans, to avoid touching them until they are actually used. Finally, aggressive coalescing helps reclaim small blocks and keep large blocks available.

Blocks too big to fit in a segment are allocated as a contiguous sequence of segments; the header of the first segment in the sequence is of class HeapHugeseg. Memory wasted in the last segment is much less than might be feared; any pages not touched are not even assigned by the operating system, so the average waste for huge blocks is only half a virtual-memory page.

Dispatching for deallocation is simple and quick:

```
void operator delete(void* ptr)
{
  long header = (long)ptr & MASK;
  ((HeapSegment*)header)->free(ptr);
}
```

HeapSegment::free() is a virtual function, so each segment type handles deallocation its own way. This allows different Heaps to coexist. If the freed pointer does not point to allocated memory, the program will most likely crash immediately. (This is a feature. Bugs that are allowed to accumulate are extremely difficult to track down.)

The classical C memory management functions, `malloc()`, `calloc()`, `realloc()`, and `free()` can be implemented on top of HeapAny just as was the global operator new. Only `realloc()` requires particular support.

The only remaining feature to implement is the function `Heap::of(void* ptr)`. We cannot assume that ptr refers to heap storage; it may point into the stack, or static storage, or elsewhere. The solution is to keep a bitmap of allocated segments, one bit per segment. On most architectures this takes 2K words to cover the entire address space. If the pointer refers to a managed segment, `HeapSegment::owned_by()` reports the owning heap; if not, a reference to the default global heap may be returned instead. (In the LISP community, this technique is referred to as BBOP, or *big bag o' pages*.)

PITFALLS

Where we depart from the principles of good design previously mentioned, we must be careful to avoid the consequences. One example is when we allocate a page to hold a small block: We are investing the time to get that page on behalf of all the blocks that may be allocated in it.

 If the user frees the block immediately, and we free the page, then the user has paid to allocate and free a page just to use one block in it. In a loop, this could be much slower than expected. To avoid this kind of thrashing, we can add some hysteresis by keeping one empty page for a size if there are no other free blocks of that size. Similar heuristics may be used for other boundary cases.

Another pitfall results from a sad fact of life: Programs have bugs. We can expect programs to try to free memory that was not allocated, or that has already been freed, and to clobber memory beyond the bounds of allocated blocks. The best a regular memory manager can do is to throw an exception as early as possible when it finds things amiss. Beyond that, it can try to keep its data structures out of harm's way, so that bugs will tend to clobber users' data and not the memory manager's. This makes debugging much easier.

Initialization, always a problem for libraries, is especially onerous for a portable memory manager. C++ offers no way to control the order in which libraries are initialized, but the memory manager must be available before anything else. The standard iostream library, with a similar problem, gets away by using some magic in its header file (at a sometimes intolerable cost in startup time) but we don't have even this option, because modules that use the global operator new are not obliged to include any header file. The fastest approach is to take advantage of any nonportable static initialization ordering available on the target architecture. (This is usually easy.) Failing that, we can check for initialization on each call to operator new or malloc(). A better portable solution depends on a standard for control of initialization order, which seems (alas!) unforthcoming.

DIVIDENDS

The benefits of careful design often go beyond the immediate goals. Indeed, unexpected results of this design include a global memory management interface, which allows different memory managers to coexist. For most programs, though, the greatest benefit beyond better performance is that all the ad hoc apparatus intended to compensate for a poor memory manager may be ripped out. This leaves algorithms and data structures unobscured and allows classes to be used in unanticipated ways.

THE DIFFICULTIES OF USING OBJECT-ORIENTED TECHNIQUES: PERCEPTIONS OF C++ DEVELOPERS

Steven D. Sheetz

INTRODUCTION

Professional developers that use C++ were asked to identify issues, ideas, or concepts that they believe are difficult to understand about using object-oriented (OO) programming techniques. They organized these concepts into categories based on the similarity of the concepts, rated the importance of the categories for understanding OO programming techniques, and defined causal relationships between the categories. The result is a representation of the perceptions of what is difficult about using OO techniques that includes potential problems to be avoided and focuses attention on issues perceived as being important. The concepts generated by the developers identify specific difficult issues. The categories represent a higher level of mental organization of the difficulties of using OO techniques. Cognitive maps derived from the causal relationships show the interactions of the categories and imply ways to manage the difficulties by influencing categories rated as most important for understanding OO techniques. Implications of the study for adopting OO techniques are discussed.

Object-oriented (OO) analysis, design, and programming techniques are being considered by many information systems (IS) organizations (Booch, 1991; Borgida, 1985; Coad and Yourdon, 1991a, 1991b). However, researchers have suggested that the difficulties of adopting and learning OO techniques are substantial, and that decisions to adopt OO techniques should be made with caution (Fichman and Kemeer, 1991; Rosson and Carroll, 1990). Identifying issues perceived as contributing to the difficulties of understanding and using OO techniques provides a basis for revealing common pitfalls and applying training resources where they can be most effective.

This study examines perceptions of what is difficult to understand about using OO systems development techniques from the perspective of professional developers who use C++. A focus on the perceptions of what is difficult to understand about using OO techniques provides a basis for identifying the issues that might be addressed to improve the efficiency and effectiveness of using OO techniques.

A cognitive mapping approach was used to capture the perspectives of the participants. Cognitive mapping is a research method that uncovers an individual's perceptions of his or her environment (Weick and Bougon, 1986). The cognitive maps were collected using the software tools provided by a Group Support System (GSS).

This section presents the importance of OO systems and the need for identifying the problem(s) to be addressed to improve the OO system development process from the perspective of OO developers. The next sections provide background on the difficulties of learning OO techniques and the methodology used in the study to derive cognitive maps representing the perceptions of the participants. The difficulties of using OO techniques reported by developers that use C++ are then presented followed by a discussion that highlights implications of the study for OO developers and their managers.

Importance of OO Techniques

Information systems organizations are considering OO techniques as a potential solution to the perennial problem of delivering timely and cost-effective systems that meet users' needs (Kalakota, Rathnam, and Whinston, 1993; Scholtz et al., 1993). Leading Information Systems journals, for example, Communications of the Association of Computing Machinery (special issues in September 1992 and September 1993), and the popular press, for example, Business Week's Cover Story (Verity and Schwartz, 1991), are promoting object-orientation as a potential solution for what currently ails software development. But, adopting OO techniques is potentially a difficult process. From the perspective of an IS organization, adopting OO techniques requires revising or replacing many current (and successful) practices, for example, structured programming and relational database design. This limits the appeal of untested techniques. IS researchers recognize this issue.

> *For object orientation, the rival entrenched technology is not just a language generation or a database model, but the entire procedural paradigm for software development. It is therefore difficult to imagine a more compelling instance of prior technology drag in software engineering (Fichman and Kemerer, 1993, p. 19).*

The difficulty that experienced developers have had learning OO techniques is another issue that has the potential to influence the widespread adoption of OO techniques.

Learning OO analysis, design, and programming techniques has been described as a difficult process (Rosson and Carroll, 1990; Vesey and Conger, 1994). As such, it is important to discover what is difficult to understand about OO systems to aid adoption of this solution to the software crisis. Representing professional developers' views of the difficulties of using OO systems analysis, design, and programming techniques contributes to our ability to address the issues that are most important for understanding and using OO techniques.

OO systems analysis and design techniques are intended to provide problem-oriented representations that reduce the mapping required from problem constructs to computational structures (Booch, 1991; Coad and Yourdon, 1991a, 1991b). Proponents of these approaches claim that software developed in this way will be of high quality resulting in higher usability (due to the match of the software with the users conceptualization of the problem) and maintainability (due to the reduced mapping from problem constructs to computational structures) than software designed using other techniques. Researchers of OO system development methods believe in the the ability of OO techniques to create a direct model of a problem domain (Rosson and Gold, 1989; Rosson and Alpert, 1990). However, as Kent (1978) pointed out,

> *A model is a basic system of constructs used in describing reality. ... [It] is more than a passive medium for recording our view of reality. It shapes that view, and limits our perceptions. If a mind is committed to a certain model, then it will perform amazing feats of distortion to see things structured that way, and it will simply be blind to the things which don't fit that structure.*

Thus, to understand what contributes to the difficulty of using OO techniques requires investigating what users of OO techniques perceive as contributing to the difficulty of developing OO systems. That is, we must discover their mental models of the difficulties of using OO systems development techniques. Their mental models are based on their experiences and hence, perceptions, of using OO techniques. Although their model may be incomplete, based on incorrect assumptions, or simply naive, the difficulties of using OO techniques for the developers is based on their mental model (Norman, 1988). Consequently, identifying existing difficulties in understanding OO systems is a necessary step in defining what should be addressed to control the inherent or essential complexity in OO systems. For as Brooks (1987) states, "complexity of software is an essential property, not an accidental one."

A focus on identifying and understanding the issues that contribute to the difficulties of using OO techniques is appropriate for a previously little explored area where the most important problems to be studied have yet to be determined. Identifying perceptions of what is difficult to understand about OO systems provides a basis for identifying the characteristics of OO systems that should be controlled to effectively and efficiently develop OO systems.

BACKGROUND

Difficulties of Learning OO Techniques

Few studies have addressed the issues of the difficulties of learning OO techniques. Recent articles indicate that novices have more problems learning OO methods than process-based methods (Vessey and Conger, 1994), experienced programmers have problems learning Smalltalk (Carroll, Brown, and Dibello, 1992; Nielsen and Richards, 1989; Rosson and Albert, 1990), teaching OO concepts before OO languages is desirable, and the use of OO environments should be limited in early learning stages (Rosson, Carroll, and Bellamy, 1990). Addressing this issue requires understanding what OO developers believe is difficult about using OO techniques.

A study of experienced developers as they learned Smalltalk identified several problems with their learning process (Campbell, Brown, and Dibello, 1989). First, they had a need to understand in detail every method that executed when they used the class library. This indicates that these experienced developers were not initially able to realize the benefits of encapsulation provided by OO languages and environments. Other experienced system developers also reported a difficulty getting to specifics of the code as a problem (Nielsen and Richards, 1989). The second problem dealt with mastering the syntax of Smalltalk. The third problem dealt with understanding the Smalltalk class hierarchy. The experienced developers preferred to learn the hierarchy by reading the code. There is a large amount of code in the hierarchy, and a learning by reading approach seems to be an unneccesary use of resources. Nielsen and Richards (1989) describe a similar problem associated with Smalltalk being too large and generalized for novices. For example, the large number of possible data structures may overwhelm the novice, however the experienced developer may see this variety as powerful. The fourth problem was a need to perform coding experiments and observe the results. The final problem was associated with the use of analogies to experience with other programming languages. Using analogies is beneficial where the analogy matches with the issue from an OO perspective, but can be detrimental if the analogy is poor.

The process of OO design also has been studied (Rosson and Gold, 1989). In this study experienced OO designers solved a problem and described what they were thinking throughout the design process. The study revealed several approaches used to create OO designs. First, designs were driven by the problem domain knowledge of the designer. Both information and behavior mapping lead to the identification of more abstract class hierarchies. Second, designers used metaphoric extension of the problem to identify requirements by allowing objects to be viewed as an organization of intelligent agents. Rosson and Gold indicate that identifying useful organizational metaphors may be an important part of OO design. Third, most of the OO designers used anthropomorphism to extend and evaluate their designs. The approaches described by the designers are consistent with many popular OO methodologies.

This research attempts to provide guidance for potential adopters of OO techniques. However, there remains a great deal to learn about what makes using OO techniques difficult.

COGNITIVE MAPPING METHOD

Importance of Understanding Difficult Issues

Defining the correct problem has been identified as essential for the efficient use of organizational resources. Research has been criticized for focusing on problem solution rather than problem identification (Weick and

Meader, 1993). This is consistent with the idea that we should know what needs to be managed before selecting measures to use for managing. Determining the concepts perceived as causing the most difficulty of understanding contributes directly to the problem-identification process. To investigate problems in the appropriate context requires uncovering the perspectives of people that work in that environment, that is, developers of OO systems.

Cognitive Mapping For Revealing Difficult Issues

Cognitive mapping is a set of approaches for studying and recording people's perceptions about their environment. These perceptions are recorded graphically in the form of a "mental map" that shows concepts and relationships between concepts. Many cognitive mapping techniques (Axlerod, 1976; Bougon, et al., 1977; Bougon, Komocar, and Ross, 1990; Bougon, 1992; Eden, 1992; Eden et al., 1992; Fiol and Huff, 1992 Finch et al., 1989; Huff, 1990) consist of three major steps: (1) eliciting concepts, (2) refining concepts, and (3) identifying assertions that concepts are connected by causal relationships. A *cause* map, a special type of cognitive map, is built by connecting concepts to each other by arrows; the arrows represent assertions that one concept affects another concept. Additional steps are necessary for the derivation of *group* maps. For example, Delphi panel techniques include steps to reconcile or combine individuals' idiosyncratic representations (Montazemi and Conrath, 1986; Zhang et al., 1992). By looking at the views of others and reconsidering their own views, members of a Delphi panel can move toward consensus (Dalkey and Rourke, 1971). GSS provide tools necessary to implement the procedures of both cognitive mapping and consensus building techniques. Thus, cognitive mapping procedures can be combined with a Delphi panel approach using a GSS. A focus on perceptions of what is difficult about using OO techniques is the final component necessary for identifying the problems associated with using OO techniques.

The Self-Q technique for cognitive mapping has been used in a variety of domains and is consistent with other cognitive mapping approaches. Thus, it provides a useful basis for a cognitive mapping approach implemented with a GSS. The Self-Q technique consists of the following steps:

◆ Self-questioning to identify concepts associated with a domain.

◆ Grouping the concepts from self-questioning into categories.

◆ Developing or defining the categories.

◆ Ranking the categories by importance.

◆ Determining relationships between categories.

The GSS approach for investigating perceptions of OO system complexity was an adaptation of these.

Group support systems (GSS) have become a well-established area of research in information systems (Anson et al., 1992; Davis et al. 1992; Hoffer et al, 1990; Sheetz et al., 1994). A GSS is a computer-based system that combines hardware, software, and procedures to structure and support group activities. For example, an automated agenda provides structure since participants know that specific activities will be conducted in a specified order during a GSS session, for example, elicit concepts, refine concepts, and identify relationships between concepts. Each activity could be supported using a tool provided by the GSS, for example, electronic brainstorming to elicit concepts, a categorizing tool for classifying/refining the concepts, and a matrix tool for identifying relationships between categories.

The GSS used in this study was the VisionQuest software of Intellect Corp. VisionQuest uses the concept of a dialogue to structure group interaction. A dialogue consists of a coordinator, an agenda, and a list of participants. The agenda is simply a list of tools to structure the group interaction. The dialogue coordinator determines which VisionQuest tools will be used to put together the agenda, depending on the nature of the task. Like most GSSs, VisionQuest allows participants to enter their ideas simultaneously and anonymously. Individual inputs can be aggregated and displayed.

The steps in the Self-Q technique were implemented with the VisionQuest software. Additional activities were included for the group to reach consensus. The resulting GSS agenda included the ability to develop a set of agreed-on categories as the basis for individual cognitive maps and facilitates the process of combining individual maps to represent group perspectives .

Table 10.1 shows the steps in the GSS session, including a brief activity description, the time required for each step, and the VisionQuest tool used for each activity. Throughout the session, the facilitator (the author) provided procedural guidance only, for example, administrative activities such as reading instructions and keeping time. At no time did the facilitator provide feedback on group responses. Details of each GSS activity follow.

TABLE 10.1 PROCEDURES FOR THE GSS APPROACH TO COGNITIVE MAPPING

Activity	Description	Time	VisionQuest Tool
Eliciting concepts			
Introduction	System use, informed consent form, framing statement, and stall diagram.	10 Min.	Brainwriting
Concept identification	Elicit characteristics, concepts, or issues that contribute to (increase or decrease) techniques. the difficulty of using OO	40 Min.	Brainwriting
Refining concepts			
Category identification	Elicit categories that organize the list of concepts by similarity.Agree on definitions and names	20 Min.	Verbal, Compactor
Concept categorizations	Participants place the concepts into the top ten categories.	25 Min.	Compactor
Discussion of concept	Participants discuss placements. Categorizations	5 Min.	Compactor
Category rating step 1	Participants rate each category on a seven-point scale from important to extremely important.	5 Min.	Rating
Discussion of category ratings	Group means are calculated and discussed.	15 Min.	Verbal
Category rating step 2	Participants rate each category on a seven-point scale from important to extremely important.	5 Min.	Rating
Discussion of category ratings	Group means are calculated and discussed.	15 Min.	Verbal
Category rating step 3	Participants rate each category on a seven-point scale from important to extremely important.	5 Min.	Rating

continued

Activity	Description	Time	VisionQuest Tool
Defining relationships			
Relationship identification	Participants are individually presented a comparison matrix of the categories in a rating task. Rating is on a scale of -3 to +3 from strongly negative influence to strongly positive influence of one category on another category.	30 Min.	Scoring
Debriefing	Participants enter comments on the GSS procedures and results of the process.	10 Min.	Brainwriting

Introduction

Each data collection meeting began with a 10-minute introduction of the facilitator and participants. The participants were trained on the GSS software. The purpose and domain of the study were presented.

Concept Identification

This activity was supported using a Brainwriting exercise. Brainwriting is a VisionQuest tool that implements electronic brainstorming by allowing each participant to privately key in comments, which are then displayed on a public and all individual screens. Participants were asked to generate items that represented characteristics, concepts, or issues they believed contributed to OO system complexity.

Category Identification

The purpose of this activity was to determine a set of categories, including definitions, that contain the set of concepts developed in the previous activity. This activity was supported with a combination of Brainwriting and Compactor tools. The Compactor is a tool in the VisionQuest software that supports the process of converging from a large number of concepts into a smaller set of categories. This process requires that category definitions be specified before concepts can be placed into categories by participants. The categories and their definitions would then be used for the next activity where participants place the concepts into the categories.

Participants viewed the concepts from the previous Brainwriting exercise and verbally suggested categories. The facilitator wrote the group's suggested category names on a chalkboard and revised them until the group reached agreement. Agreement was defined by there being no further comments on the list of categories when participants were asked to add to, modify, or delete categories on the list. The facilitator recorded the categories and definitions, as agreed on by the participants, in the Compactor tool.

Concept Categorization

This 45-minute process attempted to validate the categories identified. This activity was supported with the Compactor tool. The categories identified in the previous step were used to group the items from the concept identification step. Each participant individually placed each concept into one of the categories based on the similarity of the concept to the category definition and to other concepts placed in the category by that participant. If most of the concepts fit well into a category, that is, were placed in that category by a majority of participants, then face validity for the categories as a set is increased. In other words, there would appear to be agreement on the meanings of the concepts and the categories.

Category Rating

The purpose of this activity was to determine the amount of consensus on the relative importance of the categories. This activity was supported using the Rating tool, with three ratings rounds intended to be the equivalent of a Delphi panel process. Ratings were measures of the importance of a category to the difficulties of using OO techniques using a scale of (important) to 7 (extremely important). This scale is appropriate since the categories are derived from the "important" concepts and therefore a scale anchored with "not important" is likely only to compress ratings into the upper portions of the scale. The participants rated each of the categories individually and the mean ratings were then discussed. Another rating exercise was conducted with the group results of the first rating exercise displayed on the public screen. The discussion and rating steps then were performed a final time.

Relationship Identification

Relationships were identified using an influence matrix implemented using the VisionQuest Scoring tool. Participants rated each cell in the matrix on a scale showing the influence of the category in each row on the category in each column. The rating scale ranged from a strongly negative influence (-3) to a strongly positive influence (+3). These relationships provided the final component required to produce a cognitive map of the group's perceptions of the difficulties of using OO techniques.

REPORTED DIFFICULTIES OF USING OO TECHNIQUES

C++ Programmers Views

The results of the study are presented in terms of the concepts, categories, and cognitive maps generated by the C++ developers that participated in the study. 12 OO system developers that use C++ completed the procedures previously defined to identify what they believed was difficult about using OO techniques. The participants were experienced with structured programming techniques, averaging eight years of system development experience. They had varying levels of OO experience averaging two years and ranging from less than one year to over five years. Each participant completed the agenda with a group of other OO developers.

Nine groups of developers completed the study. Most participants were in groups that mixed both Smalltalk and C++ developers. Thus, the categories identified by the groups were influenced by people with OO experiences in addition to C++ programming.

Difficult Concepts Identified

Concept level data results from the concept identification and concept categorization procedures. Participants identified 262 concepts in the electronic brainstorming sessions averaging of 22 concepts per participant. Some examples of these concepts are presented in Table 10.2 which includes five of the concepts generated by each of the 12 participants.

Concepts placed in each category were consistent with the definitions determined by the group during the session. This is an indication of internal validity of the experiment, that is, the participants accomplished the assigned task and grouped similar concepts based on the definitions.

TABLE 10.2 EXAMPLES OF DIFFICULT ISSUES IDENTIFIED

Abstraction is difficult.

Desire to make programming constructs match analysis constructs.

Still focusing on programming, not engineering.

"Iterative hacking" characteristic of most OO development processes.

Many techniques encourage enlargement of probability space beyond what's feasible.

Domain object identification/granularity.

Change impact in deep inheritance hierarchies.

Decision on whether to subclass or to delegate.

Object dependency analysis.

High-level design/specification versus implementation detail/language capability.

Uses versus inherits.

Evaluating a design.

Having to redesign the base class to accommodate the derived classes.

Difficult to combine objects from multiple sources with multiple world views.

Testing objects that use lots of other objects.

Initially moving from a procedural mindset to an object-oriented one.

Defining the object specifications well.

Management not understanding the need for more up-front design time.

Bad code can be written in OO languages just as well as procedural.

OO really is a long-term solution, many times it ends up being more costly in the short term.

continued

Knowing what is available to reuse.

Sharing code/ideas/designs among programmers during development.

Estimating development resources required—people, time.

Determining what is a "good" design, implementation.

Knowing whether to / how to decompose complex problem domain concepts into many or few, simple or complex objects.

When inheritance is better than delegate relationships.

An object that has too large of an inheritance tree is difficult to reuse.

Adapting new object software to interface with legacy systems.

The whole issue of Quality Assurance is more complex.

The purist of OO are the root of most of the technology's problems.

Level of granularity to decompose into objects.

Ability to merge OO architecture with user interface.

Unlearning traditional programming techniques.

Multitude of "mine's better" vendors in marketplace.

Clients lack of understanding of OO technology...if you aren't a developer, you seldom see the benefits of the technology.

Lack of a single common terminology across languages.

Lack of a simple comprehensive design methodology.

Management has absolutely no idea what OO really is.

Bridging the conceptual gap between real world objects and OOP objects.

Trying to understand control flow of messages (goes one place one time and another place the next time).

Inability for large groups to agree on definition of "object".

Lack of stable technology, for example, C++, OODBMSs.

Using objects in business (re)engineering.

continued

Object collaboration—encapsulation and coupling.

Building an appropriate incentive model to drive reuse, both individually and corporately

Deciding whether a concept should be represented as an attribute or another object.

Knowing when to create an abstract superclass.

Use of word "object" to mean either "class" or "instance".

Developing repositories of reusable objects.

Choosing an OO language and environment.

Managing documentation or information of object methods and attributes for use in subclassing.

Coordinating use of objects (classes) between large number of developers.

Determining which languages, environment best suits the application.

Subclassing from a library of classes (no source code) and trying to "guess-stimate" how the superclass functions.

Having a consistent way of communicating or drawing OO designs and/or hierarchies.

Distributing system intelligence among objects.

Documenting the flow in the system (message passing) .

Balancing object size with inheritance diagram size (width and depth).

Keeping a high-level perspective during analysis—objects are more bottom-up

Maintaining a class library and encouraging reuse of it

Categories of Difficult Issues

The categories identified represent a level of abstraction that shows how the participants organize the difficulties of using OO techniques. This organization reveals major issues perceived as important by the participants. Thus, categories perform a central role in organizing and understanding the views of the participants and form the basis for the cognitive maps.

Each group of participants identified a set of categories. The set of categories identified by a group represents the shared views of the OO developers in that group. The nine groups identified a 70 categories, which were evaluated to identify ideas or themes that were identified by more than one group of developers.

The sets of categories identified by the groups were highly consistent, showing many common themes across groups. These common themes were used to combine the categories identified by the groups into a set of overall categories that seem to be shared across groups. This was done using the category definitions provided by the participants. The process resulted in eight overall categories that were shared by most groups. This set of overall categories of difficult issues included *Modeling and Design, Education, Implementation, Management, Reuse, Technology, Organization Issues,* and *Traditional Versus OO.* Table 10.3 shows that the categories identified by the groups were consistent with the overall categories. An X in a cell of the table shows that the group in that column independently identified a category consistent with the overall category in that row. The table shows the consistency of the set of overall categories with the categories identified by each group. For example, Group 1 identified categories that were consistent with six of the overall categories. Similarly, the table shows the overall categories that were most commonly identified. For example, the overall *Management* category was identified by eight of the nine groups. The large number of X's indicates that the views of the groups were similar. All groups identified the *Modeling and Design* category and most groups identified the *Education, Implementation, Technology, Management,* and *Reuse* categories. Only three groups defined the *Organization Issues* and *Traditional versus OO* categories.

The categories and definitions provided by the groups were combined to create the set of overall categories. The definitions of the overall categories are the category names and definitions identified by the groups. This results in an organization of the categories that reveals the similarities of perceptions of the groups. This organization is presented in Tables 10.4 a–10.h. These tables show the mapping of each category identified by the groups of OO developers to its corresponding overall category. This mapping provides a basis for discussing the similarities of the categories identified by the nine groups of OO developers.

At least one category that was consistent with the overall *Modeling and Design* category was identified by all nine groups. The category names and definitions provided by the groups that were included in the overall *Modeling and Design* category are presented in Table 10.4a. This overall modeling and design category contains issues associated with the problem domain requirements, finding objects and relationships between them, creating abstractions of the problem, mapping the analysis to a design, and knowing that a design is complete and/or high quality.

TABLE 10.3 CONSISTENCY OF OVERALL CATEGORIES AND CATEGORIES IDENTIFIED BY THE GROUPS

Category Name	Group Number								
	1	2	3	4	5	6	7	8	9
Modeling and Design	X	X	X	X	X	X	X	X	X
Education	X	X		X	X	X	X	X	X
Implementation	X	X	X		X	X	X	X	X
Technology	X	X	X	X		X	X	X	X
Management	X	X		X	X	X	X	X	X
Reuse	X		X	X	X		X	X	
Organization issues				X		X			X
Traditional versus OO	X					X			X

An *Education* category was identified by eight of the nine groups. Table 10.4b presents the category names and definitions provided by the groups that were included in this overall category.This category includes issues associated with learning OO concepts/principles, training on OO tools/techniques, mentoring, and informing developers and management on the costs/benefits of using OO techniques.

The overall *Implementation* category was identified by eight of the nine groups. This category contains issues associated with programming standards, interface issues, using OO languages, and testing. Table 10.4c presents the category names and definitions provided by the groups that were included in this overall category.

A *Technology* category also was identified by eight of the nine groups. Table 10.4d presents the category names and definitions provided by the groups that were included in this overall category. This category includes concerns about OO languages, selection of methodology, interfacing to non-OO systems, OO environments, "pure" OO concepts, and current marketplace evaluation of products.

A *Management* category was identified by eight of the nine groups. Issues associated with this category include project management, the development process, OO life cycle, integrating work, and human resource management. Table 10.4e presents the category names and definitions provided by the groups that were included in this overall category.

A *Reuse* category was identified by six of the nine groups. Issues associated with reuse included understanding existing code/designs/analyses, finding objects to reuse, and creating objects for reuse. Table 10.4f presents the category names and definitions provided by the groups that were included in this overall category.

A category associated with *Organization Issues* was identified by three of the nine groups. These issues were associated with effects of adopting OO techniques on the organization, business process reengineering to take advantage of OO, investments required to adopt OO techniques, and accounting for costs and benefits. Table 10.4g presents the category names and definitions provided by the groups that were included in this overall category.

A category associated with issues pertaining to the transition from traditional structured development techniques to OO, and tradeoffs between traditional and OO techniques was identified by three of the nine groups. This overall category was named Traditional versus OO. Table 10.4h presents the category names and definitions provided by the groups that were included in this overall category.

TABLE 10.4A MODELING & DESIGN CATEGORY AND SUPPORTING GROUP CATEGORIES AND DEFINITIONS

Category Name	Definition
Modeling and Design	*Abstraction:* Issues associated with defining and assessing the quality of a set of abstractions. Should this be one concept or two is part of the object here and over there. (1)
	Modeling: How do you know your model is complete. Converting requirements into a model. Discovering objects and how do you associated behaviors with objects, i.e., assigning behaviors to objects. (2)
	Modification of Design: Adding/changing existing code or designs. (3)

continued

Category Name	Definition
Modeling and Design	*Imperfect Map:* Mapping the problem to the analysis, analysis to design, and design to the implementation. (3)
	Process Issues: Introducing OO company wide leads to the need for business process reengineering, and the impacts that result from BPR. OO allows high level ideas to implemented faster which impacts the processes down stream, e.g., implementation and config management. (4)
	Analysis/Mapping: Identifying relevant objects/concepts/mechanisms in the problem domain. (5)
	Design: Using the constructs identified in analysis and converting them into something that can be coded. Adding the implementation specific domain objects to problem domain objects. (5)
	OO Design: All issues relating to how to design the architecture including different methodologies, implementation strategies. (6)
	Analysis and Design: Choosing, using, and understanding OO methodologies and modeling, both for a single project and across projects. (7)
	Detailed Design: The definition of the attributes and how the smaller nitty gritty things fit together, how data is transferred, defining all the methods. Ownership issues, e.g., two objects communicating who owns the buffers. Transition from high level abstract design to what is inside your objects, looking inside the blobs. Detailed class design. (8)
	Problem Definition: Understanding the problem and the parameters to it. (8)
	High-Level Design: Design of objects, the communication between high-level objects. Identifying high-level objects. The relationships between objects, for example, how they relate to the problem definition and each other, at a purely abstract level. (8)
	Designing Objects and Relationships: Designing objects and relationships between objects including class and instance relationships (isa, hasa). Designing hierarchies to maximize reuse. (9)

TABLE 10.4B EDUCATION CATEGORY AND SUPPORTING GROUP CATEGORIES AND DEFINITIONS

Category Name	Definition
Education	*Language/Tools:* Problems with learning and using OO languages and tools. (1)
	Training: Training programmers, management, analysts. Developing mentors. Consistent training. (2)
	Education Issues: The need for education. Dealing with the paradigm shift. Mentoring. How to educate, hard to take people with years of structured experience and convert to OO. Costs of education, budgets are 1/3 of what is necessary. Learning organization. (4)
	Education: How do you learn about the concepts in the other categories, for example, OO concepts, analysis/mapping, etc. (5)
	OO Concepts: Understanding OO constructs, such as, multiple inheritance, message passing, metaclasses, event driven programming, object as a programming unit. (5)
	Educating Developers: All issues related to developer training, includes tools, development techniques, and how the political environment works. (6)
	Education: Converting the masses through education and mentoring. Exposing the benefits of OO versus traditional techniques. (7)
	OO Principles: The concepts that you need to understand to use OO techniques, such as, inheritance, encapsulation, polymorphism, class, object, and so on. (7)
	Training/Learning: Bringing developers up to speed. Not only the tools but the OO concepts. (8)

TABLE 10.4C IMPLEMENTATION CATEGORY AND SUPPORTING GROUP CATEGORIES AND DEFINITIONS

Category Name	Definition
Implementation	*Concurrency:* Less structure in communication allows unexpected results and dynamic communication. (1)
	Polymorphism: Overloading, overriding, delegating, and other issues associated with deciding what function use. When to use what. (1)

continued

Category Name	Definition
Implementation	*Programming Issues:* Standards (defining and enforcing). Knowing what is good programming, looking for existing code, knowing what is out there. (2)
	GUI: The end product, what the user sees of objects (front end). (2)
	Testing: How to test the model, the code, unit/integration/system testing, method testing, assuring your objects work the way they were designed. (2)
	Testing: Testing an OO implementation. (3)
	Implementation Difficulties: The difficulties of implementing using an OO language, includes implementing not only OO designs, but using OO languages in general. (3)
	Implementation: The best way to code your design or how to code. How to apply the OO concepts. (5)
	Interfaces: Interfacing to existing systems and persistence and especially to other non-OO technologies. (5)
	User Interface: User interface design issues, how to tie it to your architecture, and tool issues (what kind of tools to you need to build). (6)
	Programming: Mapping of principles and design to actual code. Maintaining the paradigm in the face of reality. (7)
	Implementation: Implementing the OO concepts in a particular language. Language peculiar issues. Going from the abstract the actual implementation. (8)
	Standards: Documentation, coding, design, and testing standards, including the level of quality and performance, e.g., memory and speed. (8)
	Implementation: Implementation issues including anything that relates to languages and development environments. OO and nonOO actual implementation issues. (9)

TABLE 10.4D TECHNOLOGY CATEGORY AND SUPPORTING GROUP CATEGORIES AND DEFINITIONS

Category Name	Definition
Technology	*Performance:* Problems associated with the tools and the programmers and the number of operations. Perception that OO is slow. (1)
	Tools: CASE, diagramming tools/notation, languages, GUIs, platforms, OS, interfaces to batch/DBs. (2)

continued

Category Name	Definition
Technology	*Documentation:* Of any of your tools programming language, methodology, models, GUIs, updating documentation. (2)
	Methodology: Who's to use, when to use, what is the difference between methodologies, how strictly do you follow them. (2)
	Standard Methodology: The lack of a standard method. Existing OO methods may be more similar than advertised. (3)
	Technical Issues: Language choice, methodology specification, architecture, looking broadly at the technologies available, tools. Defining what is "real" OO technology. Integrating other technologies, CBR, neural nets, genetic algorithms, or legacy system issues. (4)
	Marketplace: The directions of the industry, including products, industry focus (what's currently being developed), and how the industry views products (e.g., rating of C++, SmallTalk, many available platforms). (6)
	OO Technology: Specifics about different languages, environments, Dbs. Mapping the OO principles to tools. How is technology changing and dealing with the coming technology. Choosing a specific implementation. (7)
	Tools and Environment: Selection adoption and self-defense from your tools and environment. Political problems. (8)
	Understanding OO Technology: Understanding OO technology and techniques so that they can be used most effectively and properly. Knowing what does and does not exist, knowing what tools and techniques adhere to true OO principles. (9)

TABLE 10.4e MANAGEMENT CATEGORY AND SUPPORTING GROUP CATEGORIES AND DEFINITIONS

Category Name	Definition
Management	*Process and Management:* OOA, D, and P processes as well as project management. (1)
	Management Interaction: Project management, getting management to buy into the OO paradigm, task planning, managing iteration. (2)
	Management Downstream: Project management and definition. How you approach project management, for example, gantt w/ 15 milestones versus 150 milestones. How to assign a team member to a portion of the project. Different SDLC. (4)

continued

Category Name	Definition
Management	*Project Management:* Managing people and the development process. (5)
	OO Project Management: All issues related to managing OO projects. Includes integration of other peoples work, roles, and deliverables. (6)
	Management Issues: Impact of OO technology on how projects and businesses are run, such as schedule impact, need for training. (7)
	Project Management: Estimating, setting up a methodology, assigning work, deciding if we should purchase things and what we want to develop on our own. Human resources management. (8)
	Management Aspects: How to manage a project, split the work among teams, life cycle to use, timeframes, schedules, how to know when to iterate (start/stop), knowing the difference between prototypes and reality. (9)

TABLE 10.4F REUSE CATEGORY AND SUPPORTING GROUP CATEGORIES AND DEFINITIONS TABLE

Category Name	Definition
Reuse	*Reuse:* Reusing class libraries and other existing stuff, designing for reuse, and finding the thing you want to reuse. (1)
	Understanding Existing: Understanding existing OO analyses, designs, or code. Lots of methods, superclasses, and useclasses. (3)
	Development Issues: Finding object definitions, managing class hierarchies; analysis and design process, implementation, testing, certification, reuse. (4)
	Reuse: Everything having to do with reusing code/design/analysis in a new situation (other than the one for which it was originally built). (5)
	Reuse: Understanding and achieving the benefits of reuse. We generally know what we want, but it is unclear how to get there. (7)
	Maintenance: Maintenance of objects and classes including the production code but also the documentation so that it can be reused. Code that exercises the object to test changes. (8)

10.4G ORGANIZATION ISSUES CATEGORY AND SUPPORTING GROUP CATEGORIES AND DEFINITIONS

Category Name	Definition
Organization Issues	*Organization:* How the adoption of OO affects current organization structures or vice versa. The people aspects of the organization as it relates to responsibilities. Like the role of a DBA has changed in the world of OO. (4)
	Management Upstream: Accountability in a financial sense. A project that creates original classes versus a project that reuses many objects and gets credit. Must have champion. HRM issues. Compensation of OO people. (4)
	Business Issues: Accounting, costs (short term and long term), benefits (standlt), and mapping of costs to benefits. Legal issues. (4)
	Communication: Having infrastructure to support rapid and frequent communication as necessary. Technologies to support communication (email, lotus notes). How to emphasize (force) communication. High bandwidth communication, lots of information fast. (4)
	Client Relations: All issues related to the education of the client of the benefits and on the OO development process and managing client expectations. (6)
	Understand OO Philosophy: Understanding OO philosophy including knowing what OO development will do and won't do for you, understanding the scope of OO. Understanding the investments that must be made, for example, time, money, training, upfront investments, long-term values. (9)

Category importance ratings indicate the participants' perceptions of the relative contribution of the categories to the difficulties of using OO systems development techniques. Table 10.5 presents the categories in rank order of the mean category importance ratings and the ratings of each category by each participant. The ratings of the participants show that a moderate level of agreement was attained by the participants. This agreement is significantly different from zero agreement, with a Kendall coefficient of concordance of .44, $p < .01$ (Siegel and Castellan, 1989).

Review of Table 10.5 shows that the participants believe that issues associated with modeling and design are the most important contributors to the difficulty of using OO techniques. Education and implementation also ranked as important contributors to the difficulty of using OO techniques. The category definitions for these categories in Tables 10.4a–10.4c show the most important issues are associated with understanding the problem and mapping the problem to an OO representation, the next most important issue is learning the OO techniques, which is followed by using OO languages and environments to implement computer systems. The high ranking given to the education category indicates that more training and learning is desirable from the perspective of the participants. These developers perceive organization and culture issues as unimportant.

TABLE 10.4H TRADITIONAL VERSUS OO CATEGORY AND SUPPORTING GROUP CATEGORIES AND DEFINITIONS

Category Name	Definition
Traditional versus OO	*New/Good?:* A perception that OO is good because it is new and the structured techniques are bad because they're old. (1)
	Fear Unfamiliar: Fear of the new untested stuff. Risk managers look for proven technology that will accomplish the task. (1)
	Traditional versus OO: All issues including religious beliefs, for example, performance. Tradeoffs (where traditional approaches may be better than OO). Benefits and detriments of both traditional and OO approaches. (6)
	Cultural Aspects: Programmer and manager mindsets, including for example, design, code reuse, and interaction/team dynamics. Expectations that come from the image that people try to sell about OO (hype), which could be different from reality. (9)

TABLE 10.5 RATINGS OF CATEGORY IMPORTANCE

	Participant Number												
Category Name	1	2	3	4	5	6	7	8	9	10	11	12	Avg
Modeling and Design	7	7	6	3	7	5	5	5	6	7	5	7	5.8
Education	4	6	0	7	6	7	5	5	7	6	5	4	5.2
Implementation	5	6	4	6	6	6	4	7	2	1	4	3	4.5
Technology	2	3	4	6	0	4	2	5	3	4	5	6	3.7
Management	6	6	0	4	3	5	5	5	1	4	1	3	3.6
Reuse	3	4	6	0	2	0	0	6	5	7	7	0	3.3
Organization Issues	0	0	0	3	1	4	5	0	0	0	0	0	1.1
Traditional versus OO	3	0	0	0	0	4	2	0	0	0	0	4	1.1

Difficulties Viewed as Cognitive Maps

The relationships for a cause map of each individual's perceptions of the difficulties of using OO techniques was specified in the relationship identification step. Maps using the overall categories were derived from the individual maps and the category mapping shown in Tables 10.4a–10.4h. This was done by replacing the group generated categories in the individual maps with the corresponding overall category. In 15 cases, two or more categories from one of the individual maps were consistent with only one of the overall categories (see Tables 10.4a–10.4h to identify these instances). When this happened, the overall category assumed all the links of the two categories in the individual map. If two links were identical in direction but different in strength of effect, the higher strength number was placed on the map. If two links were different in direction both links are shown. The number of relationships identified by the individual participants ranged from 11 to 34 with an average of 23 of the 72 possible relationships.

The relationships identified by the participants show how the difficulty due to one category affects the difficulty due to other categories. An arrow indicates that the participant believed that the difficulty due to the originating category influenced the complexity of the terminating category. The direction of the effect, increase or decrease in the difficulty due to the terminating category is shown with + or - signs, respectively. Increasing means that there is a positive correlation between difficulty of the two categories, that is, an increase in difficulty due to the originating category increases difficulty due to the terminating category. Decreasing means that an inverse relationship exists between the categories, that is, an increase in difficulty due to the originating category decreases difficulty due to the terminating category. The strength of the effect is shown by a number (3 = strongly, 2 = moderately, blank = slightly).

Each map was evaluated using *givens means ends analysis* (Bougon et al., 1977). Givens are identified by having mostly outflows of causal influence, means as having about the same number of inflows and outflows, and ends as having more inflows than outflows. Cognitive centrality of a category is an indication of a focus of the participants and is defined as the sum of the inflows and outflows. The ratio of inflows to outflows is an indication of whether the node is a given, a means, or an end. Viewing the nodes in increasing order of this ratio shows the direction of causality in a cognitive map (Bougon et al., 1977; Weick and Bougon, 1986). Table 10.6

presents the number of inflows, outflows, ratio of inflows to outflows, and the total number of connections (cognitive centrality) for each category for each individual map. The table provides an overview of the relationships identified by different the participants.

A review of Table 10.6 shows that the *Implementation* and *Modeling and Design* categories are the most cognitively central categories. This seems an appropriate focus for OO developers and is consistent with the category importance ratings. These categories also represent the means of OO development and were identified as such by the analysis. *Education* and *Technology* were viewed as important categories that were influenced by using OO techniques. Thus it appears that the acquisition of expertise in this domain comes from using OO modeling and implementation techniques. This has clear implications for training techniques. *Reuse*, *Management*, and *Organization issues* also make sense as givens or inputs into the OO development process. The influence of each category is discussed in Table 10.6 and the cognitive maps are presented in Figure 10.1.

Reuse was identified as given. With all the potential advantages claimed by reuse advocates it seems reasonable that the desire for reuse is an input to the OO development process. Eight of the 12 participants indicated that this category was related to other categories. All eight of these participants indicated that including reuse concepts influences the difficulties in the other categories. For the participants that identified reuse as a category, it had a high cognitive centrality, averaging 8.5. This indicates that reuse is a very important aspect (and benefit) of using OO techniques to the participants. Most participants see reuse as increasing difficulties due to other categories. However, several participants viewed reuse as decreasing difficulties due to other categories. Intuitively, reuse would reduce the difficulties of modeling and implementation, while perhaps increasing the difficulty due to management issues. Perhaps the disagreement indicates that reuse is an aspect of OO techniques that is not completely understood by the developers.

Relationships between the *Management* category and other categories were identified by 11 of the 12 participants. Management of resources and constraints are important to the OO development process and were appropriately identified as inputs to the process. Most participants view management difficulties as influencing the *Modeling and Design*, *Implementation*, *Technology*, and *Education* categories. This perspective is encouraging for the prospects of decreasing the difficulties of using OO techniques through refined management practices.

Organization issues were seen as related to the other categories by three of the 12 participants. These participants were especially interested in organizational issues and attributed high levels of cognitive centrality to this category indicating that they believe it has potential to influence the other categories. This makes sense from the perspective of OO methodologies that recommend attempting to directly model business problems using OO techniques.

Implementation is perceived as one of the most important categories. All 12 participants indicated that this category influences the difficulty due to other categories and is influenced by the difficulty due to the other categories. This category is strongly influenced by the *Education, Technology,* and *Reuse* categories. The *Modeling and Design* and *Management* categories appear to be strongly influenced by implementation difficulties.

Modeling and Design also was identified as an important means of developing OO systems. All 12 participants indicated that this category influences the difficulty due to other categories and is influenced by the difficulty due to the other categories. This category was strongly influenced by *Implementation, Reuse, Technology,* and *Management* categories. *Modeling and Design* also influence the difficulty of education issues.

Education was identified as highly interconnected to the difficulty due to other categories. Increases in the difficulty of education increases the difficulty represented by the other categories. 11 of the 12 participants see education as influencing most categories. Education is also influenced by the need to address issues represented by the other categories, for example, *Modeling and Design, Implementation,* and *Management.* Thus, it appears that there is a need for training during the process of adopting OO techniques.

Technology was identified by nine of the 12 participants as influencing the difficulty due to other categories. Decreases in the difficulty due to the tools themselves directly reduce the difficulty of *Modeling and Design, Implementation, Reuse,* and *Education.* This represents a protechnology bias of the participants and appealing opportunities for vendors.

TABLE 10.6 SUMMARY OF RELATIONSHIPS BETWEEN CATEGORIES

Category Name	Participant Number												Avg
	1	2	3	4	5	6	7	8	9	10	11	12	
Givens													
Reuse	3,5, .60, 8	5,5, 1.0 10	3,3, 1.0 6	0,0, U, 6	4,4, 1.0 8	0,0, U, 0	0,0, U, 0	2,5, .40, 7	4,5, .80, 9	4,5, .80, 9	5,4, 1.25, 9	0,0, U, 0	2,3, .66 5.5
Management	2,6, .33, 8	6,4, 1.4, 10	0,0, U, 0	4,5, .80, 9	3,4, .75, 7	3,5, .60, 8	3,5, .60, 8	4,1, 4.0, 5	4,4, 1.0, 8	5,5, 1.0, 10	,0,5, U, 5	3,5, .60, 8	3,4, .75, 7
Organization Issues	0,0, U, 0	0,0, U, 0	0,0, U, 0	5,5, 1.0, 10	0,0, U, 0	5,5, 1.0, 10	3,4, .75, 7	0,0, U, 0	0,0, U, 0	0,0, U, 0	0,0, U, 0	0,0, U, 0	1,1, 1.0, 2
Means													
Implementation	5,4, 1.25, 9	6,5, 1.2, 11	3,2, 1.5, 5	5,5, 1.0, 10	2,4, .50, 6	4,4, 1.0, 8	5,2, 2.5, 7	2,2, 1.0, 4	3,5, .60, 8	3,5, .60, 8	4,4, 1.0, 8	3,5, .60, 8	4,4, 1.0, 8
Modeling and Design	5,4, 1.25, 9	6,4, 1.5, 10	3,3, 1.0, 6	4,4, 1.0, 8	3,3, 1.0, 6	5,5, 1.0, 10	4,5, .80, 9	5,3, 1.66, 8	2,4, .50, 6	4,4, 1.0, 8	4,3, 1.33, 7	3,5, .60, 8	4,4, 1.0, 8
Ends													
Education	3,3, 1.0, 6	5,6, .83, 11	0,0, U, 0	5,4, 1.25, 9	4,3, 1.33, 7	5,5, 1.0, 10	2,4, .50, 6	3,5, .60, 8	5,2, 2.5, 7	5,4, 1.25, 9	4,2, 2.0, 6	4,0, U, 4	4,3, 1.33, 7
Technology	3,1, 3.0, 4	5,5, 1.0, 10	2,3, .66, 5	5,5, 1.0, 10	0,0, U, 0	0,0, U, 0	0,0, U, 0	2,2, 1.0, 4	4,2, 2.0, 6	5,3, 1.66, 8	5,4, 1.25, 9	4,0, U, 4	3,2, 1.5, 5
Traditional versus OO	4,2, 1.0, 6	2,6, .33, 8	0,0, U, 0	0,0, U, 0	0,0, U, 0	5,3, 1.4, 8	4,1, 4.0, 5	0,0, U, 0	0,0, U, 0	0,0, U, 0	0,0, U, 0	3,5, .60, 8	2,2, 1.0, 4
Summary													
No. of Categories	7	7	4	6	5	6	6	6	6	6	6	6	6
No. of Links	25	35	11	28	18	27	21	18	22	26	22	20	23

Cells that contain four numbers represent the inflows, outflows, ratio of inflows to outflows, and cognitive centrality for each node. U indicates that the ratio of inflows to outflows is undefined.

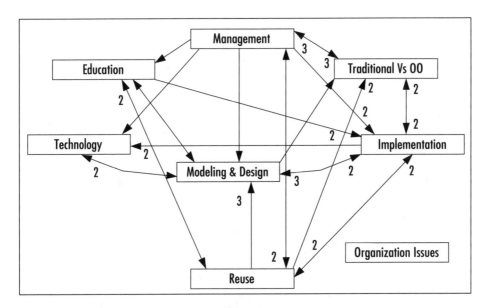

PARTICIPANT 1

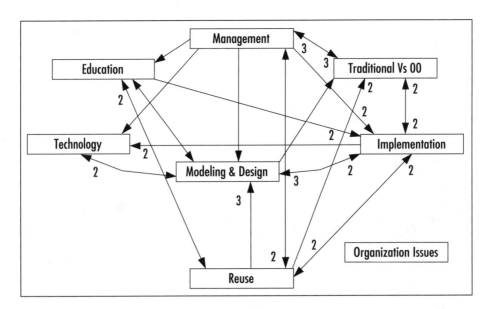

PARTICIPANT 2

FIGURE 10.1

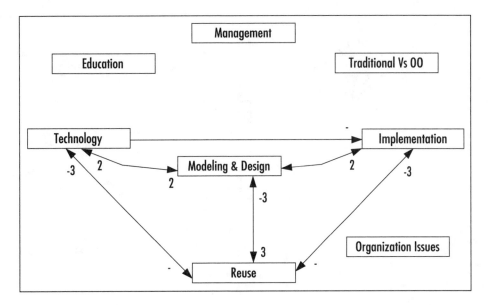

PARTICIPANT 3

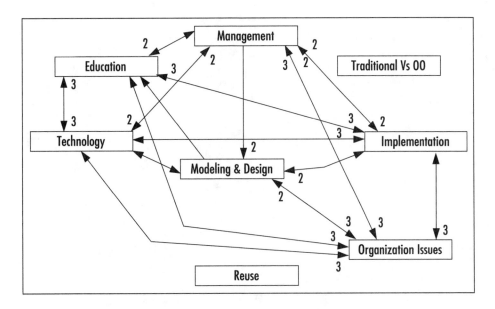

PARTICIPANT 4

FIGURE 10.1 *continued*

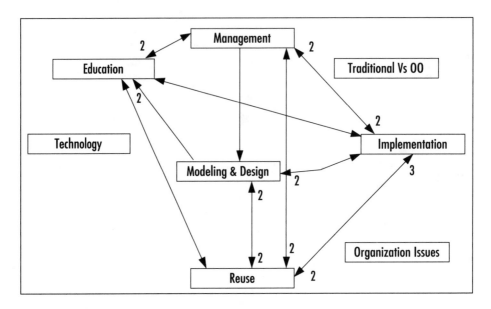

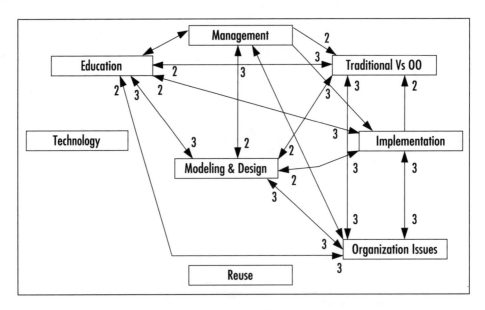

PARTICIPANT 6

FIGURE 10.1 *continued*

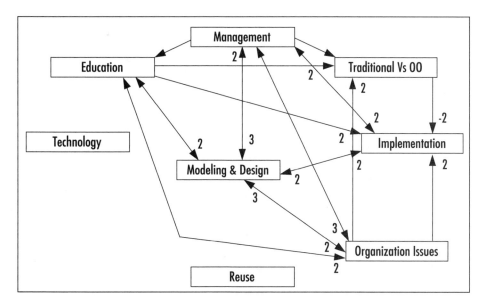

PARTICIPANT 7

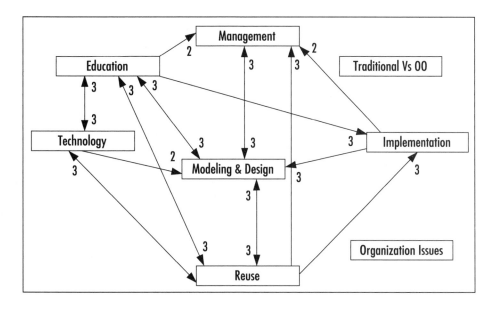

PARTICIPANT 8

FIGURE 10.1 *continued*

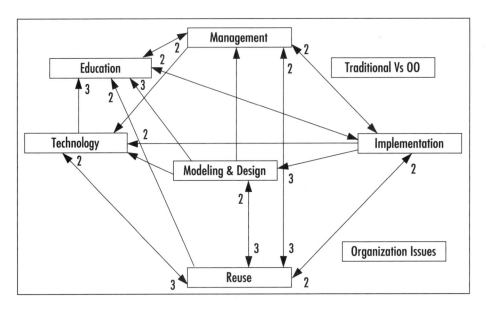

PARTICIPANT 9

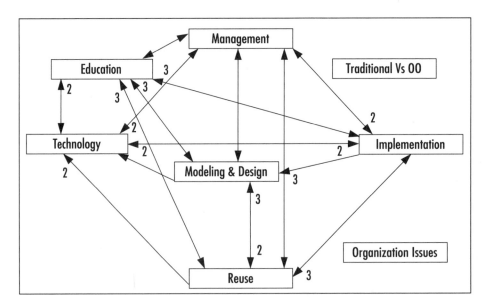

PARTICIPANT 10

FIGURE 10.1 *continued*

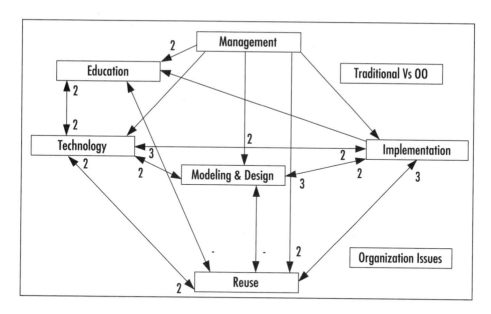

PARTICIPANT 11

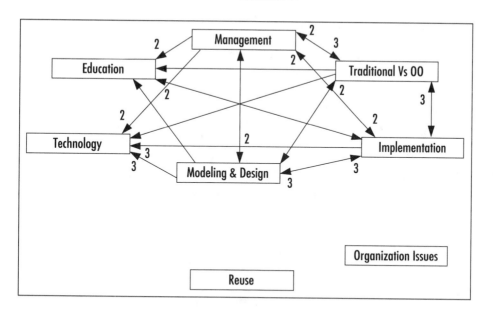

PARTICIPANT 12

FIGURE 10.1 *continued*

IMPLICATIONS AND SUMMARY

The categories identified cover a wide range of issues associated with developing software using OO techniques. Many of the issues identified apply to developing software, regardless of the techniques used. For example, modeling and design, implementation, and management issues are essential to any computer system development process. This seems to support the idea that using OO techniques is not a panacea filled with easy solutions to the software crises (Brooks, 1987). However, OO specific implications can be derived from examining the concepts, overall categories, and cognitive maps.

A need for education that addresses both modeling, design and implementation issues is seen as important in terms of the number of groups that identified those categories (see Table 10.3), the category importance ratings (see Table 10.5), and the cognitive centrality of the categories (see Table 10.6). The concepts identified (see Table 10.2) and the group category definitions (see Tables 10.4a–10.4c) provide aid in defining the specific aspects of using OO techniques that should be part of any training program. Such a training program should include an emphasis on abstraction of high level objects, identifying relationships between those objects, mapping from the problem to the analysis, the analysis to a design, identifying semantic structures (AKO, APO), testing, interfaces (GUI and to noon systems), and hands-on experiences. Education appears to be an important aspect of using OO techniques (see Table 10.5) that is seen as capable of influencing the difficulty due to other categories.

Management also is seen as having the potential to influence the difficulty due to other categories. This means that by addressing these issues the difficulty of OO development can be reduced. Managers could pursue training for themselves and developers to decrease difficulty throughout the OO development process. The participants identified several difficulties of managing an OO development process, for example, estimating, life cycle definition, iterations, and dividing work among team members.

Reuse was a concern of most of the participants. Issues associated with this category include understanding existing class libraries and finding what you want in a class hierarchy. However, the definitions provided by the groups for this category are very superficial. Perhaps this promise of using OO techniques could be defined in greater detail since it seems that it is desirable but difficult to achieve.

The identification of organizational issues such as business process reengineering and the costs/benefits of adopting OO techniques shows that the use of OO techniques is perceived as having the potential to greatly impact organizations.

The *Traditional Versus OO* category shows that the culture in the work environment has an impact on the adoption of OO techniques. A culture that encourages the value of matching the system to the problem and "trust" in objects produced by other development groups is important to realize the benefits of using OO techniques.

Limitations of the study include the small number of participants. However, a larger sample was used to develop the overall categories. Small numbers of participants are common for in-depth exploratory studies.

The difficulties of using OO techniques were obtained from 12 OO developers who use C++. A GSS approach to cognitive mapping was used to reveal both shared perceptions (overall categories) and individual views (cognitive maps) to provide an understanding of the difficulties of using OO techniques.

The responses of the developers show that they believe that OO techniques suffer from some of the same limitations of other development techniques. Modeling, design, and implementation issues were perceived as the most important aspects of OO development. Education, management, and reuse also were widely cited categories. Organizational issues and concerns about traditional versus OO show that the social environment is an important aspect of using OO techniques. This study provides a basis for a variety of future research questions that are based on the perceptions of working OO developers.

REFERENCES

1. Anson, R.G., Fellers, J.W., Bostrom, R.P., and Chidambaram, L. (1992). "Using group support systems to facilitate the research process." *Proceedings of the Twenty-Fifth Hawaii International Conference on System Sciences*, Volume IV, IEEE Computer Society Press, Los Alamitos, CA, 70–79.

2. Axelrod, R. (1976). *Structure of Decision—The Cognitive Maps of Political Elites*, Princeton University Press, Princeton, NJ.

3. Booch, G. (1991). *Object-Oriented Design with Applications*, The Benjamin/Cummings Publishing Company, Redwood City, CA.

4. Borgida, A., Greenspan, S., and Mylopoulos, J. (1985). "Knowledge Representation as the Basis for Requirements Specifications." *IEEE Computer*, 18(4), 82–90.

5. Bougon, M.G. (1992). "Congregate cognitive maps: a unified dynamic theory of organization and strategy." *Journal of Management Studies*, 29(3), 369–389.

6. Bougon, M.G., Baird, N., Komocar, J.M., and Ross, W. (1990). "Identifying strategic loops: the self Q interviews." In Huff, A. S. (Ed.), *Mapping Strategic Thought*, John Wiley and Sons, Ltd., Chichester, England, 327–354.

7. Bougon, M.G., Weick, K., and Binkhorst, D. (1977). "Cognition in organizations: an analysis of the Utrecht Jazz Orchestra. " *Administrative Science Quarterly*, 22, 606–639.

8. Brooks, F.P. (1987). "No Silver Bullets: Essence and accidents of Software Engineering." IEEE Computer, 20(4), 10–19.

9. Campbell, R. L., Brown, N. R., and Dibello, L. A. (1992). "The programmer's burden: Developing expertise in programming." In Hoffman, R. R. (Ed.) *The Psychology of Expertise: Cognitive Research and Empirical AI*, Springer-Verlag Inc., New York, NY, 269–296.

10. Coad, P., and Yourdon, E. (1991a). *Object-Oriented Analysis, 2nd Ed.* Yourdon Press, Englewood Cliffs, NJ.

11. Coad, P. ,and Yourdon, E. (1991b). *Object-Oriented Design.* Yourdon Press, Englewood Cliffs, NJ.

12. Dalkey, N., and Rourke, D. (1971) *Experimental assessment of Delphi procedures with group value judgments.* R-612-ARPA. RAND Corporation, Santa Monica, CA.

13. Davis, G.B., Nunamaker, J.F., Watson, H.J., and Wynne, B.E. (1992). "The use of a collaborative work system for the study of the key issues facing information systems managers: a comparison of issues and data collection methods from previous studies." *Proceedings of the Twenty-Fifth Hawaii international Conference on System Sciences*, Volume IV, IEEE Computer Society Press, Los Alamitos, CA, 46–59.

14. Eden, C. (1992). "On the nature of cognitive maps." *Journal of Management Studies*, 29(3), 261–265.

15. Eden, C., Ackermann, F., and Cropper, S. (1992). "The analysis of cause maps." *Journal of Management Studies*, 29(3), 309–324.

16. Finch, L., Landry, J., Monarchi, D.E., and Tegarden, D.P. (1987). "A Knowledge acquisition methodology using cognitive mapping and information display boards." *Proceedings of the Twentieth Hawaii International Conference on System Sciences*, Vol. III, IEEE Computer Society Press, Los Alamitos, CA, 470–477.

17. Fiol, M. and Huff, A.S. (1992). "Maps for managers: where are we? where do we go from here?" *Journal of Management Studies*, 29(3), 267–285.

18. Hoffer, J.A., Anson, R., Bostrum, R.P., and Michaele, S.J. (1990). "Identifying the root causes of data systems planning problems: an application of the PLEXSYS electronic meeting support system." *Proceedings of the Twenty-Third Hawaii international Conference on System Sciences*, Volume III, IEEE Computer Society Press, Los Alamitos, CA, 30–39.

19. Huff, A.S. (1990). *Mapping Strategic Thought*, John Wiley and Sons Ltd., Chichester, England.

20. Kalkota, R., Rathman, S., and Whinston, A.B. (1993). "The role of complexity in object-oriented systems development." *Proceedings of the Twenty-Sixth Hawaii International Conference on System Sciences*, Volume II, IEEE Computer Society Press, Los Alamitos, CA, 759–768.

21. Kent, W. (1978) *Data and Reality: basic assumptions in data processing reconsidered*, North-Holland, Amsterdam, The Netherlands.

22. Montazemi, A. R., and Conrath, D. W. (1986). "The use of Cognitive Mapping for Information Requirements Analysis." *MIS Quarterly*, 10(1), 44–55.

23. Norman, D.A. (1988). T*he Psychology of Everyday Things*, Basic Books, New York, NY.

24. Nielson, J., and Richards, J. T. (1989). "The Experience of Learning and Using Smalltalk." *IEEE Computer*, May, 111–116.

25. Rosson, M. B., and Alpert, S.R. (1990). "The cognitive consequences of object-oriented design." *Human-Computer Interaction*, 5, 345–379.

26. Rosson, M.B., and Carroll, J.M. (1990). "Climbing the Smalltalk Mountain." *SIGCHI Bulletin*, 21(3), 76–79.

27. Rosson, M.B., Carroll, J.M., and Sweeney, C. (1991). "A view matcher for reusing Smalltalk classes." In *Proceedings of the ACM CHI '91 Conference on Human Factors in Computing Systems*, 277–283.

28. Rosson , M.B., and Gold, E. (1989). "Problem-Solution Mapping in Object-Oriented Design." *OOPSLA-89 Conference Proceedings, SIGPLAN Notices*, 24(9), 7–10.

29. Scholtz, J., Chidamber, S., Glass, R., Goerner, A., Rosson, M.B., Stark, M., and Vessey, I. (1993). "Object-Oriented Programming: The Promise and the Reality." *Journal of Systems Software*, 23, 199–204.

30. Siegel, S., and Castellan, Jr., N.J., (1988). *Nonparametric Statistics for the Behavioral Sciences*, McGraw-Hill, Inc., New York, NY.

31. Sheetz, S.D., Tegarden, D.P., Kozar, K.A., Zigurs, I. (1994). "A Group Support Systems Approach to Cognitive Mapping." *Journal of Management Information Systems*, 11(1), 31–57.

32. Verity, J.W., and Schwartz, E.I. (1991). "Software Made Simple: Will Object-Oriented Programming Transform the Computer Industry." *Business Week*, (Sept. 30), 92–100.

33. Vessey, I., and Conger S. (1994). "Requirement Specification: Learning Object, Process, and Data Methodologies." *Communications of the ACM*, 37(5), 102–113.

34. Weick, K.L., and Bougon, M.G. (1986). "Organizations as cognitive maps: charting ways to success and failure." In Sims, H. and Gioia, D. (eds.), *The Thinking Organization: Dynamics of Organizational Cognition*, Jossey-Bass, San Francisco, CA.

35. Zhang, W., Chen, S., Wang, W., and King, R.S. (1992). "A Cognitive-Map-Based Approach to the Coordination of Distributed Cooperative Agents." *IEEE Transactions on Systems, Man, and Cybernetics*, 22(1), 103–114.

ABOUT THE AUTHORS

Bruce Eckel provides C++ training & consulting. He is the author of *Thinking in C++* (Prentice Hall, 1995), *C++ Inside & Out* (1993; 2nd ed. of *Using C++*, Osborne/McGraw-Hill, 1989) and Borland's C++ video training courses. He is a voting member of the ANSI/ISO C++ Committee. He was a columnist for *Micro Cornucopia*, C++ editor of *The C Gazette*, and is currently C++ columnist for *Embedded Systems Programming*. He has given seminars throughout the world, and is the C++ track chair for the Software Development conference.

Tim Gooch is an author and C++ programmer in the Louisville KY area. He is the Editor-in-Chief of *Borland C++ Developer's Journal*, a monthly programmer's journal published by The Cobb Group. He began using Object Oriented Programming techniques with Object Pascal on the Macintosh, and then moved to C++ on PCs using Borland C++ in 1991.

Jan Gray has a B.Math. in Computer Science from the University of Waterloo, and since 1987 has helped create development tools at Microsoft Corp. He helped write Microsoft's source control system, a prototype incremental C compiler, and C++ semantics for the Visual C++ compiler. Jan has served as a representative on the C++ standards committee and as "resident C++ apologist". He now works on incremental linking and other interesting applications of program databases. Jan is actually a repressed computer architect and spends his copious spare time creating RISC CPUs from Xilinx FPGAs.

Dr. Thomas Keffer is the President of Rogue Wave Software, Inc., a leading developer of C++ class libraries. He has been working with C++ since 1987 and is a member of the ANSI/ISO C++ committee.

Scott Meyers is the author of *Effective C++* (Addison-Wesley, 1992), co-author of *The Downloader's Companion for Windows* (Prentice hall, 1995), a columnist for the *C++ Report*, and a frequent speaker and consultant on C++ software development. He received his Ph.D. in Computer Science from Brown University in 1993, and his research on software development has been reported in technical journals and at conferences around the world. He is currently writing *More Effective C++*, to be published by Addison-Wesley in 1995.

Nathan Myers cut his C++ teeth at Mentor Graphics on cfront 1.2. He developed what became Rogue Wave's Heap.h++ product, and the Tools.h++ internationalization features. He participates on the ISO/ANSI C++ Standards committee, particularly the standard library.

Steve Ross is program manager for C++ compilers and build tools. He's also worked on the Microsoft C/C++ documentation, including the C++ Language Reference materials. Ross has been at Microsoft since 1988 as a writer on C language documentation and has driven innovations in on-line reference and documentation.

Dan Saks is the president of Saks & Associates, a C++ training and con-sulting company. He serves as secretary of the ISO+ANSI C++ standards committee. He is a contributing editor for both *The C/C++ Users Journal and Software Development*. He has also written regular columns for *The C++ Report* and *The Journal of C Language Translation*. With Thomas Plum, Dan Saks wrote *C++ Programming Guidelines* (Plum Hall, 1991) and developed *The Plum Hall Validation Suite for C++*.

Steven D. Sheetz is a doctoral candidate in Information Systems at the University of Colorado at Boulder. His research interests include systems analysis and design techniques, software measurement, and group support systems. He received a BS in Computer Science from Texas Tech University in 1984 and a MBA from the University of Northern Colorado in 1987. He has seven years of work experience as a programmer and systems analyst.

Hank Shiffman is the C++ product manager for Borland. His two decades of programming experience include everything from mainframes to micros and languages from Algol and APL to Xerox assembly. He has written about C++ for *Dr. Dobbs Journal* and *SunWorld* in the U.S., *Software Design* in Japan and *UNIXopen* in Germany.

INDEX

A

B

D

T

W

X